AF322974

A Private View

A Private View

AMERICAN PAINTINGS
FROM THE MANOOGIAN COLLECTION

Yale University Art Gallery, New Haven

Detroit Institute of Arts

The exhibition was organized
by the Yale University Art Gallery and the Detroit Institute of Arts

EXHIBITION DATES

Yale University Art Gallery, New Haven
April 3–July 31, 1993

Detroit Institute of Arts
September 11–November 14, 1993

The High Museum of Art, Atlanta
December 18, 1993–March 6, 1994

Richard Manoogian's remarks on p. 9 were taken from
American Paintings from the Manoogian Collection, exh. cat.
(Washington, D.C.: National Gallery of Art/Detroit:
Detroit Institute of Arts, 1989), p. 9.

Dimensions are given in inches, followed by centimeters
in parentheses.

Cover: John Singer Sargent,
Young Girl Wearing a White Muslin Blouse,
between 1882 and 1885 (p. 76).

Library of Congress Cataloging-in Publication Data
A Private view : American paintings from the Manoogian Collection.
        p.   cm.
    Catalog of an exhibition held Apr. 3–July 31, 1993, at the Yale University
Art Gallery; Sept. 11–Nov. 14, 1993, Detroit Institute of Arts; Dec. 18,
1993–Mar. 6, 1994, High Museum of Art, Atlanta, Ga.
    Includes index.
    ISBN 0-89467-063-8 (hc). — ISBN 0-89467-062-X (pbk.)
    1. Painting, American—Exhibitions. 2. Painting, Modern—19th
century—United States—Exhibitions. 3. Manoogian, Richard A.—Art
Collections—Exhibitions. 4. Painting—Private collections—Michigan—
Detroit—Exhibitions. I. Yale University Art Gallery. II. Detroit Institute
of Arts. III. High Museum of Art.
ND210.P75 1993
759.13'09'0340747468—dc20   93-17036
                                                             CIP

PRINTED IN THE UNITED STATES OF AMERICA

Contents

Directors' Foreword

"A Private View: American Paintings from the Manoogian Collection" is the second exhibition to focus on works drawn solely from the collection of Richard Manoogian. The first, "American Paintings from the Manoogian Collection," organized in 1989 by the Detroit Institute of Arts and the National Gallery of Art, revealed the extraordinary comprehensiveness of this great private holding. The present exhibition takes a closer look at those works which are more personal in nature, paintings that Richard and Jane Manoogian live with in their home. Some were included in the first show; others were selected specifically for this exhibition. Curators at the Detroit Institute of Arts and Yale University Art Gallery chose these examples to illuminate the more private choices of a successful American industrialist who is also acknowledged as a superb connoisseur. The collection reveals Richard Manoogian's profound belief in the unique character, diversity, and quality of American art.

The exhibition was initiated and coorganized by Helen A. Cooper, Holcombe T. Green Curator of American Paintings and Sculpture at the Yale University Art Gallery, and Nancy Rivard Shaw, Curator of American Art at the Detroit Institute of Arts. We are grateful to them, to The High Museum of Art, Atlanta, and its director, Edward Rifkin, for their interest in sharing the show with us, and to the many individuals, including the contributors to the catalogue and doctoral candidates at Yale, who worked so tirelessly to bring this project to fruition. Their names and contributions are gratefully recognized in the acknowledgments that follow.

At Yale, the exhibition coincides with Richard Manoogian's thirty-fifth Yale College reunion. It is therefore an added privilege to be able to share this beautiful exhibition with his classmates.

Above all, we are indebted to Richard and Jane Manoogian for their generous willingness to part with these cherished works of art.

MARY GARDNER NEILL
The Henry J. Heinz II Director
Yale University Art Gallery

SAMUEL SACHS II
Director
Detroit Institute of Arts

Preface

Several years ago Richard Manoogian was asked why he collects American art in particular. "Consciously or unconsciously, collecting American paintings is important to me in a special way," he replied. "Those from an ethnic background like mine often have a great appreciation for America because of the opportunity this country has created for their families. The result is a deep love for one's country and a particular appreciation for the period in which the country grew and expanded. A love for one's country also instills a desire to give something back to it. I have lent paintings to many exhibitions. To some extent my collecting has been driven by wanting to share my paintings with others as a way of giving something back to the country that has been so good to our family."

Mr. Manoogian began collecting American art seriously in the 1970s after he became a trustee of the Detroit Institute of Arts and was also appointed to the White House Preservation Committee and the Fine Arts Committee at the State Department. His business interests regularly took him to New York and other major cities, where he would steal an hour or two away from meetings to visit museums and galleries, a practice he continues to the present day, often making a special trip somewhere to see just a single work of art.

His first acquisitions were in the field of contemporary art, as he was drawn to the color and form in works by Jackson Pollock, Frank Stella, Franz Kline, and David Smith. Ultimately, however, he found his greatest collecting pleasure in nineteenth-century American art: landscapes that reflect the energy of a young and growing nation; genre pictures that record a now vanished way of life; trompe l'oeil still lifes that, in their precision and detail, celebrate the skill of the master craftsman; light-filled impressionist views. It is an art that speaks of the goodness of life and the perfection of nature.

The Manoogian Collection is broader and larger than most present-day American collections. It follows in the proud tradition of earlier private collections of American art formed by Luman Reed and Robert Gilmor in the first half of the nineteenth century, Thomas B. Clarke at the end of the century, and Maxim Karolik in the mid-twentieth century. Like those notable predecessors, Richard Manoogian has championed the art of his own country with unflagging enthusiasm, knowledge, and loyalty. His collection is remarkable for its range and diversity. While it is principally nineteenth-century in date, it spans the period from the early nineteenth to the early twentieth centuries and includes superb objects from every decade. It ranges from creations by the best-known artists — such as Thomas Cole, Albert Bierstadt, Thomas Moran, Raphaelle Peale, Martin Johnson Heade, John Singer Sargent, William Merritt Chase, and Childe Hassam, many of whom are represented in the present exhibition — to works by lesser-known artists — such as Samuel Carr, Robert Spear Dunning, Otis Kaye, and Otto Stark, whose abilities are just now being recognized. What unites these works of art is their exceptional quality.

Although he has said that his desire is to build a comprehensive collection — and the collection as it exists today has largely achieved this goal — Mr. Manoogian admits that his acquisitions are dictated more by his passion for a particular work of art than by a systematic approach to filling gaps. While he has sought the advice of curators and listened to the arguments of dealers, in the end he has relied on his own "eye" and on the taste and judgment of his wife, Jane. They have brought together what appeals to them on an aesthetic and emotional level, and in doing so have created a collection of great beauty, to which this exhibition eloquently attests.

Visitors to the major 1989 exhibition of the Manoogian Collection organized by the National Gallery and the Detroit Institute of Arts may be surprised by the intimacy of the present selection. In choosing the thirty-seven works of art for "A Private View: American Paintings from the Manoogian Collection," we focused primarily on the art that the Manoogians live with in their home, on those objects that seemed best to reflect their individual and personal taste. Generally smaller in size and more intimate in scale than many of the works in the earlier exhibition, they have a vivid, life-affirming quality. Hung in prominent spots throughout the house or in out-of-the-way alcoves, each painting, watercolor, and pastel reveals Richard and Jane Manoogian's taste for objects that convey a sense of serenity and the optimism and promise of an earlier age.

HELEN A. COOPER
NANCY RIVARD SHAW

Acknowledgments

Both this catalogue and the exhibition draw on the efforts of many individuals. We owe warmest thanks to Greer Allen and Ken Scaglia, who designed the catalogue, and to Barbara Wells Folsom, who edited the manuscript. The superb photographs were produced by Dirk Bakker. We owe particular thanks to Joan Barnes, Registrar of the Manoogian Collection, who was unfailingly helpful and gracious, and to Carl Anderson of Masco Corporation, who assisted in handling and shipping the works.

At the Yale University Art Gallery, we are indebted to Susan Frankenbach, Registrar, who worked with Suzanne Quigley, Head of Registration and Exhibitions at the Detroit Institute of Arts, in handling the many details. Richard Moore, Operations Manager, and his staff—Burrus Harlow, Nancy Valley, and Maishe Dickman—were helpful in every way. Sarah Buie's sensitive exhibition design allowed the works of art to be seen to great advantage. Beverly Rogers, Administrative Assistant, handled myriad details with care. Janet Dickson, Curator of Education, and Janet Gordon, Associate Curator of Education, organized a rich menu of public programs built around the exhibition; Marie Weltzien, Public Relations Coordinator, brought the exhibition and programs to the attention of a wide public.

At the Detroit Institute of Arts we are grateful to Barbara Heller and her conservation staff—particularly Alfred Ackerman, Valerie Baas, and Thomas Dickenson—who performed such treatment of the collection as was necessary for exhibition. James W. Tottis, Assistant Curator of American Art, assisted with general administrative details.

Special appreciation goes to Robin Jaffee Frank, Assistant Curator of American Paintings and Sculpture at Yale, who was involved in the project from the beginning, and whose help during every phase of the catalogue's production has been invaluable. We want also to thank the Yale graduate students and interns who researched the material and wrote catalogue entries: Julia Alexander, Brian T. Allen, Bethany Astrachan, Martin A. Berger, Beth A. Handler, Alison Tilghman, Karl Emil Willers, and Mary Adair Woodall.

H. A. C.
N. R. S.

Contributors

Julia Alexander

Brian T. Allen

Bethany Astrachan

Martin A. Berger

Helen A. Cooper

Robin Jaffee Frank

Beth A. Handler

Nancy Rivard Shaw

Alison Tilghman

James W. Tottis

Karl Emil Willers

Mary Adair Woodall

Childe Hassam

1859–1935

County Fair, New England

1890
Oil on canvas
24 1/4 x 20 in. (61.6 x 50.8 cm)

Hassam has the reputation of being the American artist who most consistently followed the style of the French Impressionists in his own works. *County Fair, New England* well represents the kind of Impressionism he favored following his three-year stay in Paris, from which he returned in the fall of 1890. While in France, unlike most of his American compatriots studying there, Hassam avoided Giverny, the country retreat of the quintessential French Impressionist, Claude Monet. Although he never studied with the Impressionists, by the second year of his Parisian stay Hassam had begun to experiment with their sketchy brushwork and light palette.[1]

Hassam and the other Americans who consciously adopted Impressionism differed from their French contemporaries, who had by the 1880s increasingly moved away from figure painting. Hassam and his colleagues remained steadfastly attached to the figure in their images. Only in the late 1890s did the Americans begin to abandon the figure in order to focus on landscape. Thus, in terms of subject matter, *County Fair* more closely resembles early French Impressionist pictures from the late 1860s and early 1870s, in which artists like Monet chose to paint bustling crowds in congenial settings rather than unpopulated landscapes. Hassam's painting, both stylistically and compositionally, provides a good example of this "American" tendency to combine French techniques with an attachment to subject matter. The artist used his newly discovered impressionist techniques to glorify a typically American—more specifically, New England—subject: the county fair held in front of the town's meetinghouse.

Hassam had spent his childhood and adolescence in Dorchester, Massachusetts, where the New England landscape and customs dominated his early experiences. First as an illustrator and later as a painter, he was dedicated to capturing the beauty and character of his native region and its people. In writing to a friend, he described the impact of the New England architecture on his childhood and his vision of life:

[the white churches of New England are] masterpieces of architecture; and the white church on Meeting House Hill [in Dorchester] as I look back on it was no exception . . . unconsciously, I as a very young boy looked at this New England church, and without knowing it, appreciated partly its great beauty as it stood there against one of our radiant New England clear blue skies.[2]

In *County Fair*, a festive, well-dressed crowd is massed in front of a typical Protestant church. Red, white, and blue banners and flags adorn the plain white facade. Although a specifically New England atmosphere pervades the picture, Hassam does not particularize the building: no element of the church's architecture—its square spire, its triangular pediment, the plain rectangular windows, and the brightly whitewashed clapboard facade—endows it with any individual character. By not identifying the building through the inclusion of architectural details, Hassam transforms this simple church into a symbol of the essential, clear, and powerful beauty and traditions of New England.

The scene's "American-ness" is underscored by its primarily red, white, and blue palette. While the community church, the tightly packed crowd, and the patriotic colors convey continuity and strength, Hassam's quick brushwork and broken color imbue the setting with flickering light and movement. Glistening gold and red leaves, created by thick daubs of pure color, cover the grass in the foreground. The figures in the crowd are patches of primarily blue and white pigment. The white tent at the right seems to dissolve under bright sunlight. The white meetinghouse, the very foundation of the community, shimmers and seems to fade in and out of the clear, light-blue sky behind it. Flags and banners, symbols of celebration and the history of America, are rendered by strokes of red, white, and blue paint. Short, vivid brushstrokes fuse to make the entire image a glowing representation of a passing moment. Although the painting glorifies the solidity of American life and culture, the impressionist techniques Hassam used to describe this image serve to enhance its beauty, even its power, by evoking the immediacy of the moment.

JULIA ALEXANDER

1 Ironically, by the time of his return to New York in 1890, Hassam had so thoroughly incorporated these "impressionist" techniques into his own style that he began to be seen as a close follower of Monet; throughout his life the American vehemently refused to acknowledge this association with the older French artist. See Adeline Adams, *Childe Hassam* (New York: American Academy of Arts and Letters, 1938), 48.
2 Quoted in ibid., 90.

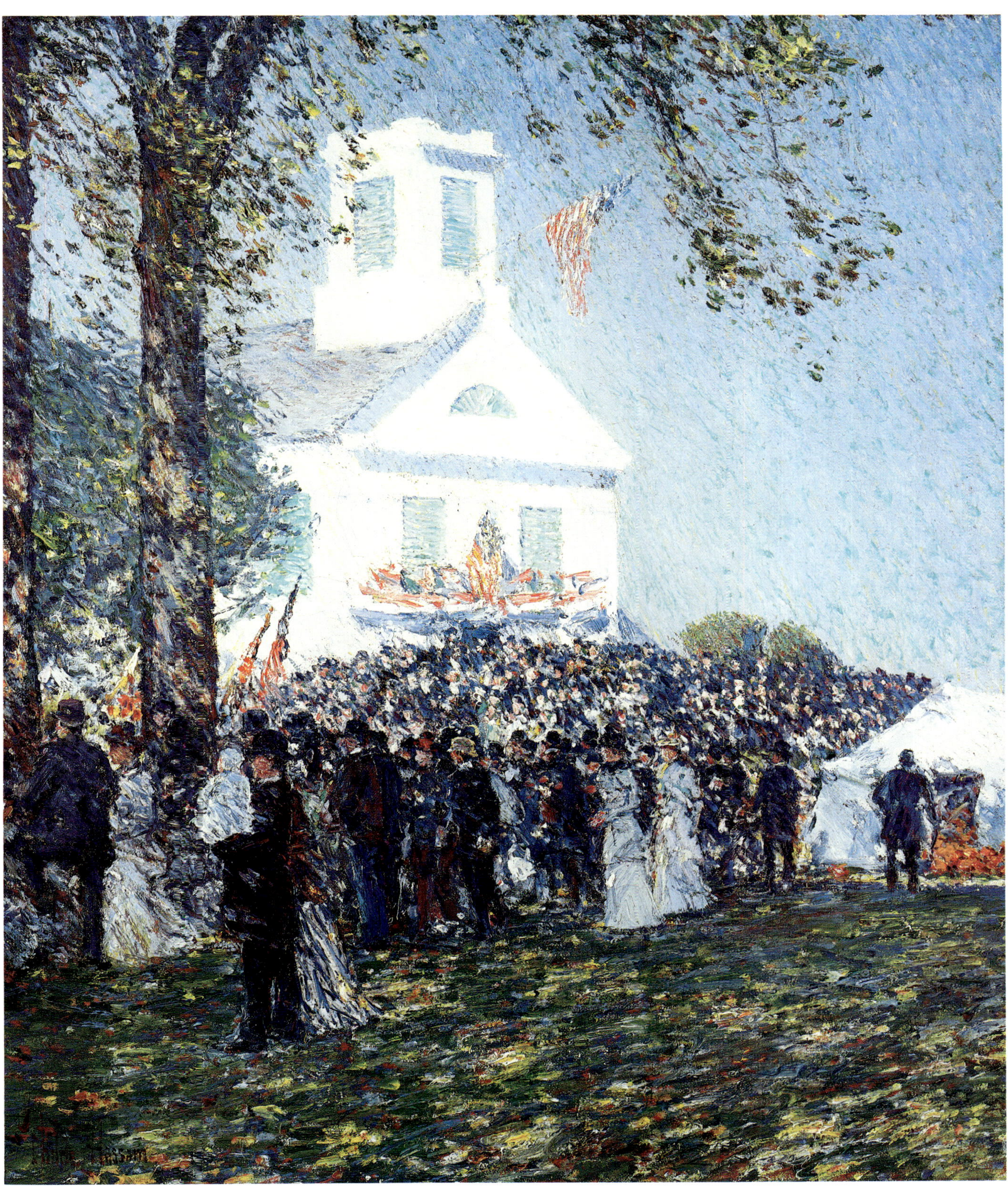

William Glackens

1870–1938

Little May Day Procession

1905
Oil on canvas
25 x 30 in. (63.5 x 76.2 cm)

While Robert Henri, John Sloan, George Luks, Everett Shinn, and the other Ashcan artists were engaged in immortalizing the lower classes of New York City, Glackens's attention was drawn to the leisure activities of the emerging middle class. He felt that the new realism, expounded by Robert Henri, need not be expressed solely through scenes that looked to the alleys or tenements for inspiration. Instead, he expressed his version of this new realism in his views of the parks and cafés frequented by New Yorkers. This attraction to the world at play is conveyed in his 1905 painting *Little May Day Procession*, one of three works he painted that year documenting the May celebration. The others were *Maypole, Central Park* (Private Collection) and *May Day, Central Park* (The Fine Arts Museums of San Francisco).[1]

New York's Central Park was the location for the popular turn-of-the-century spring event of May Day, which served as the inauguration of the more hospitable seasons. For New Yorkers, it provided the ideal natural setting for this spring festival. The park had been designed by Frederick Law Olmsted with assistance from Calvert Vaux in 1858. Olmsted had been a bit of a soothsayer with his pre–Civil War prediction of the important role the park would play for future generations.[2] Glackens was naturally drawn to such a place, and an event such as May Day provided the perfect opportunity to paint the populous in a park setting.

From the time of his marriage to Edith Dimock in 1904 and throughout his career, Glackens was extremely interested in parklike settings for his outdoor subjects. Examples range from his work in the Luxembourg Gardens to the multitude of beach and resort scenes he painted. During this early period his work was still influenced by Henri; however, his style gradually changed after his 1906 trip to France, where the work of Pierre-Auguste Renoir was to have a profound effect upon his canvases.

For Glackens, Central Park provided a suitable backdrop for the urban tableaux of his early career. In *Little May Day Procession*, the rich greens and saturated yellow tones of the foliage serve as a perfect foil to the bright white garments of the foreground figures. The participants in the parade are depicted in blue, while the focal point of the celebration, the girl carrying the multicolored maypole, is dressed in white. This palette is basically repeated in Glackens's other two May Day paintings and is similar to the Luxembourg painting of the following year. The loose, quick brushstrokes typical of these canvases endow the figures and foliage with a sense of motion.

Glackens's interest in Central Park began about 1904 and continued for approximately ten years. *The Drive, Central Park* (Cleveland Museum of Art), *Central Park, Winter* (The Metropolitan Museum of Art), and *Skaters in Central Park* (Mount Holyoke College), all demonstrate his obsession with the pleasanter side of park life. The importance of the May Day paintings for Glackens is evident in a series of letters he wrote to his wife, Edith. On April 25, 1906: "Weir has been around to see me about the sale for the benefit of the San Francisco artists. I have promised to contribute a picture and frame." He continues, "I don't mind giving the picture but I hate to part with a frame. . . ." On May 1 he again wrote to Edith: "I haven't as yet decided on what picture to send. I was thinking of sending the other May Day, the one with the procession. I have been trying to paint one. A Washington Square with the fountain." Then, on May 2, he wrote, "I have decided to send *The Little May Day Procession* and have been gilding one of those old Curly frames."[3] It is clear that Glackens wished to be represented by a park scene. In the end, he could not paint one to his satisfaction in time for the exhibition and auction at the American Art Galleries. Therefore he chose this work, emblematic of his early style, to be shown alongside those of his contemporaries.

JAMES W. TOTTIS

1 All three canvases bear the same dimensions, 25 x 30 inches.
2 In discussing his plans for the park, Olmsted wrote: "The time will come when New York will be built up, when all the grading and filling will be done, and when the picturesquely varied, rocky formations of the Island will have been converted into formations for rows of monotonous straight streets and piles of erect buildings. There will be no suggestion left of its present varied surface, with the single exception of the few acres contained in the Park. Then the priceless value of the present picturesque outlines of the ground will be perceived, and its adaptability for its purpose more fully recognized." Elizabeth Barlow, *Frederick Law Olmsted's New York* (New York: Praeger Publishers, 1972), 21.
3 Ira Glackens, *William Glackens and the Ashcan Group: The Emergence of Realism in American Art* (New York: Crown Publishers, 1957), 65.

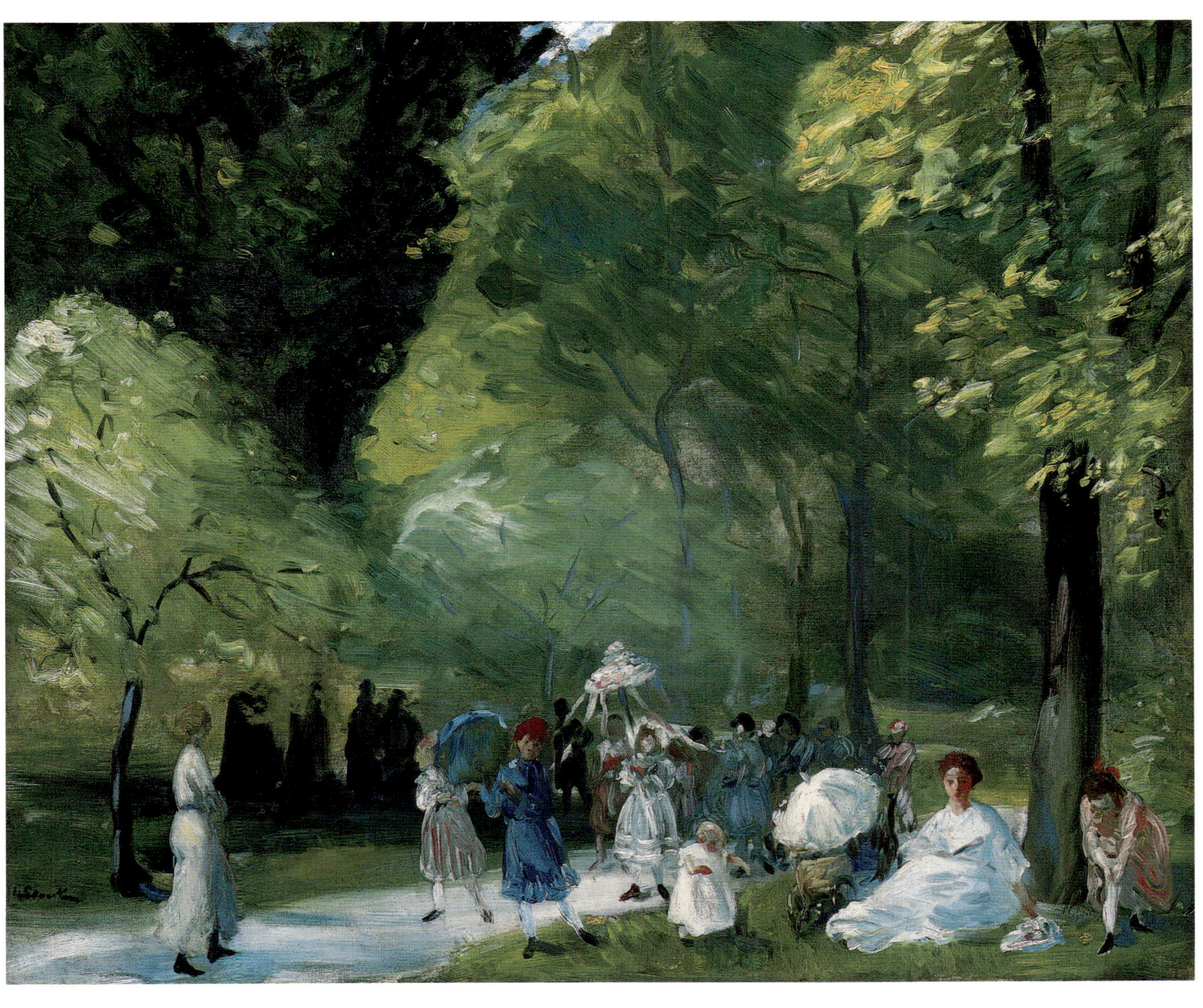

Samuel S. Carr

1837–1908

Picnic Scene in the Woods

n.d.
Oil on panel
9 ³/4 x 18 in. (24.8 x 45.7 cm)

Little information exists about Carr's life and training. Born in England, he emigrated to the United States before 1865, when he enrolled in a mechanical-drawing class at Cooper Union, New York City. Never married, he lived in Brooklyn with his sister and brother-in-law, apparently making a living through his art. During his lifetime, his paintings were exhibited at the Brooklyn Art Club, the Brooklyn Art Association, and the National Academy of Design.[1]

Picnic Scene in the Woods can be understood in the context of the nineteenth-century French tradition of the *déjeuner sur l'herbe*, or luncheon-on-the-grass pictures. In its admirable rendering of light filtering though a canopy of leaves, Carr's canvas bears a strong relationship to advanced European painting of the period. The grassy slope in this picnic scene, striated with alternating patches of sun and shade, indicates a concern with the specific effects of daylight and shadow in the open air also found in paintings by the French Impressionists and the Italian Macchiaioli. Carr's studied attention to the intricacies of costume underscores the significant role played by dress in defining the social class, respectability, and prestige of the painting's figures. The clothing not only establishes the bourgeois status of the individuals, but situates them in opposition to the rural setting. The marked difference between the looser execution of the picnic site and the meticulous definition of the figures' apparel also suggests an incongruity between the two.

Within Carr's Edenic scene of an afternoon picnic, the mythologies of unbridled sexuality are humorously played out against societal restrictions and the conventions of family life. In the far background, the image of a young girl on a swing—a traditional reference to sexual release—suggests an erotic subtext; the stance of the man in the distance opening a wine bottle as he holds it between his knees has obvious libidinous implications. The couple in the right foreground appear to be courting; their mutual attraction is humorously suggested by the phallic position of the gentleman's cane stuck in the fork of a nearby tree. The woman actually fondles a leaf directly in front of her male companion's groin, enforcing a sense of the pair's illicit desires. Admittedly outlandish to the point of bawdy humor, concealed allusions to erogenous body parts positioned at the painting's center hint at this image's natural and fleshy eroticism, symbolically obscured or even constricted by the mores of society.

The composition itself suggests the theatrical stage, while its division into paired groups mimics the classical dramatic structure of various actors in dialogue. Arranged symmetrically in the foreground, conversational duos play off each other to create a narrative progression. The intimately confiding pair of women and the romantically charged twosome of opposite sexes convey dissimilar moods—one pair of figures is somber and the other sporting. In an admirably succinct manner, a mix of vaudevillian slapstick and romantic melodrama is presented. The theatrical is embraced and encourages a consideration of the politics of gendered relations.

Through a compositional format remarkably akin to the techniques of realist cinema, *Picnic Scene in the Woods* suggests a space and reality beyond the painted image. Almost three times as wide as it is tall, the painting incorporates into its static frame the perspectives that film makes available in cinemascope or by panning the camera from side to side across a panorama. Cinematic images can also exploit an extended depth of field photography. Using camera lenses having a wide range of focus, extreme foregrounds and backgrounds can be juxtaposed within a single shot. Carr's pictorial exactness gives a similar impression of seeing far into the distance with great clarity. The deep and expansive natural space of *Picnic Scene in the Woods* surrounds and engulfs the painting's figures. The wooded grove dominates, covering far more of the painting's surface area than other pictorial elements. This prevailing presence of the landscape focuses attention on the confrontation between urban figures and rural setting, between the restrictions of civilization and the freedom of nature.

However, it may not be society's suppression of amorous impulses which Carr portrays here so much as the very flexibility of cultural proprieties to accommodate an essential eroticism. The complexity and ambiguity of this equation is never dismissed or forgotten in this work. In a manner more congruent with early-twentieth-century film technique than late-nineteenth-century avant-garde painting practice, Carr's work, with its oddly cohesive mixture of realism and theatricality, simultaneously embraces Impressionism's pictorial ambitions while rejecting—or even contradicting—many of its specific formal solutions.

KARL EMIL WILLERS

1 The available information on Carr's life is summarized in *S. S. Carr: American, 1837–1908*, exh. cat., with an essay by Deborah Chotner and foreword by Charles Chetham (Northampton, Mass.: Smith College Museum of Art, 1976).

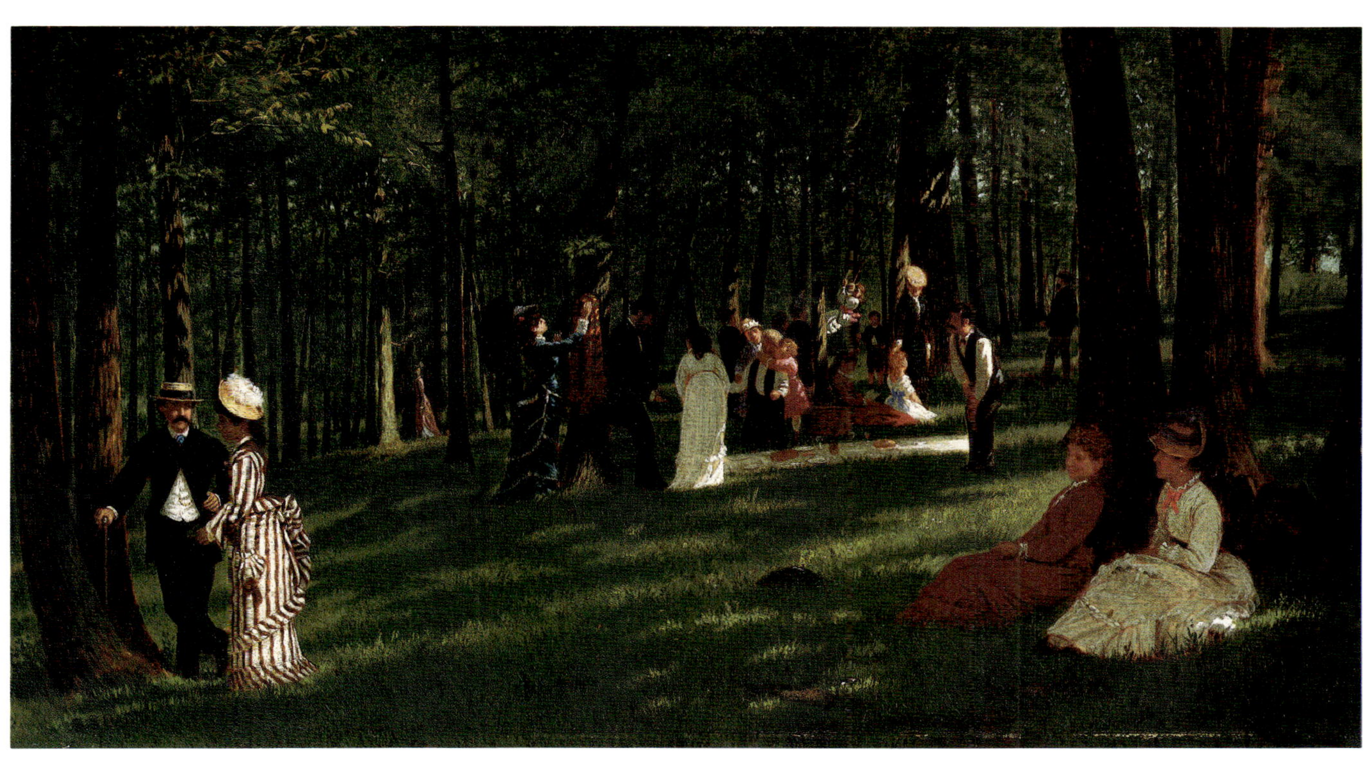

Robert Lewis Reid

1862–1929

Reverie

1890
Oil on canvas
11 ⁷/₈ x 20 ¹/₈ in. (30 x 51 cm)

Broadly and loosely painted, *Reverie* stands out in Reid's oeuvre as an exploration of new techniques and perhaps even as a harbinger of the decorative style so characteristic of his mature work. It is one of the few known works executed between the time of his return from Paris to New York in 1889 and the beginning of his commitment to mural painting in 1892–93.[1]

In 1880 Reid began his art education at the School of the Museum of Fine Arts in Boston, and after going to New York for a year, in 1885, he left for four years of study in Paris. His paintings from his early career and before 1890, the year in which he painted *Reverie*, exhibit an academic and traditional sensibility. Especially during his years in Paris from 1885 to 1889, Reid had apparently conformed to a conventional aesthetic of solid figures placed in a realistic setting, often evoking sentimental themes. By the time of his return to the United States from France in 1890, however, the artist clearly had moved away from these traditional subjects and methods of painting which had been encouraged by his French teachers at the Académie Julian, Gustave Boulanger and Jules-Joseph Lefebvre. *Reverie* represents one of Reid's earliest attempts to incorporate impressionist techniques into his own work.

Like many of his painter friends from his Boston years—such as Frank Benson or Edmund Tarbell—Reid often depicted women at leisure in an outdoor setting. *Reverie* belongs to this group of images so popular with the American public during the 1880s and 1890s. Yet, more so than many of his American colleagues (and, in fact, more like the French Impressionists), Reid chose here to employ broken brushstrokes and bright, shimmering colors in order to create an atmosphere of spontaneity and intimacy. Unlike the French artists who, by the 1890s, increasingly had moved to landscape as their primary motif, Reid, like many of his compatriots also toying with impressionist techniques, retained a strong sense of the figure.

In *Reverie* the artist placed his fashionably dressed model in the center of his composition among three birch trees that divide the image into three sections: the outer two, empty and quiet; the central one, sheltered and focused. The middle area of the composition thus becomes a serene nest into which the figure, a beacon of color, immediately pulls the viewer's eye. Although Reid placed her in the center of the canvas, thereby making her the focal point, he did not distinguish the sitter's facial features. Rather, through thick brushstrokes, he transformed her into a soft cloud of pink, a flowerlike figure at one with the landscape. Calmly poised in the cool shade of the birch trees that protect her from the emptiness of the outer edges of the canvas, she becomes a physical representation of private, self-absorbed contemplation. Just adjacent to her head and directly in the center of the canvas, a bright patch of blue draws the viewer's eye away from her and out through the dense, overhanging leaves. The figure itself thus leads the spectator's eye to this patch of bright light and, perhaps, even encourages it to move beyond the foreground to the distant and unclear horizon.

In *Reverie*, unlike in his later, more decorative works, Reid did not confine his sitter to the role of mere decorative element in the composition. Rather, he assigned her a specific and even crucial role in the viewer's participation in and enjoyment of the work. Paradoxically, the woman's act of reading roots her in her physical environment yet at the same time transports her to a higher state of contemplation; similarly, her image first entices the viewer deep into the image and then guides him out again to contemplate his own reveries.

JULIA ALEXANDER

1 H. Barbara Weinberg, "Robert Reid: Academic 'Impressionist,'" *Archives of American Art Journal* 15 (January 1975): 11; William H. Gerdts, *American Impressionism* (New York: Abbeville Press, 1984).

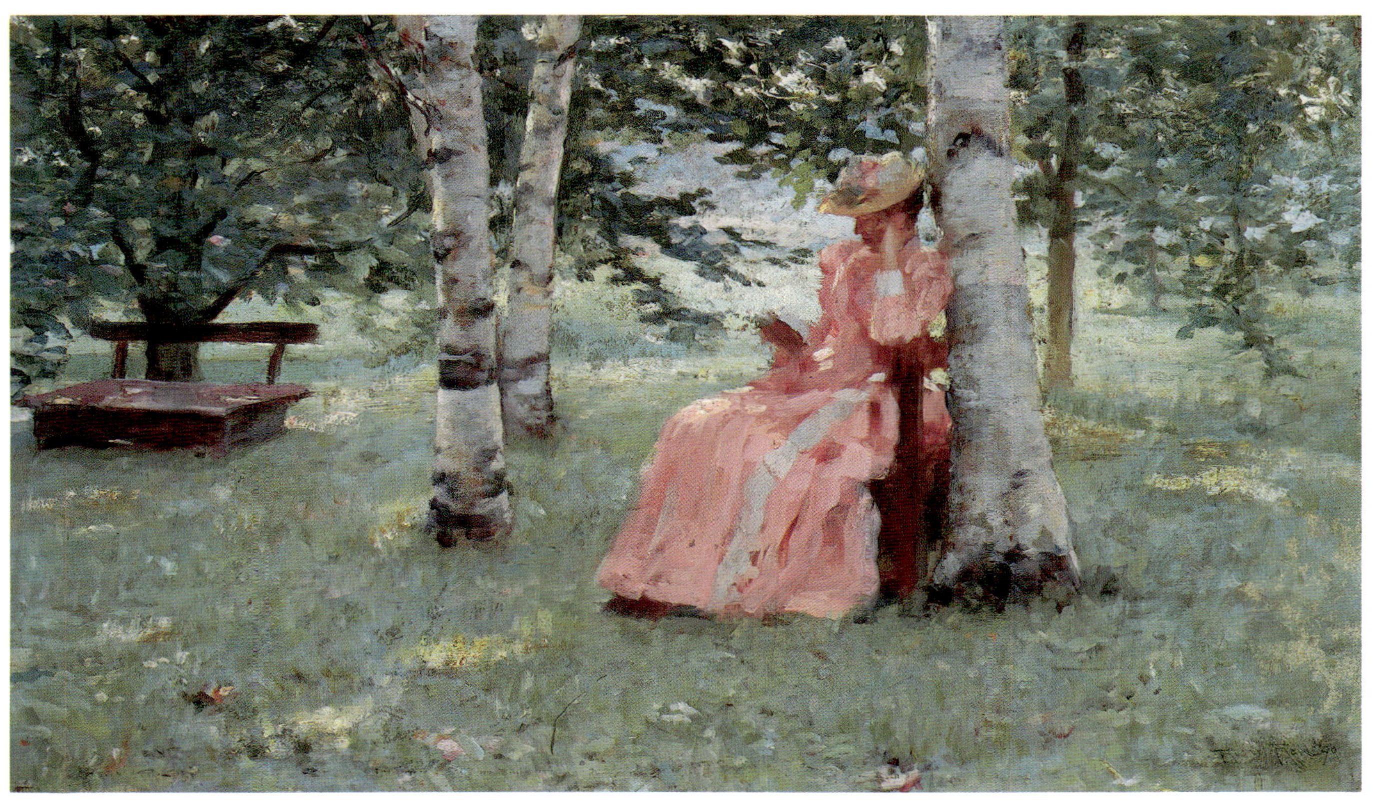

Reverie 19

Childe Hassam

1859–1935

A Paris Nocturne

1889/1890
Oil on canvas
27 1/2 x 20 in. (70 x 51 cm)

Throughout his career, Hassam sought to capture on canvas not only the everyday aspects of city life but also the particular characteristics of the specific culture he was depicting. His three-year sojourn in Paris between 1886 and 1889 proved especially fruitful in providing him with stimulating views of European city life. In addition to depicting a Parisian street-scene, *A Paris Nocturne* combines traditional, academic techniques with the more innovative impressionist style. Furthermore, this combination of pictorial styles with its theme of urban leisure activity and nocturnal setting places the painting within a group of images portraying the moral ambiguities inherent in turn-of-the-century Parisian nightlife.

The paintings Hassam executed while studying in Paris reflect the emphasis he placed on the ability to portray figures. Not coincidentally, in *A Paris Nocturne* the artist gives the figures importance equal to, if not greater than, the urban landscape, by making them the focus of his composition and by clearly delineating their forms. In spite of his renewed interest in figures, however, Hassam did not abandon certain techniques he had favored before coming to France. In his early oils painted in Boston, he had experimented with tonalist techniques, in which washes of one or more colors seem to dominate the entire canvas; the pink, violet, and yellow tones in *A Paris Nocturne* are reminiscent of these tonalist images of the mid-1880s. Furthermore, the bright, flat color area in front of the flower-stand in the lower left half of the composition and the high contrast between the pinkish sidewalk and the dark dress of the central figure reflect Hassam's interest in strong contrasts of light and dark.

Yet *A Paris Nocturne* exhibits the undeniable influence of impressionist techniques, to which Hassam had been exposed as early as 1886 in America and, later, in Paris. The sketchy brushstrokes and broken colors of Impressionism are evident in the leaves on the trees and in the flowers and orange trees to the left of the central figure. Loose brushstrokes create the central figure's shadow, while touches of impasto represent flowers and reflections of light glimmering on the apparently wet sidewalk beneath her.

Just as he combined traditional and impressionist painting techniques in *A Paris Nocturne*, so Hassam fused academic and avant-garde subject matter. In this, he was following the lead of certain of his French predecessors and contemporaries who conflated traditionally acceptable subjects with

more ambiguous aspects of contemporary life. In the 1860s and 1870s, painters such as Edouard Manet and Edgar Degas had used scenes of everyday Parisian life as a means to further their purposely anti-academic aims. By the late 1880s, the portrayal of daily life in Paris, especially its colorful nightlife, had become a suitable subject not only for the avant-garde but for the academic artist.

Paintings of fashionably dressed women in social settings—at elegant dinner parties, having tea in their homes, or engaged in the social stroll on the boulevards—had become popular by the mid-1870s. Such images were regarded as "morally ambiguous," because the fine line between "nice" Parisian women and prostitutes or courtesans had become increasingly blurred since the beginning of the Second Empire.[1] Women of good social standing, in an extremely class-conscious society, had previously distanced themselves from those less fortunate than they through the medium of fashion. However, with the ever-growing department-store culture, which had emerged from the ready-to-wear fashion industry, physical appearance or dress no longer distinguished the "good" from the "bad." Painters like the Belgian artist Alfred Stevens or the Frenchman Jacques Joseph Tissot played on this ambiguity by depicting seemingly upper-class women in somewhat compromising settings. The European public of the fin-de-siècle eagerly devoured these somewhat licentious images, creating a huge and lucrative market for such art.

A Paris Nocturne belongs to this socially ambiguous genre. The artist presents the viewer with an open, pinkish foreground out of which rises a fashionably dressed Parisienne, the type of woman made famous by painters like Stevens and Tissot. The bright lights cast by industrial gaslight glowing in a yellow, orange, and pink speckled band above the crowd, the kiosk lit from inside, and the shining, smooth pavement dominating the foreground of the image combine to create an aura of artificiality that permeates the atmosphere. Hassam's decision to exploit the nocturnal, and therefore man-made, light heightens the enigmatic atmosphere of an everyday street-scene.

Furthermore, the figures' lack of individuality lends the setting a strong sense of anonymity. Only the women's hats display any hint of personal taste or individuality, and even these resemble one another, thereby implying the "fashionable," aspect of their dress. Although the stylishness of the dresses of the two female figures might suggest that they

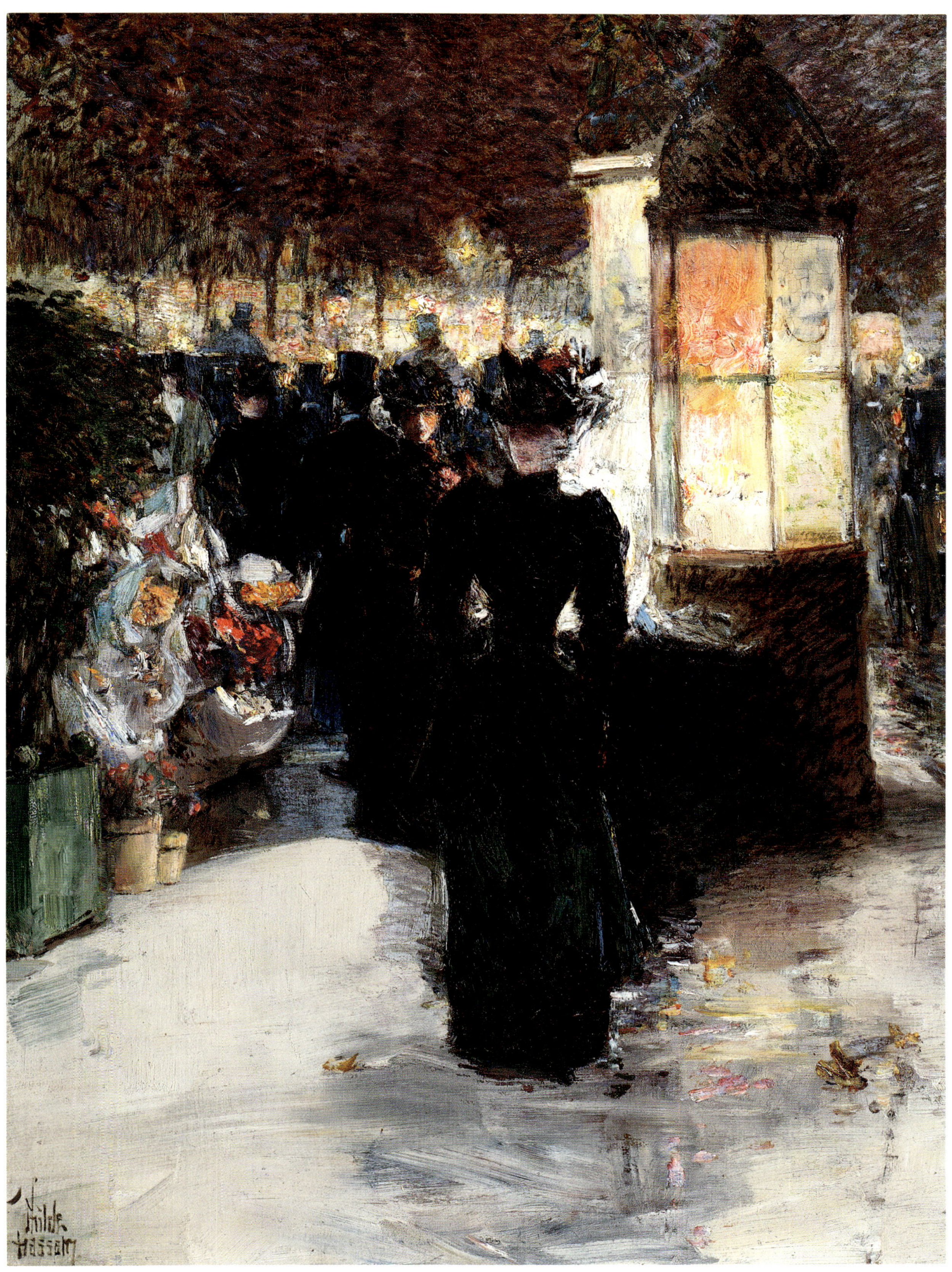

A Paris Nocturne   21

belong to the upper social classes, in fact, their apparel is an unreliable guide, as such fashions were readily available to a wide market in the department stores. Thus, the physical appearance of the central figure raises questions about her exact role in the scene.

She stands rigidly upright in a brightly lit area of the sidewalk, seeming not to be in transit from one area to another. Her solitary position and anticipatory expression, just visible behind her gauze veil, contribute to the sense that she has placed herself on display, perhaps while awaiting someone's arrival. Thrust forward by the flat and glaring bluish-pink sidewalk on which she stands, by the speckled and colored line that outlines her, and by the brilliant white light of the kiosks that silhouette her, she begins to resemble a flat, dark cut-out doll pasted in the center of the canvas. Her pink face, radiating from behind the veil, echoes—both in color and texture—one of the posters in the kiosks behind her. The woman next to the kiosk in the middle ground, who is apparently watching her, becomes yet another visual clue suggesting that, like the posters, the central figure is there to be observed. Thus, through stylistic and compositional techniques, Hassam transforms his central figure into an anonymous urban decoration much like the posters and flowers that fill the background. More than a description of urban nightlife, *A Paris Nocturne* is an image of a woman on display.

JULIA ALEXANDER

1 For a comprehensive discussion of the social history of Impressionist art, with particular attention to the depiction of women, see Robert L. Herbert, *Impressionism: Art, Leisure, and Parisian Society* (New Haven and London: Yale University Press, 1988); Timothy J. Clark, *The Painting of Modern Life: Paris in the Art of Manet and His Followers* (Princeton, N.J.: Princeton University Press, 1986).

William Merritt Chase

1849–1916

The Nursery

1890
Oil on panel
14 3/8 x 16 in. (36.5 x 40.6 cm)

The dozens of small paintings Chase executed *en plein air* in New York City's public parks between 1886 and the early 1890s were his first sustained efforts at landscape. With these works, he embarked on a new path, one that would eventually lead him from the urban gardens to the more rural setting of Shinnecock, Long Island, where he founded the first formal summer school in America where students painted out-of-doors, directly from nature.

The urban park—and, more generally, figures in an outdoor setting—had been a long-standing subject for the French Impressionists whom Chase admired. Most public gardens they depicted were populated by elegantly dressed women in self-absorbed attitudes. In Chase's painting of the Central Park nursery, the seated model wears refined attire, but her relaxed posture is unselfconscious. His "treatment of the human figure in a bright, unhackneyed fashion" was noted by a contemporary critic, who also praised Chase as a "painter who has slowly won away from entangling alliances . . . in Paris" and "struck out a line for himself." The same critic noted Chase's originality in choosing spots "rarely troubled by any but special lovers of the Park."[1] Indeed, the nursery was described as seldom frequented except by those who lived nearby. Chase's scene is not immediately recognizable as a public place and possesses the intimacy of a private garden, not unlike the suburban gardens painted by many American and French Impressionists in their own backyards.

Chase's park scenes have also been compared to images of similar subjects by the Italian landscapist Giuseppe de Nittis, a friend of Degas whose paintings and pastels had a profound impact on Chase's work in the 1880s.[2] De Nittis favored dramatic diagonals but, like Chase, stopped short of the extreme deformation of space favored by Degas in urban scenes. In *The Nursery*, Chase observes the scene from an unusual viewpoint, with the receding lines of the building on the left and the cold frames on the right halted by the background screen of trees.

While some of his park scenes depict popular forms of recreation, such as the game of lawn tennis visible in the right distance of *The Park* (fig. 1), Chase's main interest is often an isolated woman who returns our gaze. In *The Nursery*, the dresses, gloves, and hair color of the women in the fore- and middle grounds appear to be identical; only their hats are different—suggesting that the same model may have posed for both figures. The standing woman wears the same hat worn by the model in *The Park*. Since Chase often posed

family members in his park paintings, the somewhat generalized model in *The Nursery* and *The Park* may well be his wife.

In both scenes, he used a pathway to beckon the viewer toward the seated woman and into the landscape. The empty area in front of her in *The Park* is more characteristic of his compositions, inviting us to enter the space unobstructed. In contrast, the foreground placement of the figure in *The Nursery* relates the viewer to the scene with an unaccustomed directness. Here, we must first pause and imaginatively participate in the limited narrative Chase presents to us, for the model bends forward, her bouquet extending into our path. She has an assertive quality, and her preoccupied facial expression makes her seem inaccessible, like real people in an urban environment. Thus, despite the intimate nursery setting and the bouquet in her hands, which makes her a kind of modern Flora, the picture is not sentimental. At once inviting and removed, urban and rural, *The Nursery* embodies the contrasting qualities of modern life as Chase, one of the most cosmopolitan American artists, understood it.

In the late nineteenth century, the park was considered an appropriate, safe place for an unaccompanied woman. Indeed, as one female visitor's comments make clear, women went there to be alone: "When I come to my Park, and get away from people and houses and discords, I feel Nature elevate me, strengthen me, fill me with a fresh courage and faith. I feel all these things with an overwhelming intensity."[3] For Chase, as for many others, Central Park's purpose was the regeneration of the human mind and spirit. His park scenes have an arrested quality, an emphasis on quiet existence rather than action.

In *The Nursery*, the flowers in the bouquet appear freshly cut, presumably from the cold frames by the sitter herself, who wears the appropriate wrist-length protective gloves. Held in her joined hands, the bright bouquet is set off against the neutral ground and takes on extreme importance near the center of the composition. These flowers serve as the coloristic key for the whole painting, creating a harmony of red, blue, and white that moves our eye through the scene. The filmy loveliness of the women's white dresses and the trimming on the seated woman's hat resemble the white blossoms. The outdoor setting allowed Chase to create a visual equivalent reflecting popular analogies drawn between women and flowers. White, the preferred color for women's clothing in Chase's landscapes, reflects the privileged social

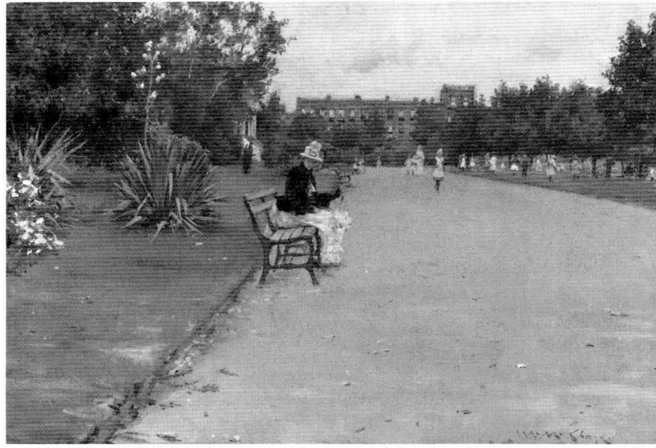

Fig. 1. William Merritt Chase, *The Park*, c. 1888,
oil on canvas, 13 5/8 x 19 5/8 in. (34.6 x 49.9 cm),
The Art Institute of Chicago, Bequest of Dr. John J. Ireland

status of the wearer, who need not concern herself with the laundering of her dress. The prevalence of women in park scenes by Chase and others suggests the social reality of men working while women enjoy idle hours; it is a world of separate spheres, in which women—like flowers—are seen as natural inhabitants of the garden, the realm of leisure and art.

Chase uses the diagonal lines of the cold frames and the spout of the watering can on the right to direct our eye toward the one man in the painting, a gardener bent over the cold frames in the distance. The plants he is nurturing will be transplanted in open borders of shrubberies in the park. The artist offers us a sequential experience, from the stooped gardener in the background, working; to the bending woman in the middle distance, admiring a large plant; to the seated lady in the foreground with her nosegay, the anticipated result of hard work and patient waiting. Chase shows the plantings in different stages of development—from the seedlings covered with protective glass, to the flowers just forcing their way out of the earth, to the beds that have gone to weed. Even the pattern of the receding frames conveys the sense of the rhythm of nature, a rhythm that life in the city tends to obscure.[4]

Chase's interest in the nursery coincided with a general upsurge in interest in Central Park's horticulture. The park's condition had deteriorated from 1875 to 1885, after which it improved, largely as a result of the efforts of the new superintendent of parks, Samuel Parsons, Jr. He was considered a "brilliant horiculturalist," and his tenure is often regarded as "a golden age of Central Park, a time when much of the vegetation had reached a well-cared for maturity."[5] Chase painted his park pictures at the beginning of this golden age.

By giving us this highly unusual behind-the-scenes view of a public place, Chase reveals that Central Park itself was a creative process, the nursery supplying the colors and textures with which the gardener, like a painter, continually transformed an imaginative vision into tangible reality. Indeed, Central Park's landscape architect, Frederick Law Olmsted, compared himself to an artist whose work remains forever unfinished: "It is a common error to regard a park as something produced as complete in itself, as a picture painted on canvas. It should rather be planned as one to be done

in fresco, with constant consideration of exterior objects, some of them quite at a distance and even existing as yet only in the imagination of the painter."[6] Here that sense of ongoing process is evident not just in the subject depicted, but also in the the looseness of Chase's rendering. Visible strokes of paint give life and feeling to the canvas. Chase's painting, like the largely artificial landscape design of Central Park, is a celebration of nature without being natural itself.

While many of his park settings correspond fairly closely to actual sites, others are known to be have been considerably altered. *The Park*, for example, is a composite view of Central and Prospect parks.[7] Chase may have altered the site in *The Nursery* as well.[8] The nursery was located in the northeast region of the park, between Harlem Meer and East Meadow. In Chase's painting, the red building on the left was probably used for storing or growing plants. A new glass conservatory was built in 1899 on the site of the present Conservatory Garden, located at 105th Street and Fifth Avenue. The old nursery beds—those depicted by Chase in 1890—were probably located slightly to the south.[9] Since there were more trees southwest of this site looking into the park, it seems likely that this is the view Chase painted in the background. Given the probable location of the building in the painting, however, we should be looking out toward Fifth Avenue.[10] He may have reversed the view to conform to his vision of the park as a place in which to escape the city.

The Nursery is thus a masterfully conceived fiction combining accurately rendered details with aesthetic invention. Taken together, Chase's park scenes do not offer historical documentation of Prospect and Central parks, but rather capture with feeling the *idea* of the urban garden, an idea more powerful than any literal transcription of the scenery would have been. No other painter has managed to represent so convincingly the elusive charm of New York's green garden at the turn of the century, that fragrant atmosphere which transports the viewer in *The Nursery*.

ROBIN JAFFEE FRANK

1   Charles De Kay, "Mr. Chase and Central Park," *Harper's Weekly* 35, no. 1793 (May 2, 1891): 328, 327.

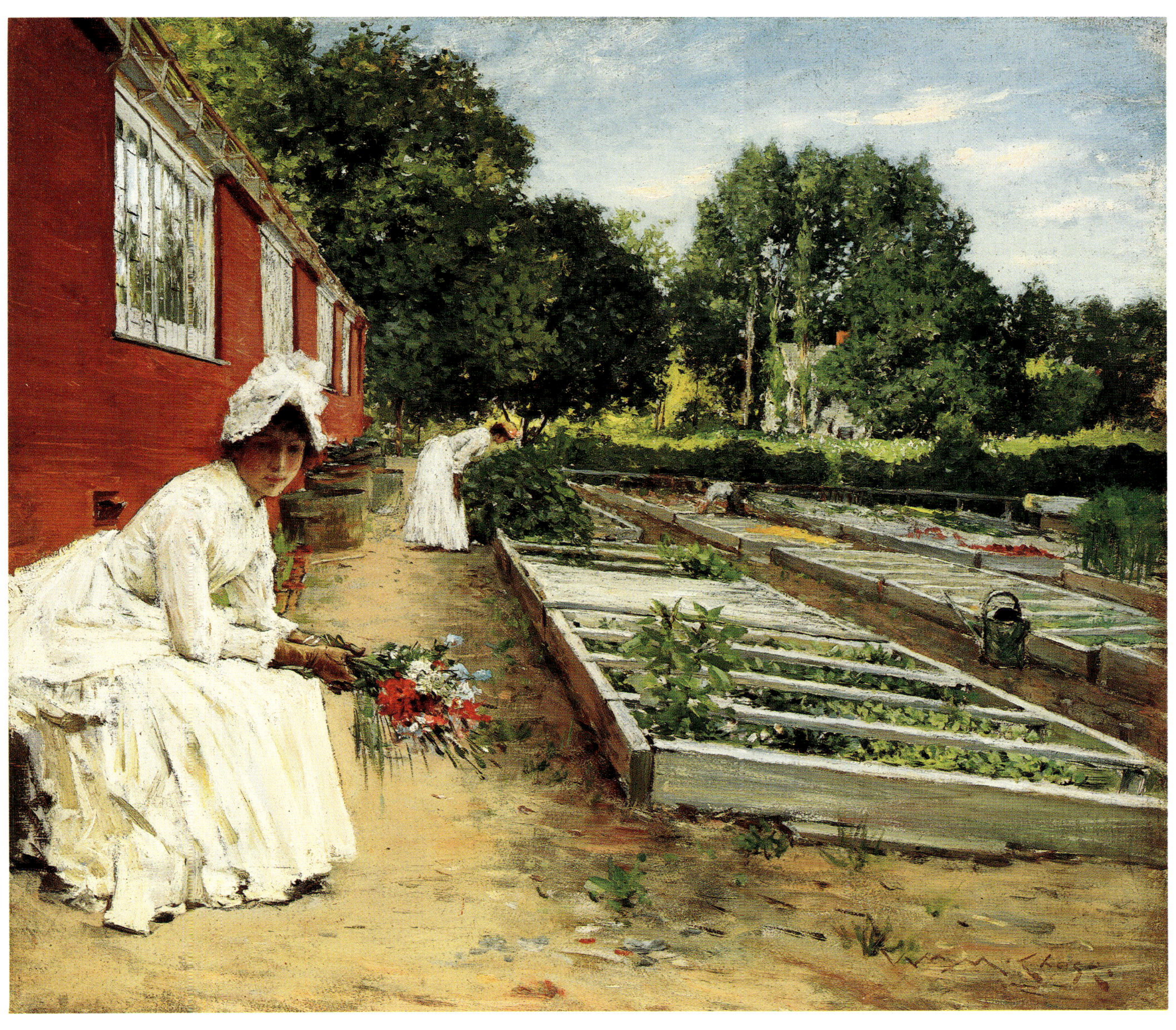

2 See Ronald G. Pisano, "William Merritt Chase, *The Nursery*," in
   American Paintings from the Manoogian Collection, exh. cat.
   (National Gallery of Art, Washington, D.C./ Detroit: Detroit
   Institute of Arts, 1989), 140–45. Pisano's entry on *The Nursery* is
   very perceptive.
3 Annie Nathan Meyer, *My Park Book*, 1898; quoted in Elizabeth
   Barlow, *Frederick Law Olmsted's New York* (New York: Praeger
   Publishers in association with the Whitney Museum of American
   Art, 1972), 112.
4 In literature and art, gardens have always been powerful settings
   for musings on human life. Chase's wife had given birth to
   three children in rapid succession following their marriage in 1886,
   around the time Chase began his paintings of New York's parks.
   This particular garden may have served as a place for the artist to
   reflect on his experience as a father, as the word *nursery* describes
   not only a place where plants are grown, but also a room set aside
   for children.
5 New York City Department of Parks and Recreation and Central
   Park Conservancy, Elizabeth Barlow Rogers, Principal Author,
   Rebuilding Central Park: A Management and Restoration Plan
   (Cambridge, Mass., and London, England: MIT Press, 1987), 56.
6 Barlow, 40.
7 Karen Zukowski, "William Merritt Chase," in *Paris 1889: American
   Artists at the Universal Exposition*, exh. cat. (Philadelphia and New
   York: Pennsylvania Academy of the Fine Arts in association with
   Harry N. Abrams, Inc., 1989), 127 and 254, n. 6.
8 I am indebted to Sara Cedar Miller, Photogapher and Historian,
   Central Park Conservancy, for discussing the location of the site
   with me and adding to my understanding of Chase's painting in
   the context of Central Park's history.
9 Louis Harriman Peet, *Trees and Shrubs of Central Park* (New York,
   1903), 325.
10 Sara Cedar Miller, in conversation.

Charles Courtney Curran

1861–1942

Chrysanthemums

1890
Oil on canvas
9 x 12 in. (22.9 x 30.5 cm)

Curran's depiction of a woman and young girl in a conservatory filled with potted chrysanthemums was painted in Paris; yet instead of a recognizable urban scene, the artist offers a private, intimate glimpse of a reflective moment. No storytelling concerns Curran or distracts us. He evokes only a mood that suggests a female, leisure-class world untouched by commercialism and industrialism. A contemporary reviewer praised Curran for selecting subjects "placid in conception, taken from everyday life. Free from the storms of passion, they are like oases in the parched desert of over-driven existence. One turns to them gratefully and sympathetically. They are mind-resters, though nevertheless they give us much for contemplation."[1] The oasis Curran created in *Chrysanthemums* and the artistic means by which he created it reveal much about the social and artistic aspirations of his era.

The same critic voiced a refrain frequently sounded in reviews of Curran's art: "The scenes which he paints are at once Ohio and Paris combined."[2] The midwestern artist's subjects and figure types were perceived as American, his technical virtuosity as French. However, the carefully controlled contours of the profiles, strong surface patterns, and harmonious arrangement of color in *Chrysanthemums* reveal an understanding of art history based on training acquired both at home and abroad.

Curran was an exceptionally fine draftsman who had studied at the Art Students League when Kenyon Cox was presiding over classes in the antique. Perhaps more than any other artist of his generation, Cox, through his teaching and writing, advocated the value of a thorough knowledge of the history of Western art—especially the precepts of classicism—for the contemporary artist.[3] By the time Curran left for Paris he was nearing maturity as a painter, having exhibited at New York's Academy of Design since 1883. In Paris, he exhibited at the Salon from 1889 to 1891 while studying at the Académie Julian with Jules-Joseph Lefebvre (1836–1912), whose receptivity to combining classical drawing with contemporary themes must have appealed to Curran. His academic study in Paris and exposure to contemporary French art confirmed the skills he had already developed and gave him the confidence to add bolder composition and color.

Throughout his career, Curran favored solidly drawn profiles, which reflected the mastery of the ideal human form he had achieved by drawing from casts, especially heads. Indeed, this process—the basis of his education at both the

League and the Académie—became the subject of *An Alcove in the Art Students' League*, painted just before he left for Paris (fig. 1).[4] In the right foreground is a plaster cast of an early Italian Renaissance bust in the Louvre.[5] Curran endowed the girl in *Chrysanthemums* with similar soft facial features radiating youthful innocence, while the stronger profile of the woman standing beside her resembles that of the adjacent Greek head. Thus, in *Chrysanthemums*, as in the earlier painting, Curran contrasted two orders of feminine beauty derived from classical and early Italian Renaissance art—but, Pygmalion-like, he transformed the casts into living models, dressed in formal daytime attire and situated in a Paris conservatory. Although his models wear contemporary dress, he made the ephemeral timeless through this subtle allusion to Athens and Florence.

Curran also conceived *Chrysanthemums* on new design principles discovered in Japanese art that suggested an approach to the depiction of contemporary life simultaneously realistic and decorative. He would have been exposed to oriental art in New York through his teachers at the League, including Cox, William Merritt Chase, and Thomas W. Dewing, who had already been to Paris, used oriental objects as accessories in their paintings, and assimilated elements of oriental design. In Paris, where the passion for oriental art was pervasive, Curran may have seen Utamaro's images of beautiful women at an exhibition of Japanese woodblock prints at the Ecole Nationale in 1890. In *Chrysanthemums*, Curran's understanding of the formal principles of Japanese prints is evident in the bold diagonal thrust of the composition, emphasized by the bars of the conservatory roof above, in opposition to the diagonal formed by the wooden box holding the pots of chrysanthemums below. To eliminate the illusion of depth, he used the repetitive bars and the profusion of flowers to create a patterned backdrop for the figures that unifies the composition on a flat surface. For him, as for many Impressionists and Post-Impressionists, the Japanese print was crucial to a translation of three-dimensional reality into two-dimensional pattern. Curran, along with other intellectuals in the closing decades of the nineteenth century, enthusiastically embraced Greek, early Italian Renaissance, and Japanese art as part of a broader cosmopolitanism in American life and art—the search for a new aesthetic in harmony with new cultural realities.

The image of female figures absorbed in quiet reflection and engaged in an aesthetic experience was explored by countless artists during the late nineteenth century. In its avoidance of sentimental anecdote, its appeal to the sensuous delight in the beautiful, its celebration of the subtle pleasures of sight and smell, *Chrysanthemums* is in accord with pictorial analogies between feminine and floral beauty by many French Impressionists and such American artists as William Merritt Chase and Childe Hassam.[6] However, Curran endows the model in *Chrysanthemums* and in another work painted in Paris in 1890, *Lady with a Bouquet (Snowballs)*, with individuality (fig. 2). The woman who posed for both images was his wife, Grace Wickham Curran.[7] In both Paris paintings, Curran not only particularized her features, but also used the reference to flowers to express faithfully the sitter's character. Grace's letters from Paris indicate a passion for ornamental flowers, as well as a knowledge of English and French gardening styles.[8]

Although the young girl posed next to Grace in *Chrysanthemums* has not been identified, in the fiction of the painting they appear to be related, and could even be read as mother and daughter because of their difference in age, physical proximity in a confined space, and equally fashionable dress. Their lack of any apparent social, emotional, or psychological bond is in accord with a typically urban demeanor akin to many of the women and children depicted by the French Impressionists, particularly Degas and Manet. This air of detachment marks Curran's painting as not only cosmopolitan but modern—fundamentally different from Victorian depictions of a woman and child, in which signs of affection would certainly have been made the subject of the painting. In Curran's own words, "The great actor does not express deep emotion by merely shouting loudly."[9] His characterization of the two actors in *Chrysanthemums* is achieved through nuance and gesture. The woman leans forward to smell a chrysanthemum held in her gloved hand; the young girl gazes down at the flowers, her youthfulness evident in her stance—a certain tentativeness in the way she touches the flower box without reaching for a flower.

The woman's charming gesture and the girl's downward gaze serve as compositional devices to bend the figures toward the flowers, but at the same time can be read as a symbolic equation between them and the flowers. The chrysanthemums emerge from their pots with their long stems gently bent; the female figures emerge from the green leaves of the tropical plant in the left foreground with their torsos gently bent. Seen against the flowers, the curls on the woman's forehead, as well as the feathers on her hat, and the young girl's soft hair brushing her shoulders, are

visually comparable to the wispy blossoms. The white flower the woman holds is in full bloom; the yellow flowers framing the girl's profile are in the process of unfolding, suggesting her progession toward womanhood. Thus the woman and child at once become the flowers and mediate our view of them.[10]

Although this conservatory may be a public place, it seems private because of the mother and child's psychological self-absorption—their seeming lack of awareness that they, like the flowers, are on exhibit in a cage of glass and iron. In *Chrysanthemums*, Curran directs our eye to the two bending figures through a series of diagonals: the long stems of the white chrysanthemums entering on the right, the side of the wooden box forming a strong diagonal in the bottom center, and the relentless rhythm of the iron bars across the top. Curran creates a tension between this containing geometric structure, a product of industry translated into art, and the living forms of the figures and flowers on display within it. This tension echoes a larger opposition between man—often the creator of both industry and art—as culture, and woman as nature.[11] Perhaps this association of women with nature in part accounts for the fact that Curran, like so many painters of women and flowers in his era, identifies in his title only the flowers—chrysanthemums—indicating that on some level they are interchangeable with the female figures.

Chrysanthemums as a subject were no doubt deliberately chosen for their fashionable aura. In American gardens, they rivaled roses in popularity.[12] A contemporary French gardening manual proclaimed that the chrysanthemum, "raised by the Chinese to a rare degree of perfection, has become all the rage in Europe ever since horticulturists have taken to sowing its seeds and developing varieties with a wide range of hues."[13]

The spate of European and American flower paintings in the latter half of the nineteenth century must be viewed in the cultural context of an unprecedented passion for cultivated nature, manifest in the rise of numerous public parks and private gardens during a period of rapid industrialization. As the leisure class grew, creating a garden as an art form became a mark of cultural status. The air of breeding displayed by the woman and girl in *Chrysanthemums* defines them as members of the leisure class. Making and contemplating ornamental gardens, like making and contemplating art, "was recognized as a civilized and civilizing activity."[14] And it was women's role to civilize. Curran's decision to

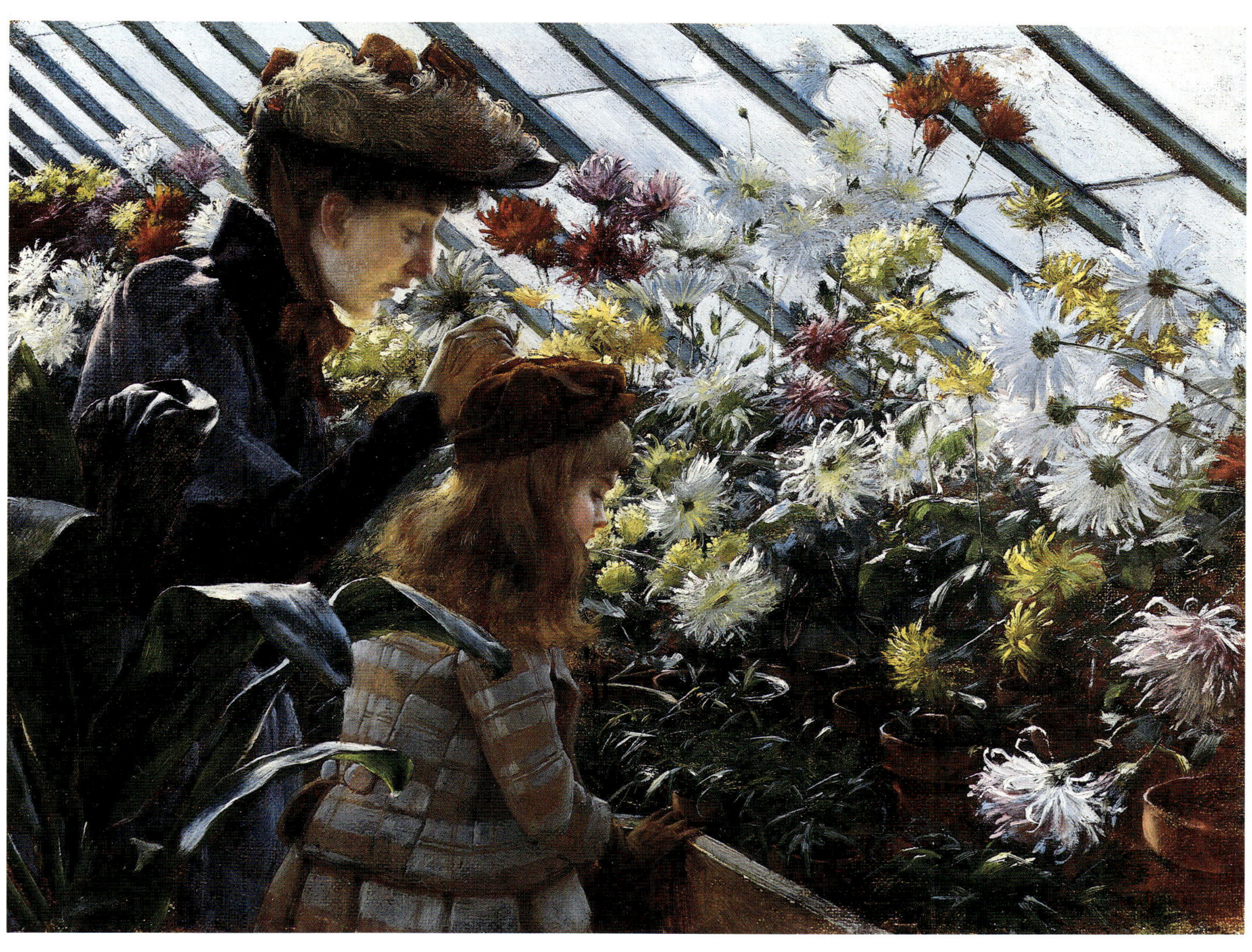

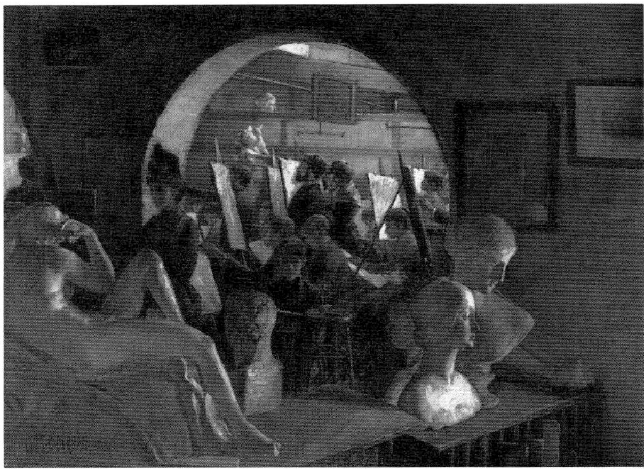

Fig. 1. Charles Courtney Curran, *An Alcove in the Art Students' League*, 1888, oil on canvas, 8 1/2 x 11 1/2 in. (21.6 x 29.2 cm), The Art Institute of Chicago, Bequest of Kate L. Brewster

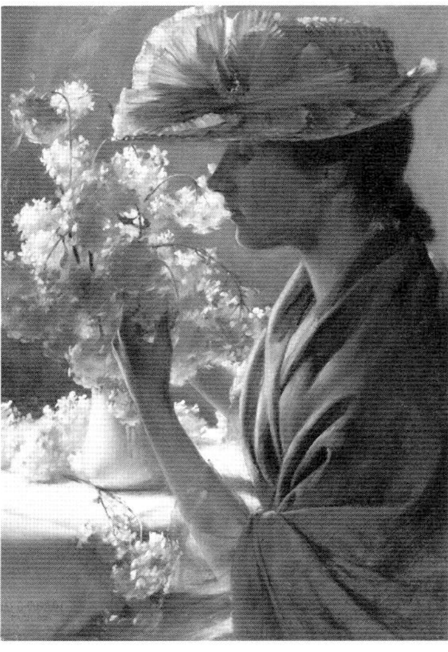

Fig. 2. Charles Courtney Curran, *Lady with a Bouquet (Snowballs)*, 1890, oil on panel, 10 1/2 x 8 1/2 in. (26.7 x 21.6 cm), Collection of the Birmingham Museum of Art, Birmingham, Alabama; Gift of Mr. W. Houston Blount, Jr.; Dr. and Mrs. Walter D. Clark; Dr. and Mrs. Orville W. Clayton; EBSCO Industries; Mr. and Mrs. Raymond Gotlieb; Estate of Mr. Clarence B. Hanson, Jr.; Mrs. W. W. McTyeire, Jr.; Estate of Mr. George H. Mathews; Mr. Joshua R. Oden, Jr.; Mr. William M. Spencer III; Mrs. Alys R. Stephens; Mr. Elton B. Stephens; Mr. Elton B. Stephens, Jr.; Mr. James T. Stephens; Mrs. Martee Woodward Webb; and Mr. Thomas M. West, Jr.

depict a woman and child in *Chrysanthemums* coincides with a cultural ideal that linked gardening with a romanticized domesticity that was promoted early in the century by such women's magazines as *Godey's Lady's Book* and later by *The House Beautiful* and *House and Garden*.

An indoor garden was viewed as an extension of the woman's household domain. Beautifying this perfumed pantry not only by her gardening but also by her feminine presence, as Curran's figures do, was in keeping with a woman's role as both interior decorator and decorative object: "[Woman's] sphere is within the household which she should 'beautify,' and of which she should be the 'chief ornament.'"[15] Unlike vegetables, grown for their utility, chrysanthemums are valued for their ornamental effect, like the attractive female figures in Curran's painting. He presents the conservatory as an experience, a place to meditate and delight the senses. The woman and child are observing, sensing, and thus participating in natural processes. But they themselves are not gardening, which involves action—getting dirt under fingernails. And they are not dressed to get dirty. Their experience is passive, not active or creative, in keeping with the ideal, but in reality rapidly changing, role of women in society.

As a setting for images of women and children in art and literature, the indoor garden also evokes the long tradition, prominent in medieval and Renaissance art, of the *hortus conclusus*, or enclosed garden of the Virgin and Child. In harmony with this Christian connotation, in *Chrysanthemums* the narrow area occupied by the figures could be read as a church aisle, with the iron columns rising to support the glass roof evoking a Gothic space, and the side of the rectangular wooden box recalling the back of a pew. Curran's visual metaphor echoed numerous verbal metaphors equating greenhouses with religious structures, referring to them as temples of flowers or naves in a church. The woman and child bow their heads in a reverent attitude, contemplating beauty as we contemplate them.

Curran revered not only beauty but science. The idea of the conservatory itself seems to be an outgrowth of a quintessentially modern desire to control nature and order our personal worlds.[16] A conservatory filled with one species in differing hues could only arise from a social structure that believed nature must be shaped. The chrysanthemums' large size and subtle color combinations celebrate mid-nineteenth-century developments in the science of horticulture, which increased their size and range of hues. More readily apparent is the triumph of science over the seasons: although the hats, gloves, and coats worn by the figures indicate that it is cool outside, inside it is perpetually warm. Thus, *Chrysanthemums* succinctly and beautifully expresses the late-nineteenth-century urban artists' relationship to nature—controlled by science, ordered by art, integrated with domestic leisure life, and mediated by women and children.

ROBIN JAFFEE FRANK

1 Gunther Teall, "Poems in Paint/The Work of Charles C. Curran," Clipping file, Detroit Institute of Arts.

2 Ibid.

3 See Kenyon Cox, "The Sculptors of the Early Italian Renaissance," *Century Magazine* 29 (November 1884): 62–66; *Old Masters and New* (1905); *Painters and Sculptors* (1907); *The Classic Point of View* (1911).

4 The title of this painting has been published as both *Académie Julian* and *An Alcove in the Art Students' League*. I would like to thank Anndora Morginson, The Art Institute of Chicago, for advising that the latter title has been confirmed by the most recent scholarship.

5 Images of this bust, Francesco Laurana's *Femme Inconnue* (Musée du Louvre), were ubiquitous in the 1880s and 1890s, as Curran would have known. A cast of it appears on a pedestal in Cox's 1904 replica of his destroyed 1887 portrait of Augustus Saint-Gaudens (Metropolitan Museum of Art). *Femme Inconnue* also served as the inspiration for Herbert Adams's bust *Primavera* (The Corcoran Gallery of Art), begun in 1890 while he and Curran were both art students in Paris. For further discussion of interest in the Laurana bust, see David C. Huntington et al., *The Quest for Unity: American Art Between World's Fairs 1876–1893*, exh. cat. (Detroit: Detroit Institute of Arts, 1983), 34–35.

6 For a discussion of the floral-female metaphor in turn-of-the-century American art, see Annette Scott, "Floral Femininity: A Pictorial Definition," *American Art* 6, no. 2 (Spring 1992): 61–77.

7 In 1907 Grace Wickham Curran became an editor and regular contributor to the arts magazine *Palette and Bench*, to which her husband also contributed. I based the identification of the model in *Chrysanthemums* on her resemblance to a model seated on the pouff in the foreground of Curran's *At the Sculpture Exhibition* (Yale University Art Gallery); see Kenneth Silver, "*At the Sculpture Exhibition* by Charles Curran," *Yale University Art Gallery Bulletin* 35, no. 1 (Summer 1974): 23, n. 10. I am immensely grateful to Mrs. Kaycee Benton, an independent scholar working on Curran, for confirming my identification and for generously responding to my other inquiries.

8 I would like to thank Mrs. Benton for sharing information on the content of Grace Curran's letters from Paris.

9 Charles C. Curran, "Class in Oil Painting," *Palette and Bench* 1, no. 2 (November 1908): 28.

10 The probability that this female-floral equation was intentional is strengthened by the fact that, while in Paris, Curran painted *The Scent of the Rose* (Private Collection), a nearly Symbolist image in which a nude woman emerges from the heart of a rose.

11 See Sherry B. Ortner, "Is Female to Male as Nature Is to Culture?" in Michelle Zimbalist Rosaldo and Louise Lamphere, eds., *Women, Culture, and Society* (Stanford, Calif.: Stanford University Press, 1974), 67–87.

12 Peter Henderson, "Floriculture in the United States," *Garden and Forest: A Journal of Horticulture, Landscape Art and Forestry*, 1 (February 1888): 3.

13 A. Ysabeau, *Le Jardinage, ou l'art de créer et de bien tenir un jardin* (Paris, 1854), 14–15; quoted in Richard Bretell et al., *A Day in the Country: Impressionism and the French Landscape*, exh. cat. (Los Angeles: Los Angeles County Museum of Art, 1984), 213.

14 Mac Griswold and Eleanor Weller, *The Golden Age of American Gardens: Proud Owners—Private Estates, 1890–1940* (New York: Harry N. Abrams, Inc., in association with The Garden Club of America, 1991), 16.

15 Thorstein Veblen, *The Theory of the Leisure Class: An Economic Study of Institutions*, New American Library ed. (New York, 1953; first published 1899), 126.

16 That desire to control nature was very apparent in Louis-Napoleon's plans for Paris. He uprooted the crowded streets to create parks, squares, gardens—pockets of fresh air that were equated, as was Central Park in New York, with health, progress, and social morality. For a discussion of the imaging of this new Paris around the time Curran was there, see "Parks, Racetracks, and Gardens," in Robert L. Herbert, *Impressionism: Art, Leisure, and Parisian Society* (New Haven and London: Yale University Press, 1988).

William Merritt Chase

1849–1916

Tired

about 1894
Oil on canvas
13 x 9 ¹/₂ in. (33 x 24.1 cm)

In this portrait depicting Chase's daughter, Alice Dieudonnée, the sympathetic response of painter to sitter is more than that of artist to model.[1] Chase has used a close-up point of view combined with the diagonal placement of the girl's upper body to bring his subject forward into our space, forcefully impressing the viewer with her emotive appeal. The diagonal slashes of paint that delineate her dress, ribbon, and arm direct attention to her face, where we are held by her intensely intimate gaze. Here the identification between artist and sitter endows the image with another level of meaning: she looks back at us looking at her. The power of Alice's gaze challenges the boundary between reality and illusion and, on one level, engages the viewer in a dialogue about making art. The forms of her head are created by a tight mosaic of brushstrokes that give her face a convincing reality in three-dimensional space, whereas the looser strokes used to form her broadly conceived dress and the pillow remain in a less defined state of becoming something other than paint on canvas. Chase's gestural strokes acknowledge the act of painting; similarly, the rectangular pillow propped up behind Alice's head serves as a frame within a frame, suggesting the artist's process of selecting a rectangular section of the visible world to record on canvas. As Alice supports her head with her hand in a time-honored gesture evoking the process of thought, the relationship in art between the mental act of conceiving an image and the physical act of painting it suggests not only the sitter's inner life but the artist's as well.

In contemporary critic Kenyon Cox's words, Chase was "a wonderful human camera—a seeing machine," whose portraits showed the external person, not the consciousness within.[2] Those who reviewed Chase's work during his lifetime often acknowledged him as a master technician but questioned whether he could convey character in his portraits, and indeed, this remains a question often asked about him. However, in *Tired*, it is precisely through his technical brilliance, especially his bravura brushwork, that he achieves a compelling characterization. Chase was conscious of the integral link between how he painted and what he hoped to convey about a sitter's personality: "Do not imagine that I would disregard that thing that lies beneath the mask, but be sure that when the outside is rightly seen, the thing that lies under the surface will be found upon your canvas."[3] His portrait of Alice is an exercise in pure painting, in which his delight in both his medium and his subject merge. Like a small jewel, the painting is opulent in its colors: sparkling pinks and whites are placed against a dusky background, and

touches of red on the pillow and tassle add the color note for which Chase was famous. Those red daubs may have a personal meaning here as well, for once, when Alice fainted during an arduous modeling session, a contrite Chase gave his daughter a charm bracelet engraved with "Little Red Note," referring to the color accent he had asked her to wear.[4]

The vivacity of Chase's portrait style in a work like *Tired* reveals his absorption of Hals's and Velázquez's gestural styles during his student days at the Munich Academy in the 1870s, combined with the light palette resulting from his later exposure to French Impressionism in the 1880s. The device of cutting off, seen in the way the frame crops the figure's left side (our right), is similar to that seen in French Impressionist paintings or in informal family photographs.

The domestic setting, as well as the cropping and free manipulation of the brush, combine to produce a slice-of-life quality—as though Chase had altered his handling in response to the informality of the moment. Most striking is his interest in capturing Alice's seemingly unposed state. Her head tilted and eyes fixed on us, she seems to be listening. The reciprocal response between artist and subject is so deeply felt that the viewer is left wondering if the contemplative spirit captured in paint is Alice's own or a projection of Chase's mood onto his daughter. In this sense, the girl becomes her father's muse, an expression of his creative spirit.

The first of nine children (one of whom died in infancy), Alice was the one Chase most often chose to depict, so that, taken together, the portraits of her from infancy through early adulthood document her father's fascination with her developing consciousness and beauty. She was born on February 9, 1887, about one year after the artist had married his model, Alice Gerson, after whom Alice Dieudonnée was named and whom she soon rivaled as most favored model. In fact, the mother is already eclipsed by her infant daughter in *The First Portrait* (The Museum of Fine Arts, Houston), in which we see the older Alice from behind, while the baby, looking over her shoulder, engages us directly. Beginning with this infant portrait and as exemplified by *Tired*, Chase almost always caught his daughter responding to someone—presumably Chase himself—outside the picture space. And as she grew older, he almost always caught her, as he had her mother before her, in a pensive mood.

In almost all his portraits of his daughter, including *Tired*, Chase created the impression of a serious child—indeed, her

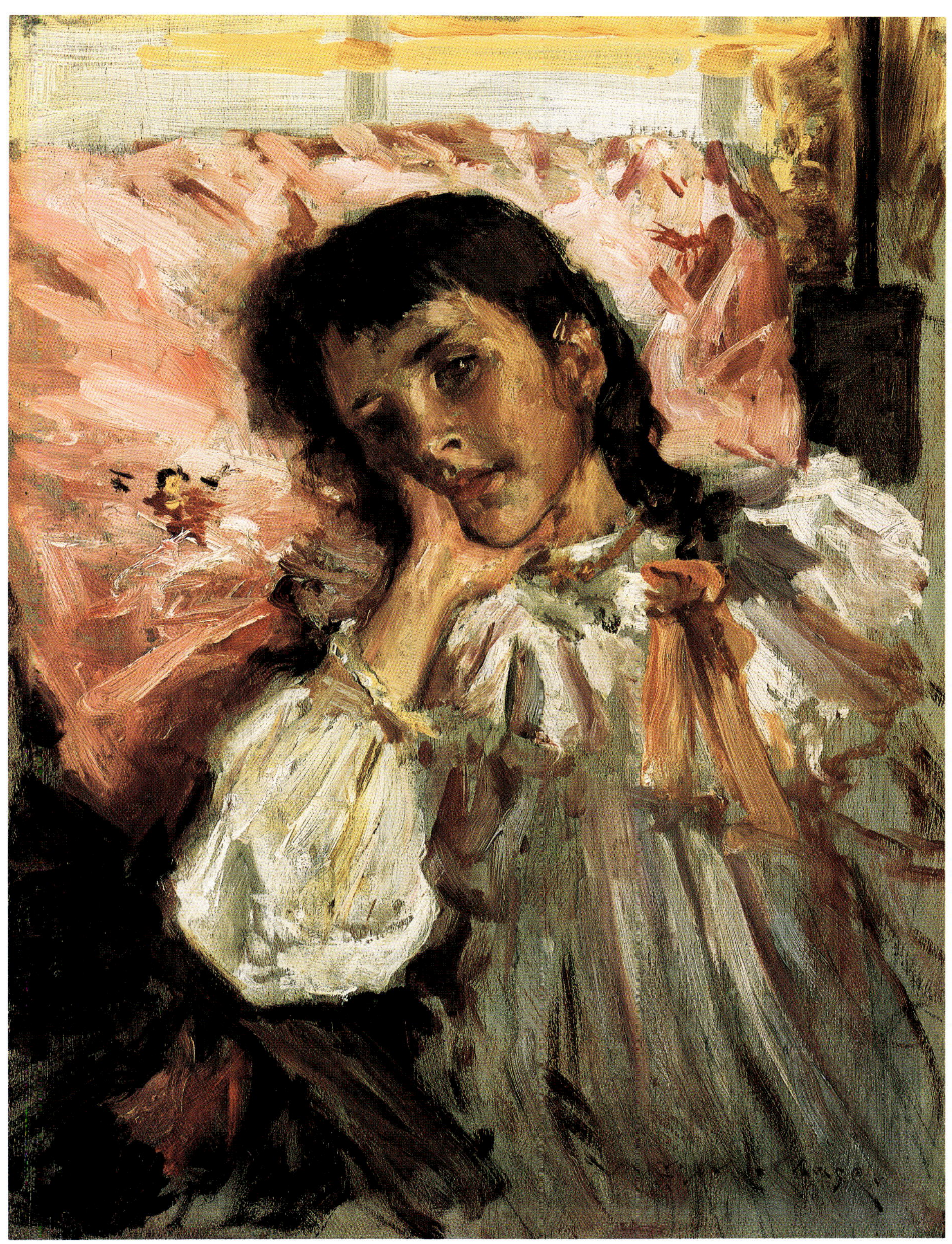

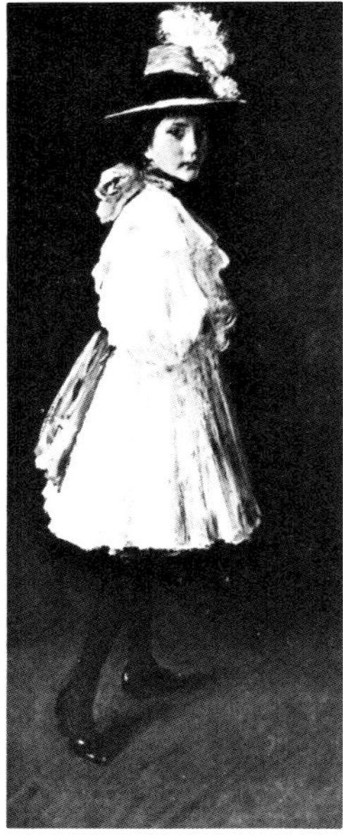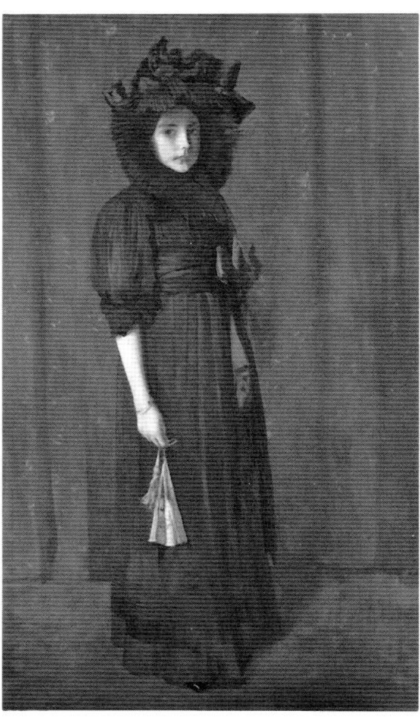

Fig. 1. *Left,* William Merritt Chase, *Alice on Sunday,* c. 1895, oil on canvas, 24 x 12 in. (61 x 30.5 cm), Private Collection. From *William Merritt Chase: Portraits,* exh. cat. (Akron, Ohio: Akron Art Museum, 1982)

Fig. 2. *Right,* William Merritt Chase, *Artist's Daughter Alice in Mother's Dress (Young Girl in Black),* c. 1899, oil on canvas, 60 1/8 x 36 3/16 in. (152.7 x 91.9 cm), Hirshhorn Museum and Sculpture Garden, Smithsonian Institution, Gift of Joseph H. Hirshhorn (photographer, Lee Stalsworth)

facial expression imparts a sophistication beyond her years.[5] In the full-length portraits of Alice, placed against a spare background, the aesthetic influence of Whistler is apparent, much as it is in Chase's full-length portraits of adult women painted from the mid-eighties through the nineties. Alice's elegant Whistlerian pose and introspective expression accelerate her maturity in *Alice on Sunday* (fig. 1), a full-length portrait in which she wears a white and pink dress strikingly similar to the one in *Tired,* a straw hat with a plume, and black stockings and shoes. One can imagine *Tired* being painted at the moment when Alice, exhausted from having to stay very still in her father's carefully directed poses while dressed in her Sunday best, loosened her belted sash and flopped onto a sofa. In no other portrait is her response to her father so seemingly frank and unaffected.

In *Young Girl in Black* (fig. 2), another Whistlerian full-length portrait, the fine dress and frilly hat donned by an older Alice belonged to her mother. Here Chase anticipated the elegant lady his daughter would become, the woman her mother already was. She was only fifteen years old when he painted *My Daughter Dieudonnée* (fig. 3), depicting her as a sultry woman seated on a wicker chair, evocatively enveloped in a large white feather boa and gazing seductively at us—or, rather, her father—from under a white plumed hat. Were these very adult accessories given to Alice by her father or did she choose them herself? Do these sophisticated and sensual images emerge from the character of the child or the mind of the artist? All are painted with great tenderness, yet there is an ambiguity about the feelings released by Chase's interpretations of Alice. As the critic John Berger has written, that ambiguity—that sense of a split identity—can be felt to a greater or lesser degree in all portraits where a female model serves as the muse for a male artist:

From earliest childhood she has been taught and persuaded to survey herself continually.

And so she comes to consider the surveyor *and the* surveyed *within her as two constituent yet always distinct elements of her identity as a woman. . . .*
One might simplify this by saying: men act *and* women appear. *Men look at women. Women watch themselves being looked at. This determines not only most relations between men and women but also the relation of women to themselves. The surveyor of woman in herself is male: the surveyed female. Thus she turns herself into an object—and most particularly an object of vision: a sight.*[6]

When asked why he chose to depict his firstborn so often, Chase responded: "Why, I don't know. She very much resembles her mother."[7] That uncanny resemblance—dark eyes, oval face, sensuous lips—as interpreted by Chase, can be seen by comparing *Tired* to *Meditation* (fig. 4), an affectionate pastel portrait of Alice Gerson at nineteen, a year before her marriage. The comparison also makes evident Chase's view of his wife as a childlike woman and, conversely, of his daughter as a womanly child. When Alice Gerson became his wife in 1886, she was twenty; Chase was thirty-seven. They had already known each other for nearly seven years, so Alice Gerson had grown from child to woman while Chase—whose first one-man show in the year of their marriage was a triumph—was emerging as a major figure on the American artistic scene. This significant difference in age and experience, compounded by inequalities between men and women both within marriage and in the larger society, probably would have allowed Chase's charming but forceful personality to dominate that of his young wife.[8] An exceptionally devoted father, according to contemporary accounts, he naturally would have exercised considerable influence over his daughter's evolving personality as well. In *Meditation,* and later in *Tired,* the similar hand-to-head poses and the pronounced directness of the gazes not only suggest that both sitters are deep in thought, but also that the object of their gazes is the artist. The viewers, placed in the position

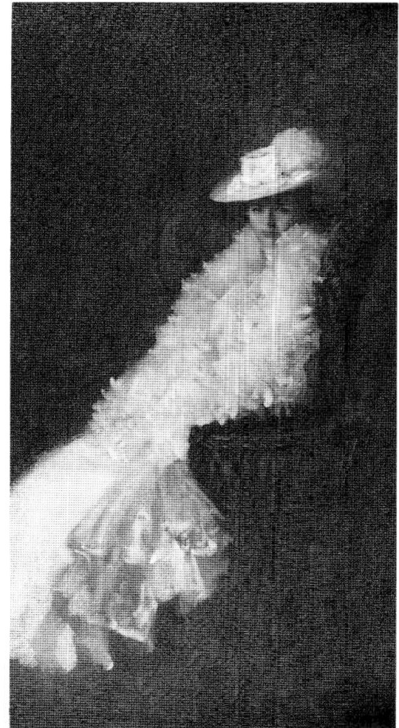
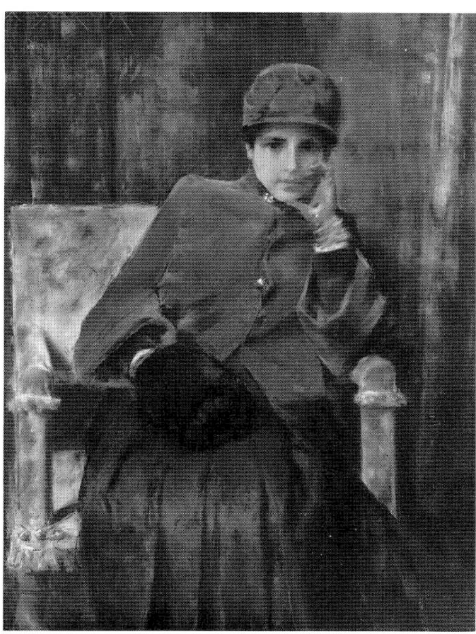

Fig. 3. *Left,* William Merritt Chase, *My Daughter Dieudonnée*, c. 1902, oil on canvas, 72 ³/4 x 36 ¹/2 in. (184.8 x 92.7 cm), The Parrish Art Museum, Southampton, N.Y., Littlejohn Collection

Fig. 4. *Right,* William Merritt Chase, *Meditation*, c. 1885–86, pastel on canvas, 26 ¹/2 x 20 ¹/2 in. (67.3 x 52 cm), Courtesy of The Jordan-Volpe Gallery, Inc.

of the artist, cannot help but feel disconcerted by the powerful intimacy of the relationship.

In *Tired*, that feeling is further compounded by the dominating vantage point looking down on the young girl, who appears to be reclining on a wooden sofa with rectangular arms and backboard.[9] The sleepiness evoked by her reclining posture and further confirmed by the title, and the looseness of the brushwork, which lends an air of dishevelment to her clothing, make her seem more vulnerable. Chase's portrait of his daughter eloquently expresses the affectionate ties of paternity, but not without a slightly disquieting intimation of sexuality, of the inequalites of age and gender inherent in their relationship, and of the intensity of the artist's gaze.

Genre artists, as well as fashionable portraitists of the day, often depicted young girls in attitudes that similarly combined childlike innocence and latent sexual promise. Perhaps this ambivalence appealed to viewers in an era in which women were counseled to remain pure and innocent, like children, but were nonetheless regarded by men as objects of physical beauty. Thus Chase's subtly evocative portrait of his daughter, although a personal response to their relationship, is also in accord with prevalent cultural perceptions. The loose rendering may indicate that he intended it for private viewing and not for public exhibition. The small scale of the canvas, allowing it to be easily held, further serves to intensify the possessive power of the viewer's gaze. A more intimate and appealing portrait cannot be found in Chase's oeuvre.

ROBIN JAFFEE FRANK

1 I am grateful to Ronald G. Pisano, who is currently working on the Chase catalogue raisonné, for pointing out that *Tired* was first exhibited in 1894; therefore, it was probably painted in 1893 or 1894. If the portrait depicts Alice Dieudonnée, as I tentatively think it does, it was probably painted closer to 1894. Chase's daughter was born in 1887: however, Chase tends to accelerate her maturity in his paintings. I extend my gratitude to Alicia Longwell, Registrar, The Parrish Art Museum, Southampton, New York, for showing me numerous photographs of Alice Dieudonnée in the William Merritt Chase Archives.

2 Kenyon Cox, "William M. Chase, Painter," *Harper's New Monthly Magazine* 78 (March 1889): 549; quoted in David C. Huntington et al., *The Quest for Unity: American Art Between World's Fairs 1876–1893*, exh. cat. (Detroit: Detroit Institute of Arts, 1983), 97.

3 Katherine Metcalf Roof, "William Merritt Chase: The Man and the Artist," *Century Magazine* 93 (April 1917): 834.

4 Keith L. Bryant, *William Merritt Chase: A Genteel Bohemian* (Columbia and London: University of Missouri Press, 1991), 167.

5 For this reason. it is difficult to determine Alice's age in undated portraits.

6 John Berger, *Ways of Seeing* (London: British Broadcasting Corporation and Penguin Books, 1972), 46–47.

7 Katherine Metcalf Roof, "William Merritt Chase: The Man and the Artist," *Century Magazine* 93 (April 1917): 840.

8 Such an age difference was quite acceptable in the mid- to late nineteenth century. Indeed, in historian Jules Michelet's bestsellers about the ideal state of marriage, *L'Amour*, 1858, and *La Femme*, 1859 (published in English translation in 1859 and 1860, respectively, in New York), the wife was much younger than the husband, childlike, and obedient. This rigid sex-role differentiation was not just a myth perpetuated by literature and art. Alice Gerson's role in their marriage was to make the Chase household a place of refuge, a counterpoint to her husband's pressing artistic and commercial affairs, according to Chase's first biographer, Katherine Metcalf Roof, in *The Life and Art of William Merritt Chase* (New York: Charles Scribner's Sons, 1917). However, it appears that Alice was the one to cope with the Chase's considerable financial pressures.

9 Alice relaxes on what appears to be the same sofa in a photograph taken c. 1900 in the Chase family home at Shinnecock, Long Island. Indeed, the tasseled pillow on the left in the photograph may be the same one placed behind her head in the painting, where the tassels are quickly brushed in the lower left-hand corner. But in the photograph, Alice, propped up on one arm, appears more alert. The photograph is in the collection of the William Merritt Chase Archives, The Parrish Art Museum (archival number 83.Stm.150).

John George Brown

1831–1913

Hiding in the Old Oak

n.d.
Oil on canvas
23 1/2 x 15 in. (59.7 x 38.1 cm)

Hiding in the Old Oak is a small study for, or a copy after, Brown's much larger canvas of the same title and subject painted in 1874 (St. Johnsbury Athenaeum). Its depiction of three young girls hiding inside the hollow trunk of an oak tree is not uncharacteristic of his oeuvre. Throughout much of his career, Brown was largely concerned with depicting children and gained a prominent reputation for portrayals of the bootblack, or shoe-shine boy, of New York's urban streets.[1] About a game of hide-and-seek, *Hiding in the Old Oak* engages the act of seeing, or—more precisely—the act of not seeing. Exactly whom or what the girls are hiding from remains a mystery. The viewer can assume the role of finder in this game, a pleasing role to play, one that emphasizes and encourages the act of viewing the work of art itself. "Looking at" the painting is shown to be analogous to the act of "looking for" the girls.

However, the reactions of exhilaration and disappointment usually associated with the event of being "found out" in such a game are absent. The painting's spectators are allowed to share in the secret of the hiding place precisely because they are not whom or what the girls are hiding from. This secretive collusion encourages the viewer to imagine the children's sense of arrested anticipation and heightened sensual awareness, an intensified state of existence characteristic of conventional descriptions of the aesthetic experience.

The girls' stares can be also be interpreted as looking out upon an unpopulated world, implying the complete eradication of the viewer's existence before the work of art. This experience of not being seen while looking at the painting gives the spectator the same sensation of being hidden that is observable in the painting itself. It is this symbiosis of affect—of feeling what one is observing being felt by others—which gives this work its unique quality and power. The unanchored movement and direction of glances create a veritable circularity of gazing out of and into the illusionistic space of the canvas only to fall back upon the viewer's act of looking. *Hiding in the Old Oak*, in this sense, is about seeing one's self in the act of looking.

The image *Hiding in the Old Oak* presents falls well within nineteenth-century gender definitions and traditional sexual roles. The girls' play involves hiding and disappearing: finding pleasure in being nonentities. Martha J. Hoppin has observed that young girls in Brown's work were more frequently pictured amid natural settings, while young boys were often the inhabitants of urban scenes.[2] Brown's image promotes and endorses sexual stereotyping by representing women as definitively natural and rural as opposed to cultural and urban, as feminine and passive as opposed to masculine and active. In *Hiding in the Old Oak*, these feminine traits impel the young women to huddle together, to "hide and seek" protection with each other.

An alternative interpretation of *Hiding in the Old Oak* points toward a politics of feminine community. The three girls are all acting together in a utopian sort of play that encourages a community of attachment and connection. This commonality of being and community of relations is an exchange between and a communing among women. The unity is supported by the absence of anyone searching for the girls; neither the title nor the picture itself introduces any activity other than hiding. The girls are a team without an opposing side.

By concealing themselves in the niche of the tree's hollow trunk, the girls also could be seen as engaging in an attempt to identify with, seek knowledge of, and create for themselves the female experience of maturity. While it can be assumed that all children may be curious about pregnancy or fantasize about giving birth, for young women reproduction represents more than mere curiosity or desire. It exists for them as a potential physical reality, a real-life option, a possibility of lived experience. *Hiding in the Old Oak* evokes three extremely profound aspects of the past, present, and future lives of the three young women. The suggestion of newborn life, of childhood play, and of adult motherhood contained in the image symbolically presents a transcendence of chronological time and conventional temporal structures.

In allegorical terms, the Muses of classical mythology were also seers of the past, present, and future simultaneously. The oak was sacred to the ruling deity, Zeus, among whose progeny were the Muses, three daughters named Melte, Mneme, and Aoide.[3] The hollow cavity of the oak in Brown's painting suggests that it has been struck by a bolt of lightning, Zeus's primary attribute. The ancient belief that oaks attract lightning may account for the tree's consecration to the father of the Muses.

Every year from 1858 (with the exception of 1871) until his death in 1931, Brown's work was included in the annual exhibitions of the National Academy of Design in New York. The iconographical attributes of ancient Greek gods and

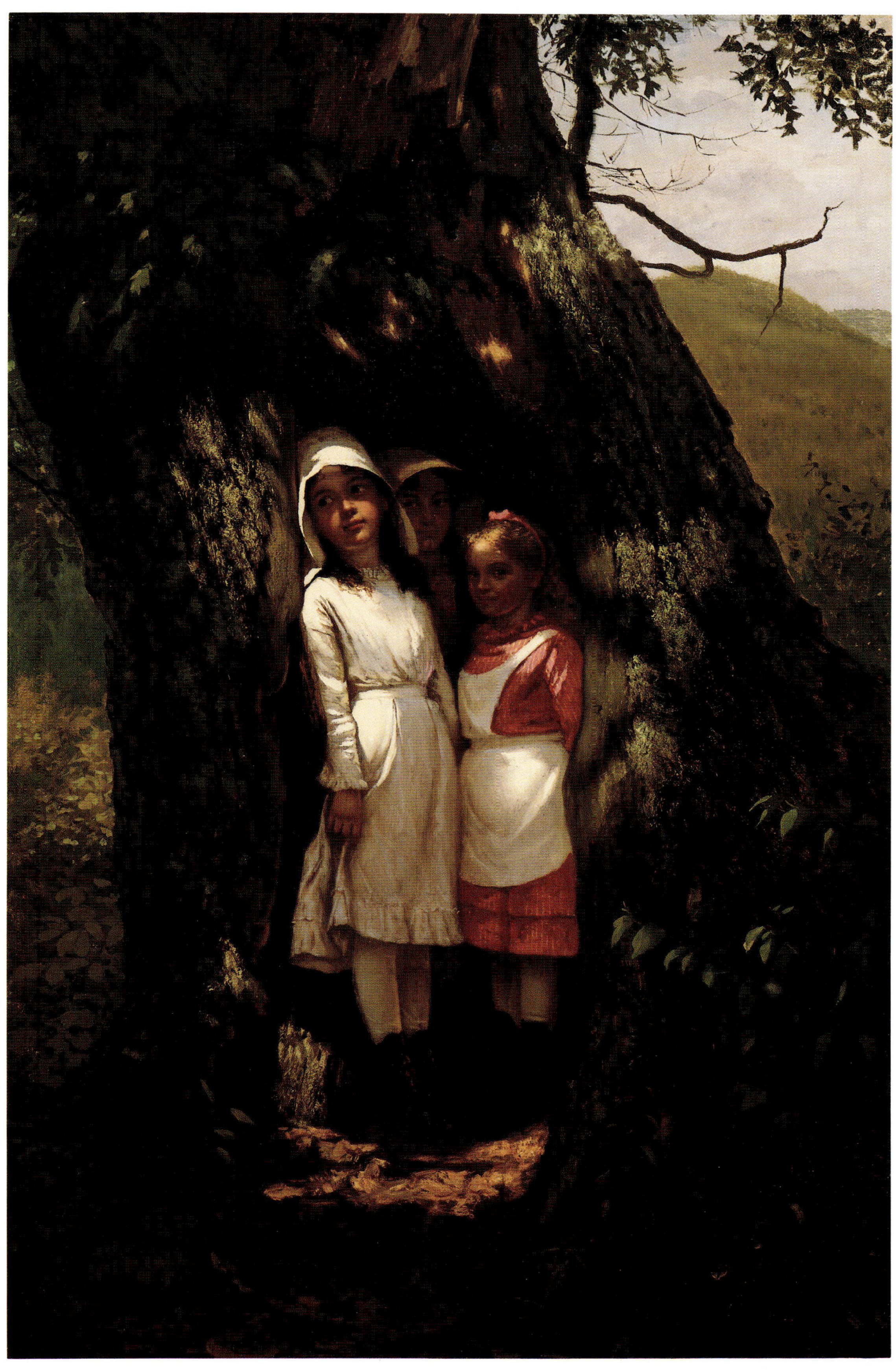

goddesses were familiar turf to the viewers, critics, and
patrons of American academic painting in the nineteenth
century. They were quick to recognize, or even prone to seek
out, such symbolism. Brown's depiction of the Muses as
three young girls can be read as an assertion of the childhood
subjects that inspired the vast majority of his artistic production. But if art's ability actually to constitute the real comes
from the Muses, then in the art of painting what the Muses
logically promote is an adamantly realist style. An appeal to
the Muses can be read as assertively substantiating the power
of realistic painting itself and supporting Brown's reputation
as a highly skilled painter in the realist mode.

KARL EMIL WILLERS

1　The most thorough source for information on other works by
J. G. Brown is Martha J. Hoppin, *Country Paths and City
Sidewalks: The Art of J. G. Brown*, exh. cat. (Springfield, Mass.:
George Walter Vincent Smith Art Museum, 1989).
2　Ibid., 17.
3　Later traditions often claimed that there were nine daughters born
to Zeus and Mnemosyne. They were Calliope (epic poetry), Clio
(history), Melpomene (tragedy), Eutere (lyric poetry), Terpsichore
(dance), Urania (astronomy and astrology), Thalia (comedy), and
Polhymnia (song and geometry).

Martin Johnson Heade

1819–1904

The Gems of Brazil

1863–64
Sixteen oil paintings on canvas,
each 12 1/4 x 10 in. (31.1 x 25.4 cm),
mounted on four panels

Heade might have been inspired to travel to Latin America by his friend Frederic Church's own importation of tropical exotica in the late 1850s, which established him as one of America's foremost artists. By 1863, Heade was in Brazil, painting this sparkling series of small hummingbird scenes, possibly numbering twenty, and in the process winning the acclaim of the Brazilian emperor, Dom Pedro II, an amateur naturalist who awarded him the Order of the Rose for his achievements. Heade intended to reproduce the paintings as lithographs in a small monograph on hummingbirds called *The Gems of Brazil*, an endeavor that concluded with no publication and the bulk of the paintings hidden, unrecognized, in private collections in Great Britain until their rediscovery in 1981.[1] Heade's early Brazilian effort led to his landscapes of hummingbirds and both orchids and passion flowers, which he first painted in 1871 and continued to produce until at least thirty years later.

The specific undoing of the *Gems of Brazil* project resulted either from the artist's rapid frustration with the inadequacies of lithographers in London, where he took the paintings for publication,[2] a lack of ready cash,[3] or the failure of the product to compete with Robert Gould's sumptuously illustrated and substantially more comprehensive five-volume *Monograph of the Trochilidae*.[4] In this respect Heade seems to have situated his project in an undesirable breach in the marketplace. On the one hand, with merely twenty images his work could not have competed with well-illustrated publications also having substantial scientific merit, such as Gould's and Jean Theodore Descourtilz's *Ornithologie brésilienne*, first published in 1842 in London and Rio de Janeiro. On the other, Heade does not seem to have contemplated an appeal to bourgeois taste such as Paul Jerrard's sentimental "candy box" book, *Humming Bird Keepsake* (1852), whose light poems by W. M. Bagley and Jerrard's own gaudy lithographs propose the hummingbird as a metaphor of flirtation, vulnerability, and love.

Heade's *Gems of Brazil* certainly possess an exotically amorous, metaphoric spirit in their depiction of pairs of iridescent birds among jungle flowers, meandering tendrils, and heart-shaped leaves and nests with both eggs and fussing fledglings.[5] Their universe, though small, dwarfs its background mountains and boughs, contributing to a sense of intimacy, the bliss of a new Eden. The delicate beauty of each work, the acrobatic movements of its subjects, and the scattered, surface-oriented composition of elements also suggest comparisons to Chinese and Japanese landscape painting, a genre of growing interest in the middle of the century, both to Europeans and to Americans. It is true that Heade claimed for his hummingbird pictures no "scientific character,"[6] but in this respect he might have done himself an injustice. Unlike even Gould, he had seen hummingbirds in their natural setting and throughout his adult life studied, cultivated, and tamed them with the vigor of "almost a monomaniac," as he described himself.[7]

Surely evident in *The Gems of Brazil* and his later hummingbird landscapes are not only Heade's personal interest but also a great sensitivity to those advancements in knowledge of natural science that occurred during his lifetime in the work of Alexander Wilson and John James Audubon in America and that of Charles Darwin in Great Britain.[8] The presentation and understanding of birds and plants as integrated elements in their natural environment was one of Darwin's most consistent themes.

The influence of Darwin on Heade's hummingbird scenes and, later, his paintings of orchids and passion flowers has been properly recognized.[9] *The Gems of Brazil* are among the earliest works of art comprehensively to present wildlife in a compatible natural setting, a presentation that Audubon, Gould, and others only occasionally undertook. Yet it is important to note that Heade's enthusiasm for Darwinism is not specifically documented in his many *Forest and Stream* articles and appears to have had its limits. Not even in *Two Fighting Hummingbirds and Two Orchids* from 1875 did Heade approach the brutal survivalism of, for instance, the German artist Max Klinger, whose fighting centaur prints, done roughly contemporaneously, suggest a man who took his Darwin both seriously and ideologically. Darwin's factual discoveries relating to the life of plants and their fertilization, rather than the overall philosophical implications of his views, were perhaps most relevant to Heade, and the artist's portrayal of flora and fauna in an interactive, atmospheric world might reflect this influence most clearly. The inclusion of at least one butterfly among *The Gems of Brazil* series further suggests at least an interest in portraying a comprehensively suitable environment. Even in this narrow respect, though, Heade's emphasis on flat surface patterns, decorative beauty, and romantic anecdote occasionally is so great that his tropical settings seem extinguished of value. Moreover, complete divorce from a natural setting is a major component of Heade's late work, his reclining flower still lifes, of which *Magnolias on a Blue Velvet Cloth* (p. 84) is an exquisite example.

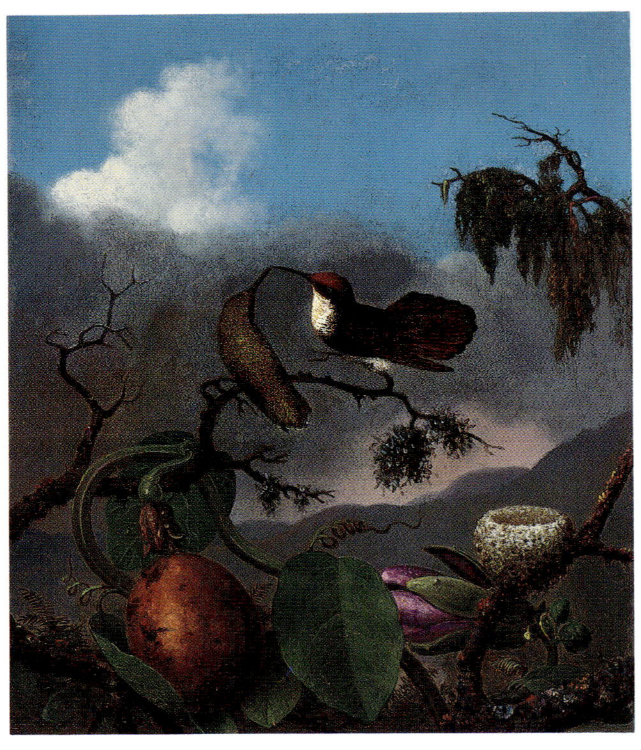
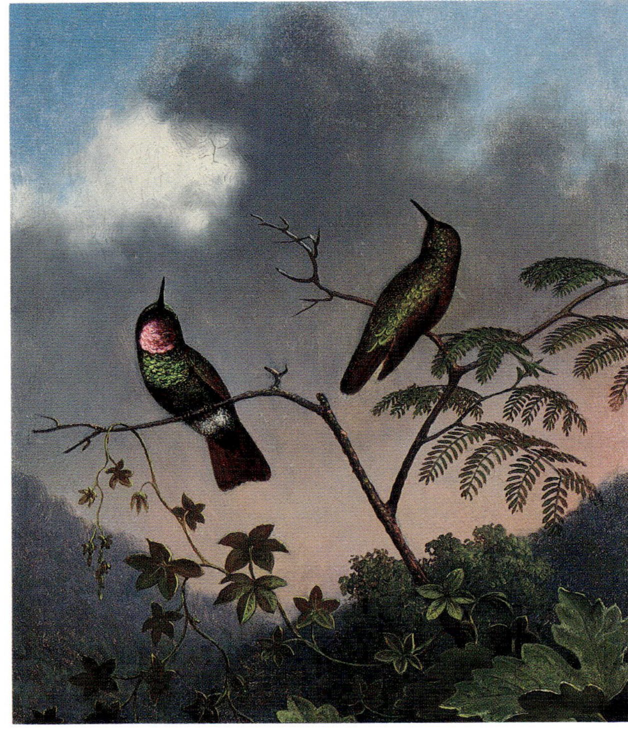
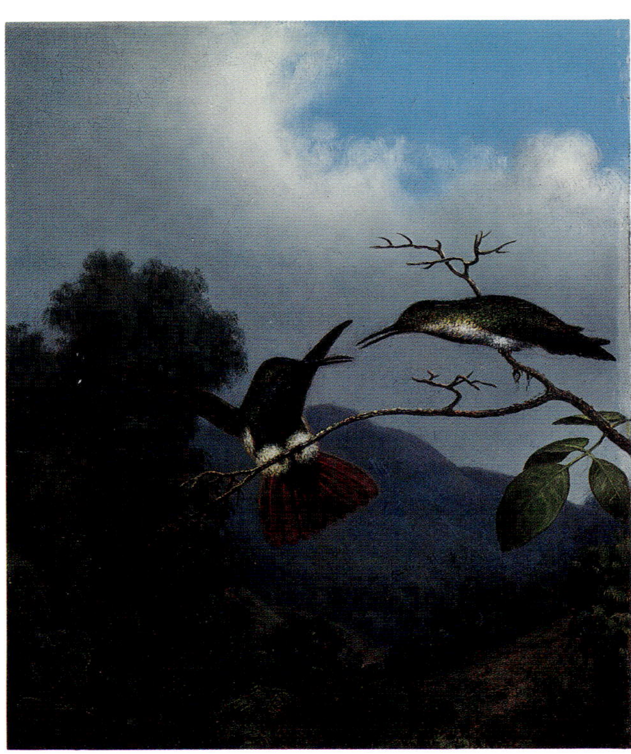
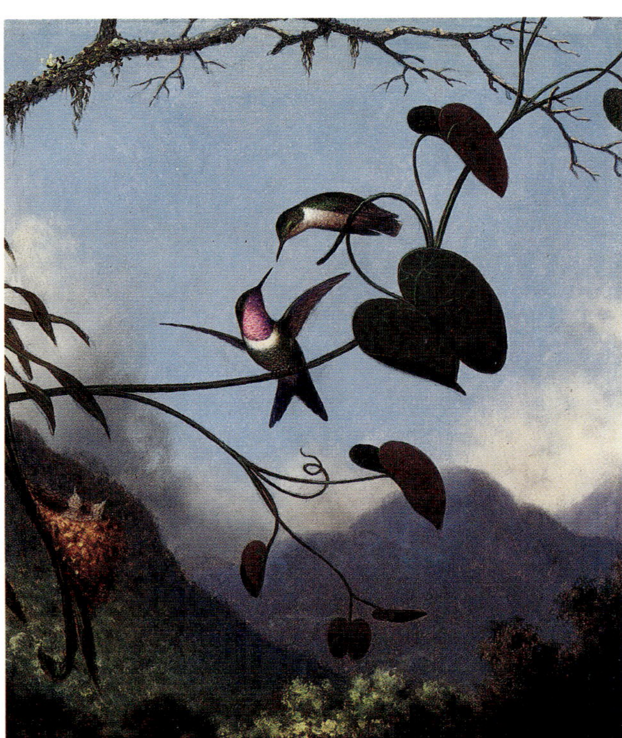

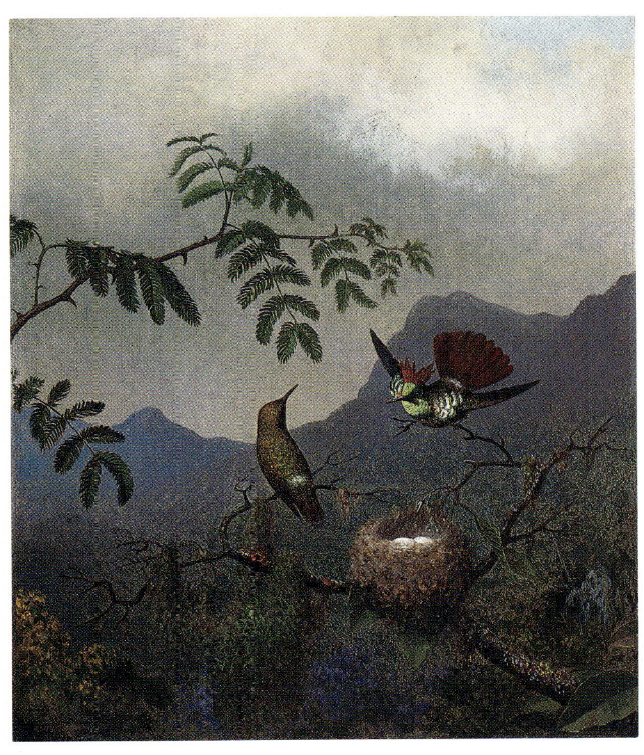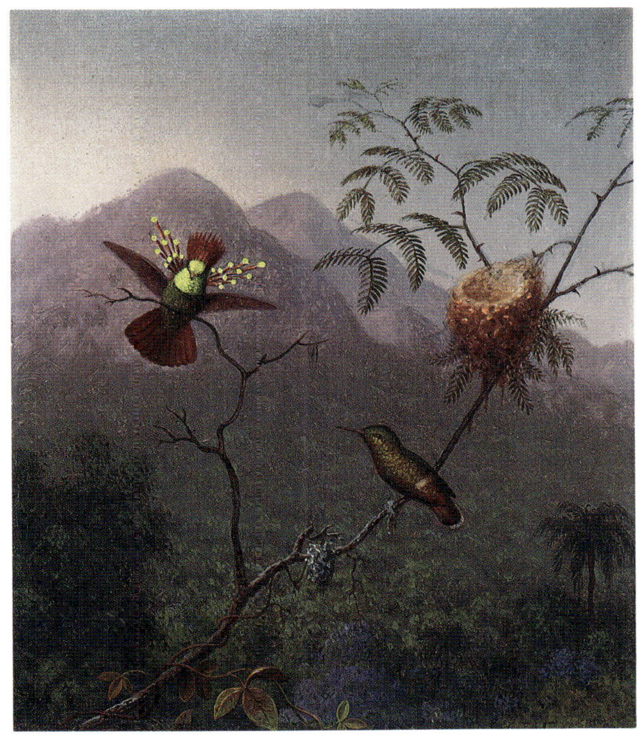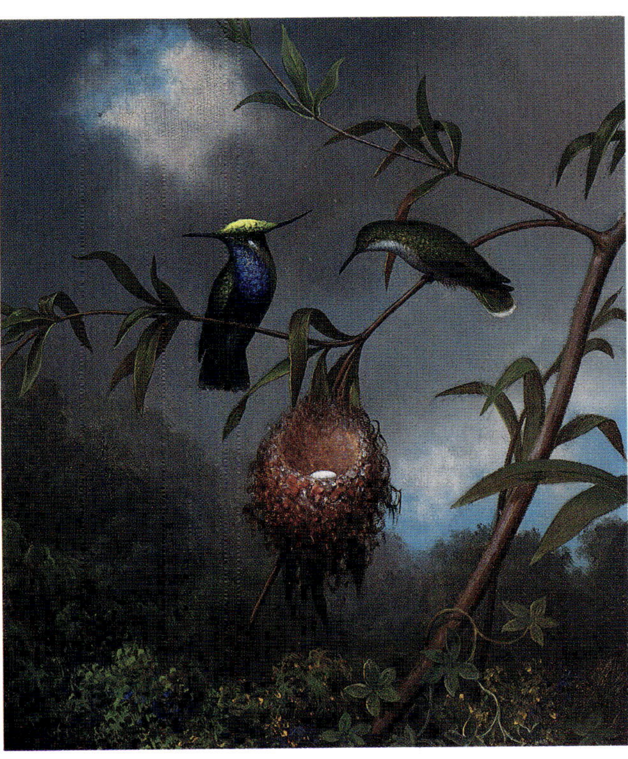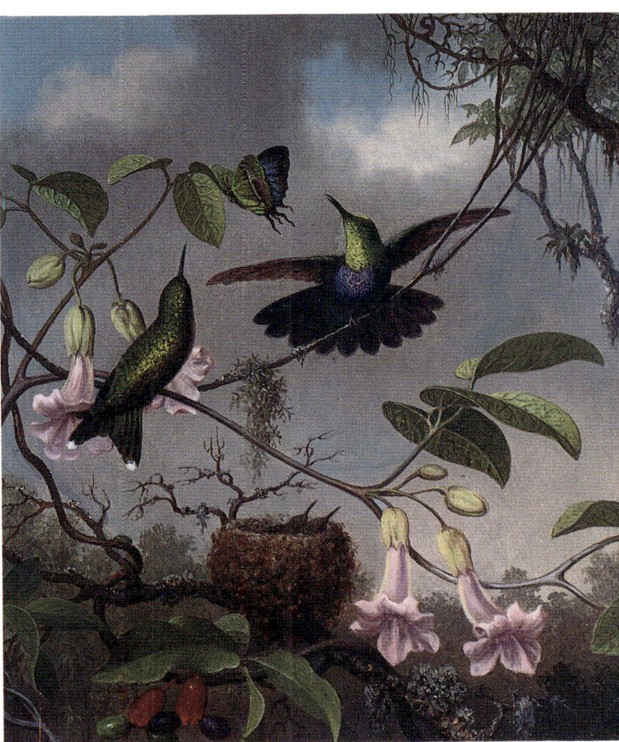

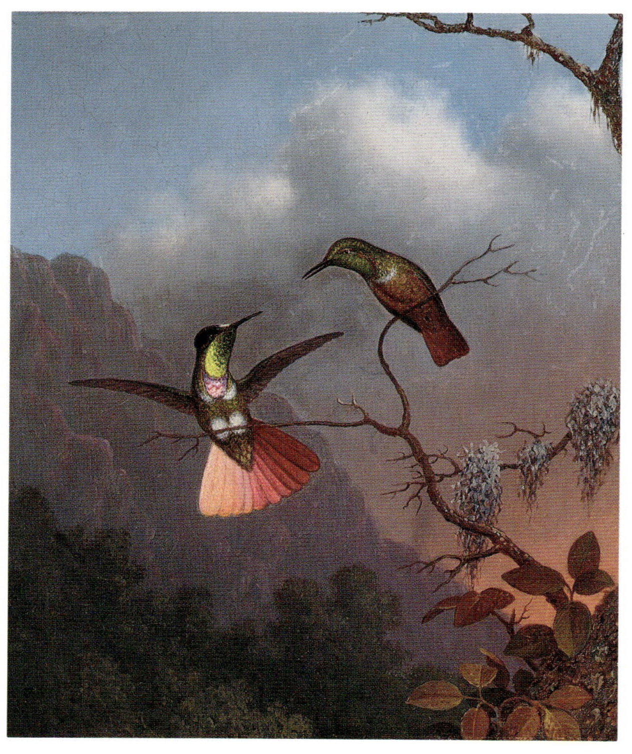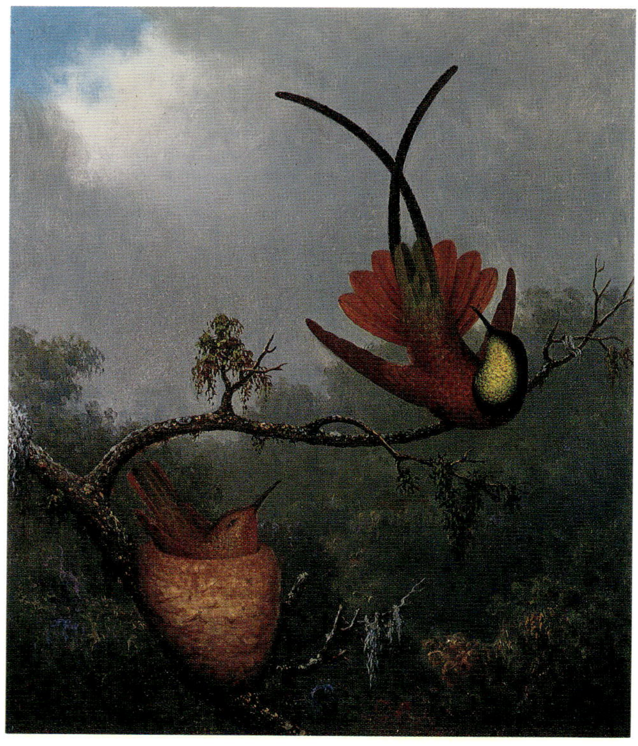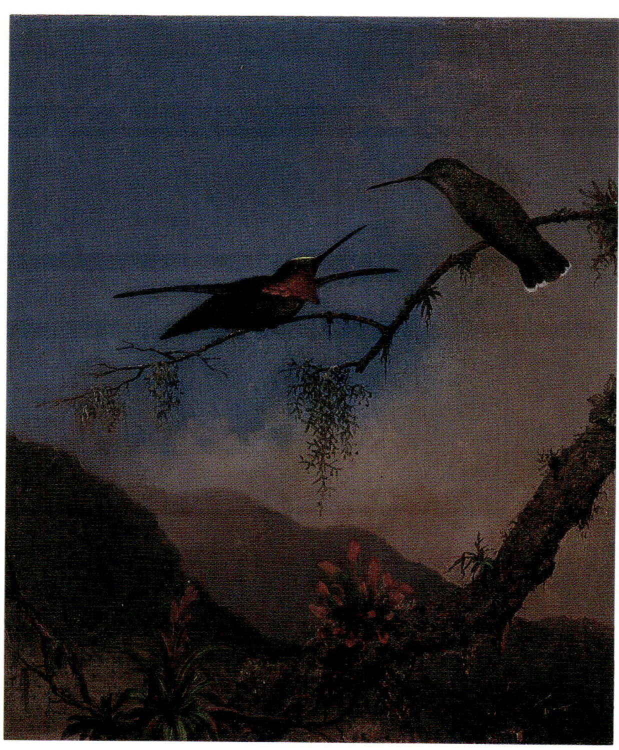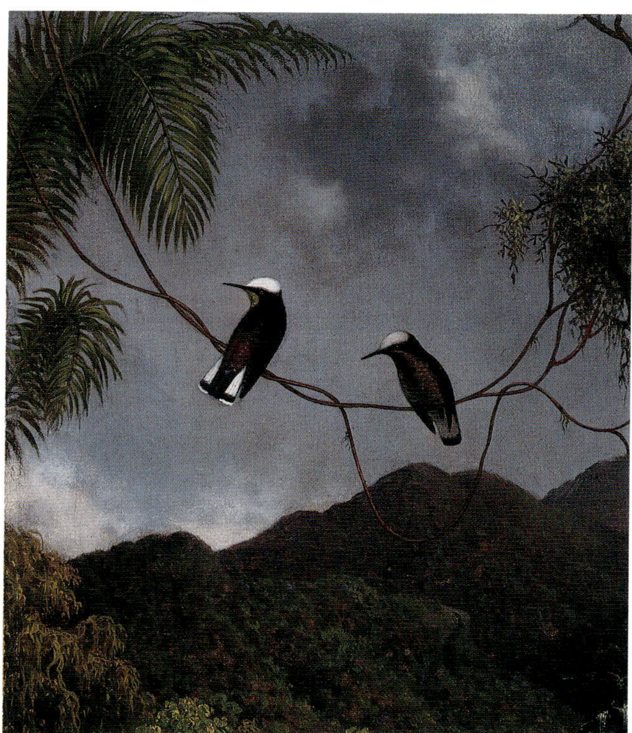

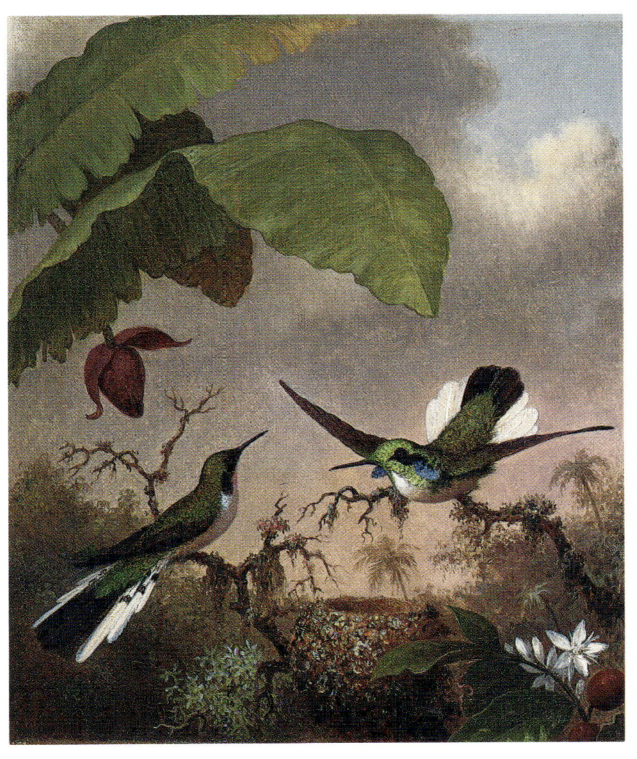 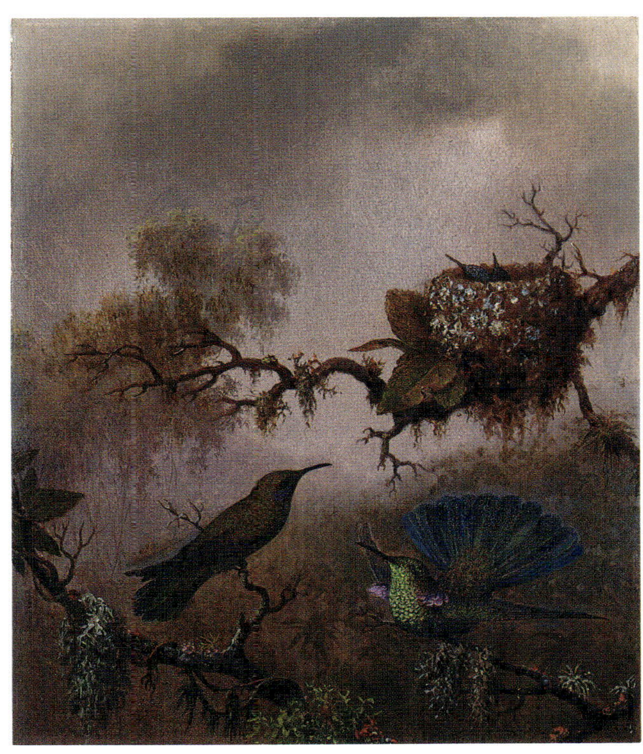

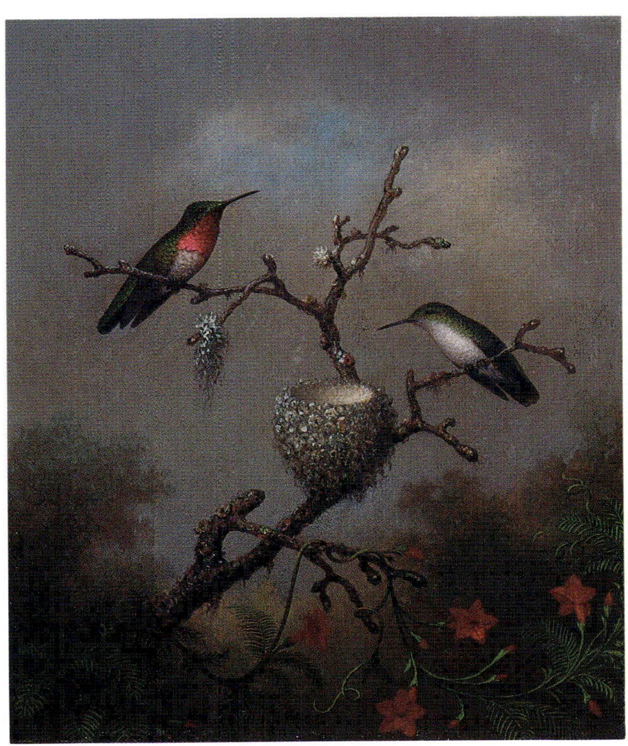 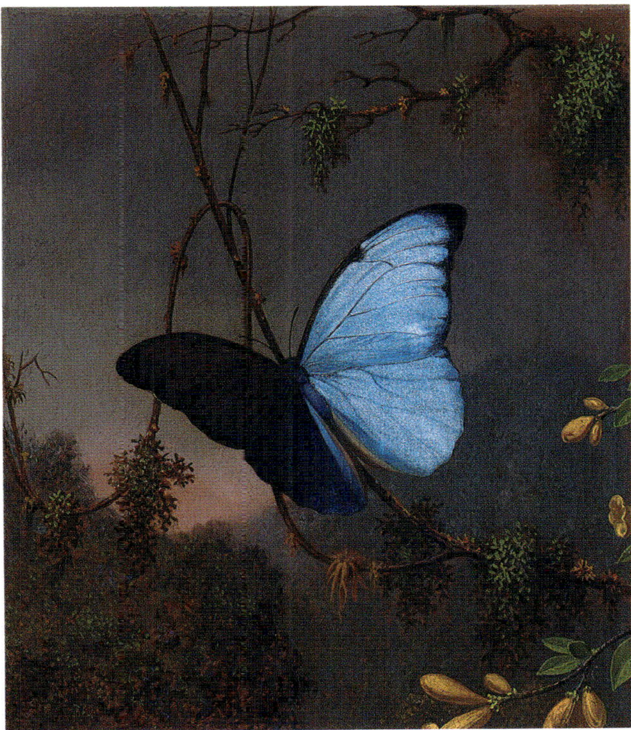

Heade's hummingbird world, a few sparring birds excepted,
radiates a sanctified harmony, a portrayal of nature as a spir-
itually instructive gift from God to man. In this respect,
these paintings depict most precisely a nature mysticism, a
transcendentalism, that relates them less to Darwin than to
the entire body of Heade's landscape work and to the luminist spirit of which he was so thorough a partisan.

BRIAN T. ALLEN

1   Heade's trip and the entire *Gems of Brazil* project is chronicled in
    T. Stebbins, *The Life and Works of Martin Johnson Heade* (New
    Haven and London: Yale University Press, 1975), 126–37.
2   These problems are discussed in Stebbins, 134–37.
3   R. G. McIntyre, *Martin Johnson Heade* (New York: Pantheon
    Press, 1948), 29–30, suggests both this and a certain lack of
    perseverance on Heade's part.
4   Gould's lithographs derive from his own drawings, prepared from
    bird skins. S. P. Dance, *The Art of Natural History* (Woodstock,
    N.Y.: Overlook Press, 1978), 111–46.
5   Heade, the hummingbird enthusiast, would probably have known
    that male hummingbirds court not through song but through
    elaborate patterns of flight. W. Scheithauer, *Hummingbirds* (New
    York, Thomas Y. Crowell Co., 1967), 48.
6   Martin Johnson Heade, "Introduction to *The Gems of Brazil*,"
    manuscript, Archives of American Art; quoted in Stebbins, 132.
    Heade was himself an amateur naturalist, whose opinions on
    wildlife are recorded in dozens of articles and letters published in
    the journal *Forest and Stream* from 1880 to less than a month before
    his death in 1904.
7   M. Heade, "Taming Hummingbirds," *Forest and Stream*, April 14,
    1892, 348: quoted in Stebbins, 129.
8   Darwin's *On the Origin of the Species by Means of Natural Selection*
    appeared in 1859, followed by *On the Various Contrivances by Which
    British and Foreign Orchids Are Fertilised by Insects* in 1862 and, in
    1876, the *Effects of Cross and Self Fertilisation in the Vegetable
    Kingdom.*
9   F. Kelly, "The Gems of Brazil," in *American Paintings from the
    Manoogian Collection*, exh. cat. (Washington, D.C.: National
    Gallery of Art/Detroit: Detroit Institute of Arts, 1989), 118, and,
    in greater detail, E. M. Foshay, *Reflections of Nature, Flowers in
    American Art* (New York: Alfred A. Knopf, 1984), 51–57.

Lemuel Everett Wilmarth

1835–1918

Apples

1891
Oil on canvas
12 x 16 in. (30.5 x 40.6 cm)

Best known for his highly detailed genre and history subjects, Wilmarth increasingly turned to still life late in his career. His earliest training was as an academic painter. After two years at the Pennsylvania Academy of the Fine Arts, he went abroad in 1858 to begin his studies with Wilhelm von Kaulbach at the Royal Academy of Munich and, in Paris, with Jean-Léon Gérôme and at the Ecole des Beaux-Arts.[1] The classicism of Kaulbach and Gérôme, their focus on the human figure, their meticulous realism in portraying genre and historical subjects, and their interest in narrative and anecdotal details[2] naturally shaped the young Wilmarth's style, and upon his return to New York in 1867, he regularly exhibited realistic genre paintings at the Pennsylvania Academy of the Fine Arts, the National Academy of Design, and the Brooklyn Art Association.[3]

In 1882, after establishing himself in the New York art community, Wilmarth purchased a farm with an orchard and vineyard along the Hudson River. He spent his summers there with his wife, Emma Barrett Higginson, returning to his Brooklyn residence in the winter months. Shortly after acquiring this property, Wilmarth began to suffer from failing eyesight that eventually prevented him from painting the intricate details of his genre works, and he began to concentrate on still-life subjects, gathering the fruits for his compositions from the trees on his farm.[4] Earlier in his career, he had occasionally exhibited still-life paintings. As early as 1868, for instance, he had submitted a still life, *Grapes*, to an exhibition at the Brooklyn Art Association. Later, in 1891, Wilmarth exhibited a work titled *Apples* at the National Academy of Design, perhaps the Manoogian still life of the same subject matter and date.[5]

In *Apples*, Wilmarth uses a conventional still-life arrangement. The shining red apples are caught in motion as they spill onto a polished wooden table, the dried leaves and stems adding texture to the composition of predominantly hard, gleaming surfaces. This composition was employed by many artists during these years, and Andrew John Henry Way, an artist and contributor to the nineteenth-century New York art journal *The Art Amateur*, described a similar method of depicting apples: "Perhaps the most picturesque effect we can give them [apples] is to place them on the polished or varnished top of a table or slab of dark-colored marble, so that we get the reflections . . . let them appear as if they were carelessly overturned from a basket."[6] Varied in size and ripeness, Wilmarth's apples are portrayed with the same strong lighting and meticulous detail of his genre paint-

ings. But he has abandoned the stiff, theatrical manner; instead, the apples are rendered with a refreshing spontaneity never found in his figural work.

A dedicated teacher, Wilmarth was appointed director of the schools at the Brooklyn Academy of Design in 1868, and during the years 1870 to 1890 he was the director and first full-time instructor of the schools at the National Academy of Design, teaching the antique and life classes. In 1875 he led a group of students to found the Art Students League of New York, where he served as the principal instructor and president until 1877.[7] Wilmarth's method of teaching logically followed the academic approach of his instructors at the Ecole des Beaux-Arts. Students spent their early training drawing from antique casts and, later, from the model. Once proficiency was achieved in this medium, they could begin to paint the figure. Wilmarth admitted, however, that the rigors of training in Europe needed to be modified in the American setting: young students would begin the study of painting before their European counterparts and would have shorter working sessions.[8] In the late 1870s Wilmarth introduced rapid sketching from the model into his life class at the academy. In contrast to laborious, timed poses, these sessions encouraged expressionism and forced the student to capture the essence of his subject with a few broad strokes.[9] His somewhat old-fashioned and stiff figural works contrast with his more freely executed *Apples*, which follows the spontaneous approach promoted in his life class. That he was willing to introduce such novel and unacademic ideas reveals Wilmarth's commitment as a teacher and his awareness of the waning influence of the academic tradition.

BETHANY ASTRACHAN

1   For biographical material on Wilmarth, I have drawn upon the following sources: G. W. Sheldon, *American Painters: With One Hundred and Four Examples of Their Work Engraved on Wood* (New York: D. Appleton and Co., 1881), 110–11; "American Painters: Seymour Joseph Guy, N.A.—Lemuel E. Wilmarth, N.A.," *The Art Journal* 1 (New York: D. Appleton and Co., 1875): 276–78; Aloysius George Weimer, "The Munich Period in American Art" (Ph.D. diss., University of Michigan, 1940), 90–94; William H. Gerdts and Russell Burke, *American Still-Life Painting* (New York: Praeger Publishers, 1971), 165–67; Dumas Malone, ed., *Dictionary of American Biography* (New York: Charles Scribner's Sons, 1936), pt. 2, 10: 312-13.

2   For information on the European academic tradition and its influence on American painters, particularly Wilmarth, see Michael

Quick, Eberhard Ruhmer, and Richard V. West, *Munich and American Realism in the Nineteenth Century*, exh. cat. (Sacramento: E. B. Crocker Art Gallery, 1978), 23–28; H. Barbara Weinberg, *The Lure of Paris: Nineteenth-Century American Painters and Their French Teachers* (New York: Abbeville Press, 1991), 87–90; H. Barbara Weinberg, *The American Pupils of Jean-Léon Gérôme*, exh. cat. (Fort Worth, Tex.: Amon Carter Museum, 1984), 66; and Lois Marie Fink and Joshua C. Taylor, *Academy: The Academic Tradition in American Art*, exh. cat. (Washington, D.C.: Smithsonian Institution Press, 1975), 55–61.

3 For a listing of works that Wilmarth exhibited, see the major indices, including: Clark S. Marlor, ed., *A History of the Brooklyn Art Association with an Index of Exhibitions* (New York: James F. Carr, 1970), 381-82; Peter Hastings Falk, ed., *The Annual Exhibition Record of the Pennsylvania Academy of the Fine Arts 1807–1870*, 3 vols. (Madison, Conn.: Sound View Press, 1989), 1: 255; Falk, ed., *The Annual Exhibition Record of the Pennsylvania Academy of the Fine Arts 1876–1913*, 3 vols. (Madison, Conn.: Sound View Press, 1989), 2: 525; Maria Naylor, ed., *The National Academy of Design Exhibition Record 1861–1900*, 2 vols. (New York: Kennedy Galleries, 1973), 2: 1044–45.

4 See Gerdts and Burke, 166–67; and Malone, pt. 2, 10: 312–13.

5 See Marlor, 381; and Naylor, 2: 1045.

6 A. J. H. Way, "Fruit Painting in Oils: II–Treatment of Pineapples, Oranges, Lemons, Bananas, and Apples," *The Art Amateur* 16 (January 1887): 32.

7 For Wilmarth's role as a teacher, see Fink and Taylor, 37, 53, 115; Eliot Clark, *History of the National Academy of Design, 1825–1953* (New York: Columbia University Press, 1954), 90–93; and Marchal E. Landgren, *Years of Art: The Story of the Art Students League of New York* (New York: Robert M. McBride and Co., 1940), 17–26.

8 See Weinberg, *The Lure of Paris*, 91, 125–27; and "Talks with Artists: I–The Life Class," *The Art Amateur* 16 (January 1887): 30–31.

9 Fink and Taylor, 55–61.

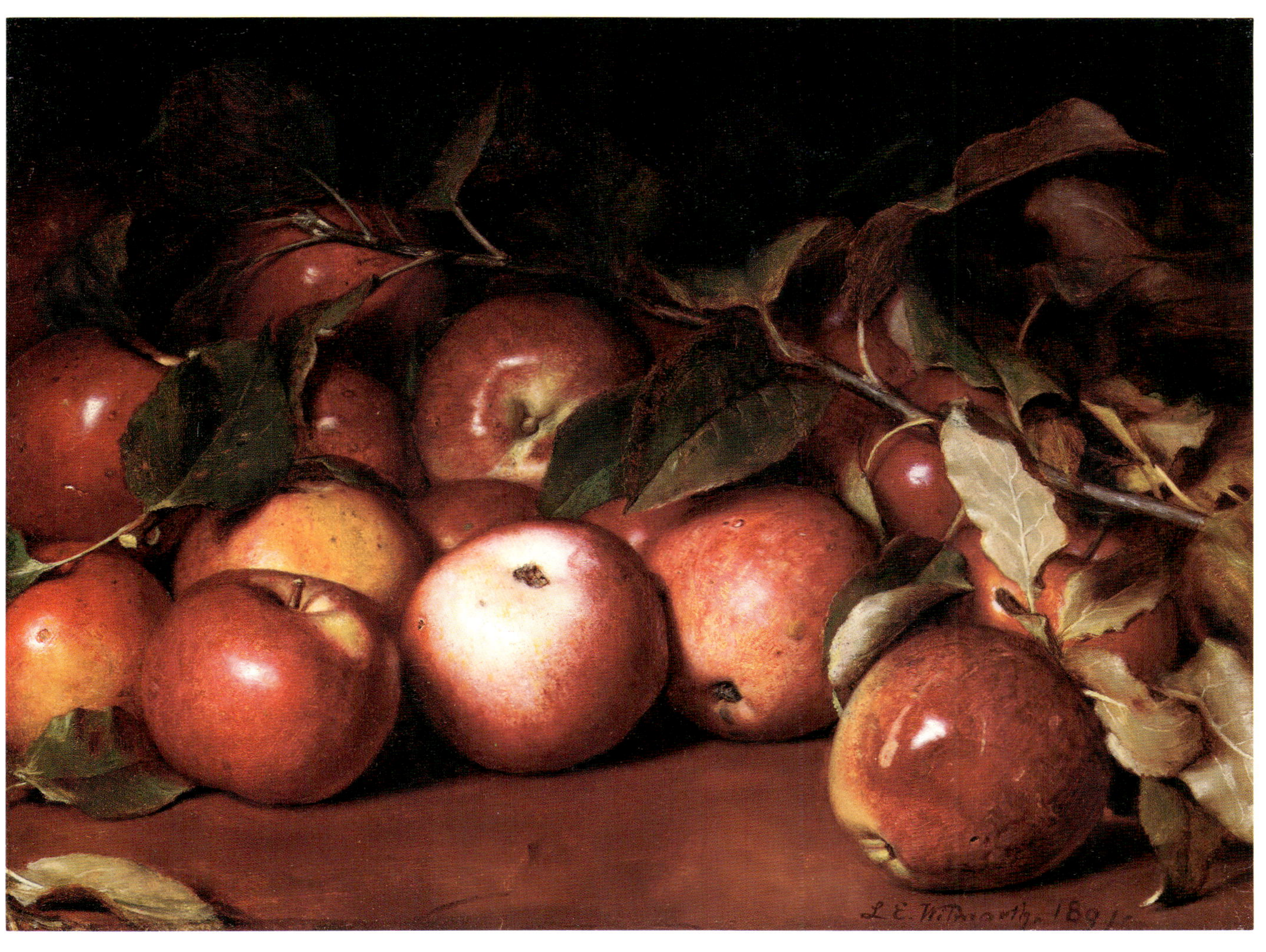

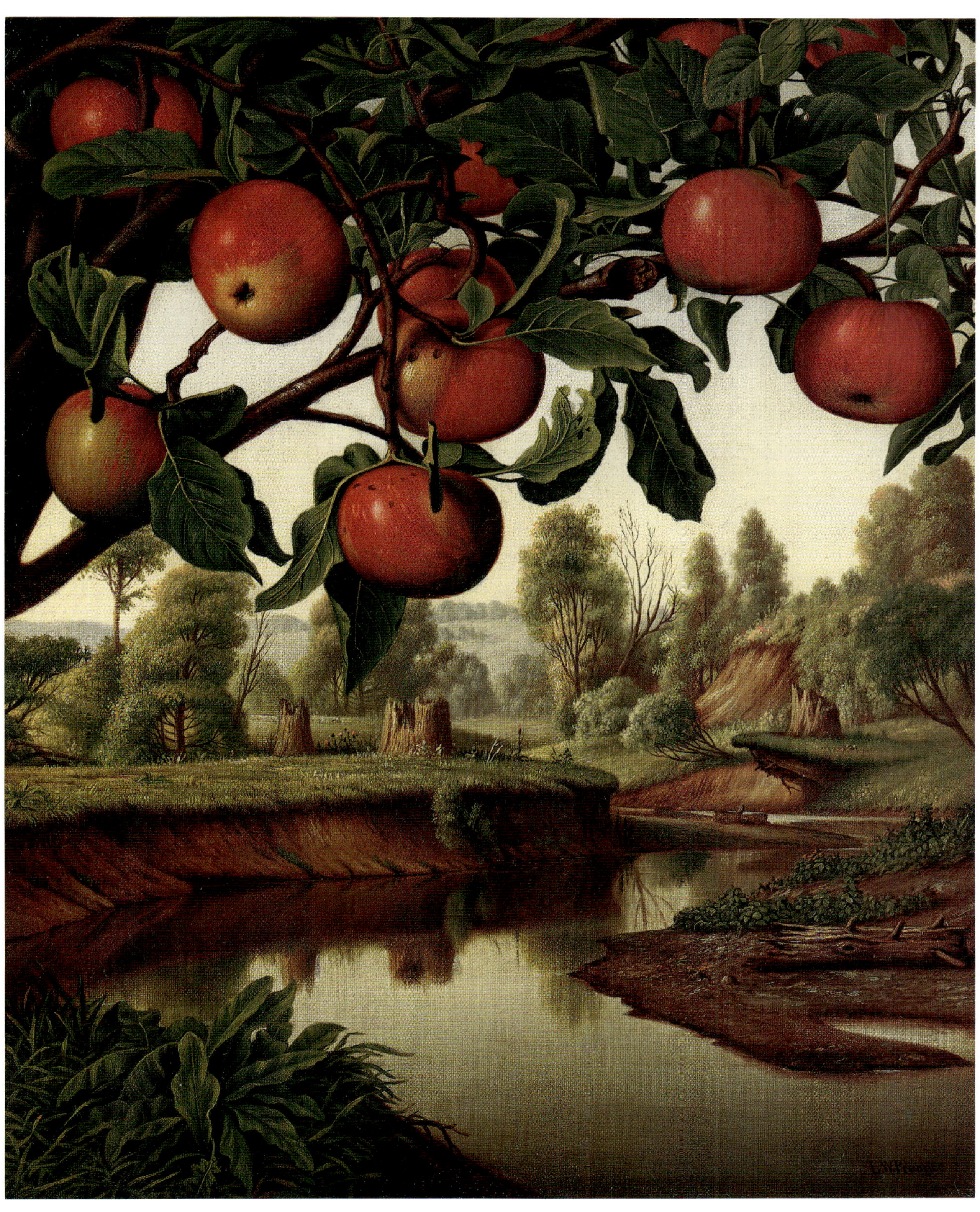

Landscape with Apple Tree   49

John Frederick Peto

1854–1907

Old Time Letter Rack

1894
Oil on canvas
30 x 25 1/8 in. (76.2 x 63.8 cm)

Whereas Peto's horizontal compositions are largely still lifes, his vertical compositions fall generally into three formats. In one, he depicted a variety of items—lanterns, knives, mugs, tin cups, corncob pipes, fishing equipment, horseshoes, or musical instruments—hanging from hooks or nails on artist's palettes, old wood boards, or the backs of doors. In another, he paints two-dimensional items, slips of paper or photographs, tacked to a flat surface and surrounded by a painted frame. And, in a third, he uses the same two-dimensional items without the surrounding frame, either tacked directly to a flat surface, in his so-called "patch" paintings,[1] or tucked into ribbons or tape tacked to a flat surface, in his so-called "rack" paintings. *Old Time Letter Rack* falls into the third category.

A flat format has been favored by trompe l'oeil painters for centuries. By eliminating depth and utilizing a two-dimensional pictorial surface, the painter can heighten the illusionism of his work, pushing the still-life objects out into the viewer's space by painting them parallel to the picture plane; thus, instead of receding, objects move forward. However, in pure trompe l'oeil—ironically—in order to deceive the eye convincingly, the painter's goal must be realism more than trickery. First, the objects must be life-size and shown in their entirety. Second, technique must be precise, and no trace of the painter's hand can be evident; objects must be rendered in a crisp, naturalistic style. Last, the background of the painting should appear to be a continuation of the viewer's space.[2]

The letter or card rack is a grid of flexible strips of ribbons or tape tacked to a two-dimensional vertical surface. Behind the bands small flat objects are held in place—tickets, envelopes, slips of paper, playing cards, photographs, newspaper clippings, postcards, pamphlets, or other handwritten or printed matter. The two-dimensionality of the letter rack makes it an ideal artistic motif for the illusionistic painter. Depictions of them appeared as early as the fifteenth century, the image probably developing out of the *cartellino*. A label or piece of curling paper painted as if it were affixed to a picture and bearing the painter's signature or an inscription, the *cartellino* is an early example of trompe l'oeil that represented paper, exploiting its flatness as an illusionistic device.[3] The letter rack also featured paper ephemera and was particularly popular in the seventeenth century, becoming the specialty of Dutch painters, who utilized a wooden background support and depicted both letter racks and *quod libet* ("what you will"), the latter incorporating small everyday objects such as

bibelots, combs, scissors, or writing implements, along with paper items, tucked into a rack. From its inception in medieval Europe to its apogee in baroque Holland, the letter-rack motif continued to be a popular subject for still-life painters throughout the eighteenth and nineteenth centuries both in Europe and in America.[4]

Here, Peto has rendered a simple grid of pink tape in the configuration of an X within a square, tacked to a black-painted old wood board. The board is composed of two planks, marred by gouges, flat-headed nails, and a faded arithmetical inscription written in chalk. A tacked-up torn green label teases the viewer with its partial words. By showing part of the label torn off, Peto records the pristine condition of the bright black paint of the board underneath in contrast to the weathered state of the surrounding area. Like the unreadable label, the illegible pasted-up newspaper clippings engender the same frustration in the viewer, who encounters only torn scraps of a story, without a headline, beginning, or end. To the right of the grid, an asymmetrical diamond shape is gouged into the splintering wood, and below it a looped string hangs from a nail. A variety of items are held in place by the tapes, some held more securely than others: a government penny postcard with bent edges; torn envelopes with partially legible handwriting; an upside-down red book with a frayed cover; an unmarked pamphlet marred by stains; an old quill pen with missing feathers; an upside-down, black and white, bust-length photograph of Lincoln; and a dark green ticket stub marked "Balcony." Just as the dark background is punctuated by areas of bright, pure color, so the flat vertical format is relieved by areas that move out into the viewer's space, casting shadows and heightening the illusion: a nail juts forward; the loosened tapes curve out limply instead of remaining taut; the glued newspaper clippings are wrinkled and pull away from the board; the folded edges of paper bend forward. Unlike pure trompe l'oeil, however, Peto's brushstroke is evident, differing from the smooth, highly finished technique that is the hallmark of true illusionistic painting. Furthermore, his interest in depicting illegible writing, bold shapes, and artistic geometries of lines and curves, squares and circles, reminds the viewer that the subject is a painting, not reality.[5] Depictions of frayed tape, torn paper, wrinkled string, rusty nails, Peto's still-life objects are old and used; they symbolize the remnants of a personal story that eludes the viewer.

Because of its false signature, this work was for a long time thought to be the work of William Harnett. Purchased as a

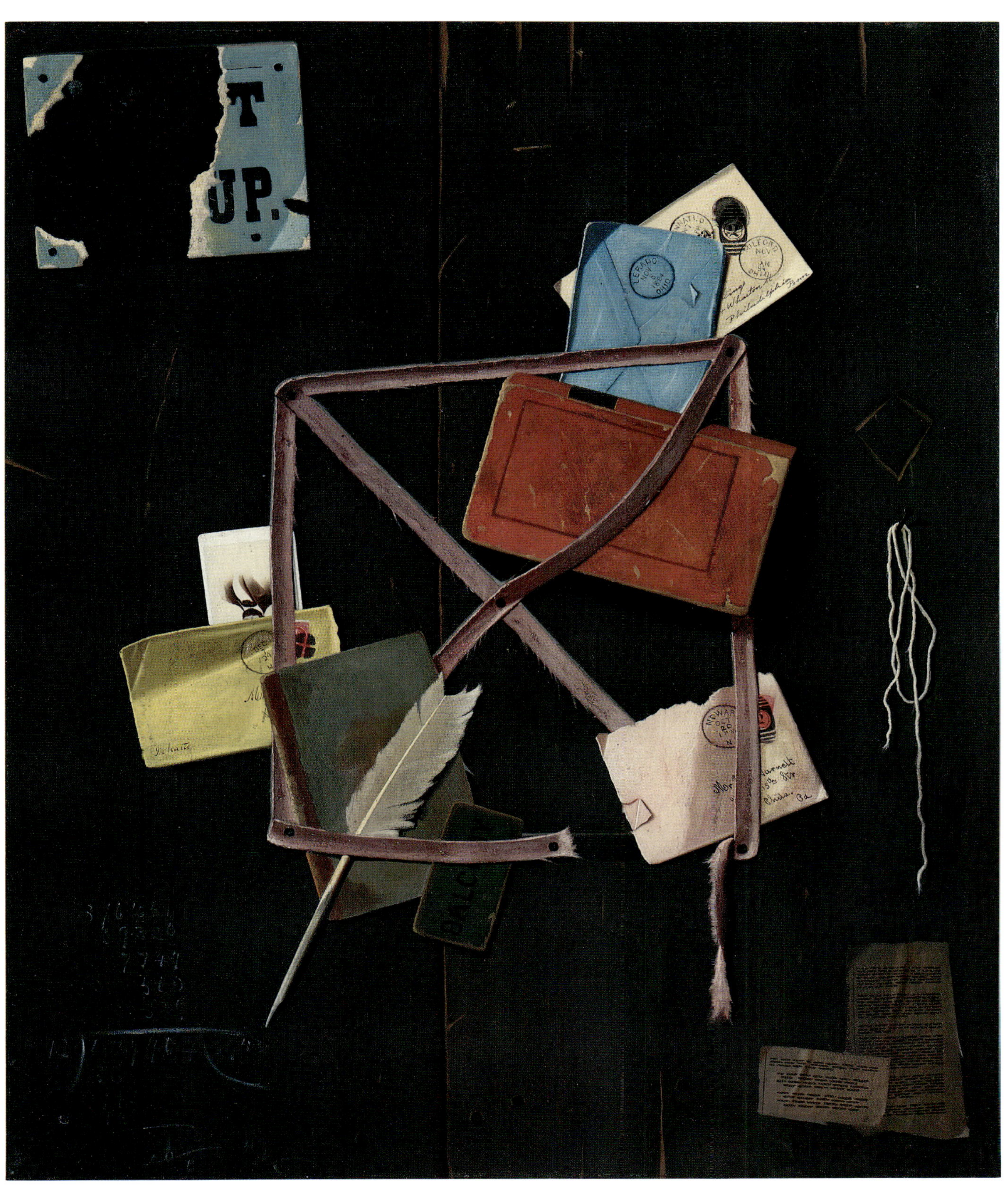

Harnett and donated to the Museum of Modern Art, New York, in 1940, *Old Time Letter Rack* was then known as *Old Scraps*. During the 1940s, Alfred Frankenstein began his research on Harnett's life and work and proved that the painting was, in fact, by Peto. He observed that each of the three addressed envelopes in the painting was in a different handwriting and medium, and that two of the handwritings were later additions that referred to Harnett or his artistic career. Furthermore, the envelope in the upper right-hand corner was painted with an 1894 postmark from Lerado, Ohio, the town Peto's in-laws were from and where he was working on a commission during that year. The date 1894 appeared on two other postmarks as well, making the connection to Harnett even more tenuous, as he had died two years earlier, in 1892. Last, the diffused lighting, the soft edges, the muted tones punctuated by areas of bright color, the emphasis on worn, discarded items, and the portrait of Lincoln,[6] a personal artistic motif that Peto frequently used—in other words, the technique and subject matter of the painting—also substantiated Frankenstein's claim that it had been painted by Peto and not by Harnett. In 1947, Frankenstein's theory was supported by Sheldon Keck, the conservator of the Brooklyn Museum, who removed the overpaint on the canvas and found a Peto signature. And in the late 1960s, Jean Volkmer, the conservator of the Museum of Modern Art, removed the lining from the back of the canvas, revealing an inscription in Peto's hand that referred to the painting as *Old Time Letter Rack*, painted in 1894.[7]

Peto essayed the letter-rack format before Harnett did. His *Office Board for Smith Brothers Coal Company* (The Addison Gallery of American Art, Phillips Academy, Andover, Massachusetts) was painted in June 1879. Harnett's first use of the rack motif, *The Artist's Letter Rack* (The Metropolitan Museum of Art, New York), is dated August of the same year.[8] Working in Philadelphia during these years, both painters mutually influenced one another, but it is Peto who is known as the "master of the rack picture";[9] he painted more than a dozen paintings in this format, while Harnett is known to have painted only two.[10] Peto's rack paintings can be divided in two periods: 1879 to 1885 and 1894 to 1904. Although not all of his early rack paintings were meant to advertise places of business, his first served mostly as commercial office boards, painted racks that incorporated items relating to a particular business, with references to its product and owner. The office boards he produced during these years were for Philadelphia businessmen and craftsmen, including the framemaker Christian Faser, editor of *The*

Philadelphia Sunday Transcript, William Malcolm Bunn, owner of *The Record*, William Miskey Singerly, and chiropodist Bernard Goldberg. Although he was sometimes commissioned by a client to paint an office board, Peto probably also painted them gratis, in the hope that the particular business establishment represented would be interested in acquiring it. Often containing explicit references and details of ownership, his early racks are typically made up of complex grid arrangements of several tapes, holding a variety of printed matter and tacked to a light-colored wood support.[11]

Peto seems to have abandoned the rack format for close to ten years, and by the time he painted the subject again in 1894, the year of *Old Time Letter Rack*, his style had changed. His rack paintings were no longer intended to adorn places of business, but instead were personal records of his own life and career—a career, marked by failure, that had vanished into obscurity. The later racks are striking in their deterioration and simplicity: the usual network of tapes, ragged and torn, has been reduced to an austere crisscross pattern perhaps influenced by Harnett.[12] Their colors have become darker, more muted, and the wood support is often painted black, brown, or dark green. Like the tapes, the objects represented—torn envelopes, dog-eared postcards, faded photographs, yellowed newspaper clippings—are characteristically frayed and worn from years of handling.[13] One scholar has referred to these items as "scraps of the artist's life," their tattered condition symbolizing the final years of a disappointed artistic career.[14]

BETHANY ASTRACHAN

1   The term "patch painting," in reference to Peto's work, is aptly defined by Alfred Frankenstein as a 'rack' picture without a rack," where objects are pasted directly onto a board without the support of tapes. *John F. Peto*, exh. cat. (Brooklyn, N.Y.: Brooklyn Museum, 1950), 18.

2   For a discussion of the characteristics of trompe l'oeil painting, see Alfred Frankenstein, *After the Hunt: William Harnett and Other American Still Life Painters 1870–1900*, rev. ed. (Berkeley and Los Angeles: University of California Press, 1969), 54; Norman Bryson, *Looking at the Overlooked: Four Essays on Still-Life Painting* (Cambridge, Mass.: Harvard University Press, 1990), 140–44; M. L. d'Otrange Mastai, *Illusion in Art: Trompe L'Oeil, A History of Pictorial Illusionism* (New York: Abaris Books, 1975), 8–25; and William Kloss, *More Than Meets The Eye: The Art of Trompe L'Oeil*, exh. cat. (Columbus, Ohio: Columbus Museum of Art, 1986), 17–20.

3 Miriam Milman defines the device known as the *cartellino*, linking these images of paper to letter-rack paintings in *The Illusions of Reality: Trompe-L'Oeil Painting* (New York: Rizzoli, 1983), 12, 60, 72–73, 83, 124.

4 For European precedents and American examples of letter-rack paintings, see Frankenstein, *After the Hunt*, 53–54; d'Otrange Mastai, 160, 176–82, 210–11, 267–73, 276; and John Wilmerding, *Important Information Inside: The Art of John F. Peto and the Idea of Still-Life Painting in Nineteenth-Century America*, exh. cat. (Washington, D.C.: National Gallery of Art, 1983), 150, 209–14.

5 Johanna Drucker discusses the anti-illusionism of the work of Peto, Harnett, and John Haberle in "Harnett, Haberle, and Peto: Visuality and Artifice Among the Proto-Modern Americans," *The Art Bulletin* 74 (March 1992): 48. Wilmerding underscores this idea throughout his book. He concludes: "Typically Peto brings us to the verge of illusionism, only to assert ultimately the primacy of paint, color, design, perception—in other words, the reality of artifice itself" (183)

6 For information on Peto's obsession with Lincoln and Civil War imagery and how this focus parallels a general fin de siècle retrospection, see Wilmerding, 13, 158, 172, 187–89, 194–204, and Frankenstein, *After the Hunt*, 107.

7 Frankenstein discusses the history of *Old Time Letter Rack* and outlines his discovery of the forgery in *After the Hunt*, 11–17. See also Frankenstein, "Harnett, True and False," *The Art Bulletin* 31 (March 1949): 38–56; and Frankenstein, *The Reality of Appearance: The Trompe L'Oeil Tradition in American Painting*, exh. cat. (Berkeley, Calif.: University Art Museum, 1970), 106. The painting is also discussed by Wilmerding, 222; and by Elizabeth Johns, "Harnett Enters Art History," in *William M. Harnett*, exh. cat. (Fort Worth, Tex.: Amon Carter Museum/New York: Metropolitan Museum of Art, 1992), 101–12. For the characteristics of Peto's style, which helped to establish the authenticity of *Old Time Letter Rack*, see Lloyd Goodrich, "Harnett and Peto: A Note on Style," *The Art Bulletin* 31 (March 1949): 57–59.

8 Wilmerding, 209.

9 Frankenstein, *The Reality of Appearance*, 96.

10 Harnett's other painting, *Mr. Hulings' Rack Picture* (Jo Ann and Julian Ganz, Jr.), was painted in 1888, nine years after his first work in the letter-rack format. See Wilmerding, 214.

11 For a discussion of Peto's patrons and his early rack paintings and office boards, see Wilmerding, 207–9, 217–20; and Frankenstein, *After the Hunt*, 102–4, 107–9.

12 Peto apparently owned a photograph of Harnett's 1879 rack painting, *The Artist's Letter Rack*. This work may have inspired Peto to use a more simplified grid arrangement in his later works. See Wilmerding, 216; and Frankenstein, *After the Hunt*, 52.

13 For a discussion of Peto's later rack paintings, see Wilmerding, 222, 230; and Frankenstein, *After the Hunt*, 108–9.

14 William H. Gerdts, *Painters of the Humble Truth: Masterpieces of American Still Life, 1801–1939*, exh. cat. (Tulsa, Okla.: Philbrook Art Center/Columbia and London: University of Missouri Press, 1981), 182. I would like to extend special thanks to Professor Gerdts for his assistance with the research on many of the still-life paintings in this exhibition and for his generosity in sharing his insights with me.

John Haberle

1853–1933

The Changes of Time

1888
Oil on canvas
24⅜ x 20¼ in. (61.9 x 51.4 cm)

Dedicated to precise, illusionistic renderings, Haberle was a master at manipulating the viewer's sense of visual reality.[1] In 1889, the art critic for the *Chicago Inter-Ocean* expressed his dissatisfaction with Haberle's *U.S.A.* (1889, Collection of JoAnn and Julian Ganz, Jr.), then on display at The Art Institute of Chicago:

There is a fraud hanging on the Institute walls concerning which it is not pleasant to speak. It is that alleged still life by Haberle, supposed by some to be a painting of money. A $1 bill and the fragments of a $10 note have been pasted on canvas, covered by a thin scumble of paint, and further manipulated to give it a painty [sic] appearance. A glass has been put over the "painting" since the writer of this picked loose the edge of the bill. That the management of the Art Institute should hang this kind of "art," even though it were genuine, is to be regretted, but to lend itself to such a fraud, whether unwittingly or not, is shameful.[2]

In response to this accusation, Haberle rushed to Chicago from New York and had experts examine the work. A declaration of authenticity was printed in the *Chicago Daily News*: "The lens was used, the paint was rubbed off, and the whole ingenious design proved really a work of imitative art, and a most excellent one. Both bills were painted, the stamp was painted, and the newspaper clipping was painted."[3]

The debate about the difference between reality and illusion succinctly describes the reactions to American trompe l'oeil painting during the second quarter of the nineteenth century. It also aptly characterizes the most successful aspect of Haberle's oeuvre, as he was devoted to exploiting the illusionistic possibilities of painting. Within the confines of this genre of pictorial deception, he consistently sought to surpass his own ingenuity, and it is precisely his flair for manipulation that helped to revivify a previously dormant tradition.

The American interest in trompe l'oeil during this period was due in part to technological and industrial developments that unleashed widespread changes in political, social, economic, and cultural structures. Most relevant here is the rise of the imitational capabilities of mass production and the faith in technology's ability to fabricate replicas of any- and everything. During Haberle's lifetime, simulation was a staple of the middle class's cultural and social diet. As a result of the rise in the availability of mass-produced merchandise, affluence was measured by plentitude. Plentitude took on distinct meaning: it was supported by the reproduction of all types of objects, ranging from paintings to furniture. Concurrently, trompe l'oeil appealed to the growing middle class: the genre represented items particular to that class in the imitational style that it desired.[4]

In art historical discourses, the still-life tradition has been denigrated and even condemned.[5] First, still life generally depicts the utilitarian, secular, and inanimate as opposed to human figures, action, and narrative, elements that give history painting its moral and philosophical meaning. Second, still life was not considered technically challenging but almost mechanical. Its emphasis on the exact transcription of objects versus inventive painterly style was unappreciated. Consequently, its perceived lack of thematic and technical sophistication placed it below portraiture, landscape, and history painting on the scale of artistic values. Indeed, such a hierarchy was established as early as the seventeenth century and has continued into the twentieth. With its commonplace subject matter and an intentionally mechanical-like painterly style, trompe l'oeil was seen as antithetical to artistic creativity and relegated to an even lower position than still life.[6]

In America, trompe l'oeil first reached a high point from 1800 to 1825, mostly in Philadelphia. Best known from this period are Charles Willson Peale's *The Staircase Group: Raphaelle and Titian Ramsay Peale* (1795, Philadelphia Museum of Art) and Raphaelle Peale's *Venus Rising from the Sea—A Deception* (1822, The Nelson-Atkins Museum of Art, Kansas City). While Charles Willson Peale was known for his portraits, his son Raphaelle is considered the earliest professional still-life painter. Yet his works never moved beyond the bounds of the genre's status.[7] In fact, despite the attention devoted to trompe l'oeil, the first half of the nineteenth century was still dominated by portrait painting, the second, by genre painting of American life, and landscape painting.[8] It was only during the last quarter of the century that trompe l'oeil became popular again, and its artistic status remained consistent. Haberle, William M. Harnett, and John Peto were the preeminent still-life painters of the later part of the nineteenth century and were partially responsible for the rise in the genre's popularity at that time.

Because of their subject matter and style, then, Haberle's paintings attracted the attention of businessmen and merchants, rather than scholars and critics. They were purchased and commissioned by entrepreneurs and exhibited in places of commerce, such as saloons, liquor stores, hotels, theaters,

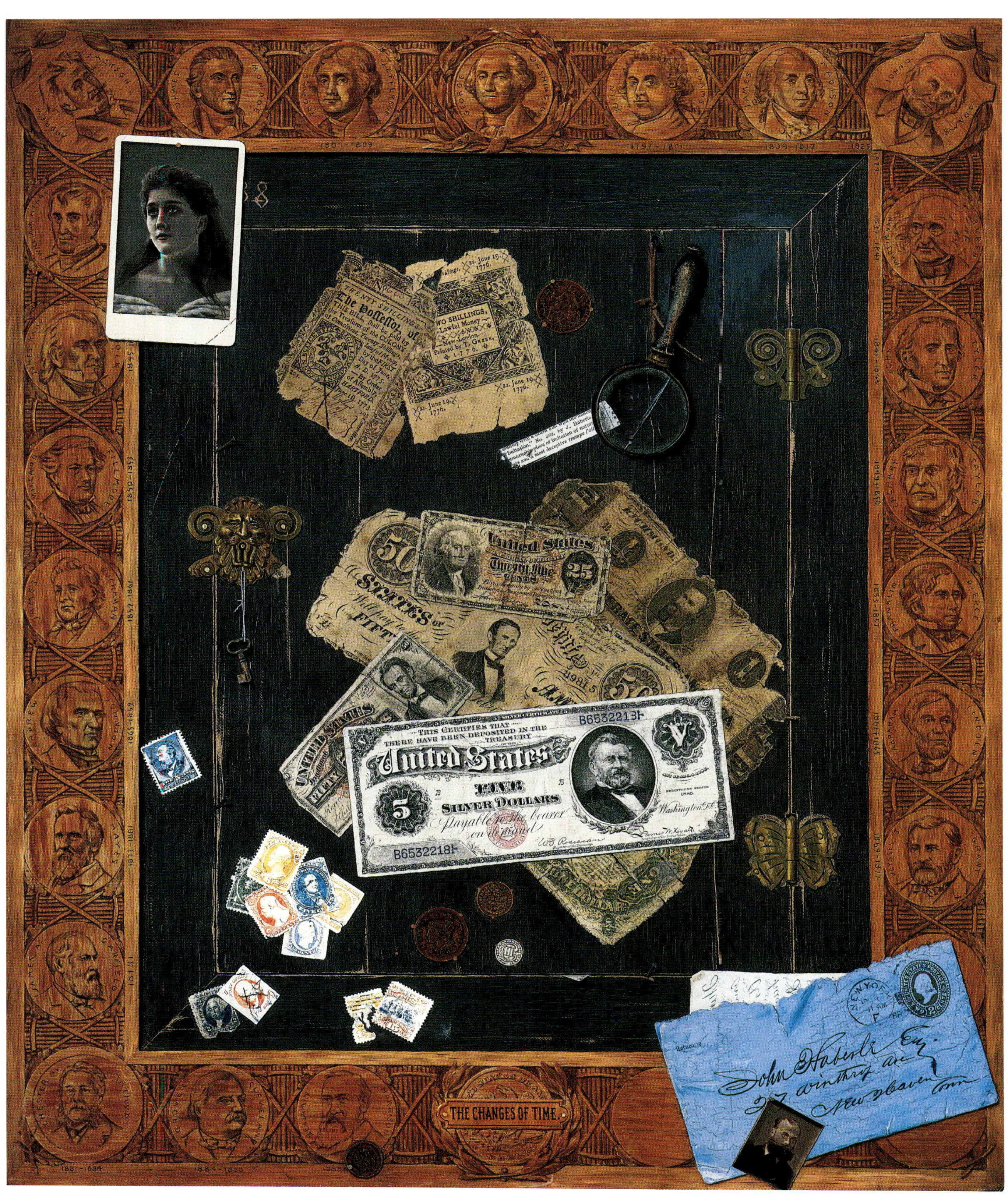

and stationery and bookstores.[9] *The Changes of Time* was first exhibited at the Pennsylvania Academy of the Fine Arts in 1889 with the high price of $2,200. It was later purchased by Marvin Preston, a Detroit businessman, and E. W. Churchill, the owner of a Detroit saloon. Along with four other paintings by Haberle, it was displayed at the saloon.[10]

Nowhere is Haberle's skill at trompe l'oeil more evident than in the witty and brazen *The Changes of Time*. Perhaps the most striking element about it is the central position accorded to paper currency, a subject that became popular for American illusionistic painters. With the rise of materialism and consumerism, monetary issues were topically important, notably the regulation and circulation of paper currency.[11] Although coinage had appeared in European painting, the depiction of paper money was a purely American phenomenon.[12] Furthermore, the flatness of paper currency lent itself to trompe l'oeil, whose effectiveness depends on the lack of pictorial depth.[13] Haberle's earliest paintings of it date from 1887.[14] Here he built upon the groundwork laid down by his contemporary Harnett, whose *Five Dollar Bill* (1887, Philadelphia Museum of Art) is the earliest known example of the paper-money genre.[15] In fact, despite warnings against counterfeiting from the Secret Service, Haberle continued to include currency in his paintings, and even to paint pictures of nothing but currency.[16]

Both the variety of paper currency represented, and the time span from which that currency is drawn—1773 to 1886—give a clever and determined overview of its history. At the center of *The Changes of Time* are six types of well-worn paper currency. The bill closest to the foreground is a five-dollar Silver Certificate bearing Grant's portrait, from an 1886 series printed in 1887. It is the newest bill in the group.[17] Beneath and directly below the Silver Certificate is the corner of a one-dollar greenback that carries a warning against counterfeiting. These bills were issued during the fiscal crises of the Civil War and were a fiat currency that could not be redeemed for precious metal. Beneath and directly above the Silver Certificate to the right are two examples of Confederate currency, a fifty-dollar bill bearing the portrait of Jefferson Davis and a one-dollar bill bearing the likeness of Stonewall Jackson. The two remaining smaller bills are twenty-five-cent and fifty-cent fractional notes. These were issued at the beginning of the Civil War as substitutes for silver and gold coins, of which there was a dearth due to hoarding. Directly above the center group are Connecticut shilling notes of 1773 and 1776, and directly below it are a variety of

coins and brightly colored postage stamps, which served as currency during the Civil War.[18]

The paper currency floats on top of a weathered cabinet door tantalizingly inaccessible: despite the brass hinges on the right side of the door, the satyr-head brass escutcheon on the left bars the cabinet from swinging open. The key that dangles from this escutcheon seems further to frustrate one's impulse to gain entry. At the same time, however, this playful inaccessibility calls attention to the flatness required for successful trompe l'oeil: regardless of the possible existence of more information behind the cabinet, a metaphor for depth, that information must remain unavailable. Indeed, the tiny corner of paper that has slipped through the crack in the bottom right-hand side of the door is ironic: the objects in the painting are all nearly paperlike in their flatness, so a cabinet full of paper only serves to reemphasize Haberle's calculated choice of flat subject matter.

On the upper right-hand corner of the cabinet door are a cracked magnifying glass hung on a nail and a newspaper clipping. Haberle regularly included newspaper clippings in his paintings. His clippings are distinguished from renderings by other artists by the legibility of their texts and their references to the success of other paintings by Haberle. This clipping reads: *"entirely with the brush and with the naked . . . e(ye) . . . 'Imitation', No. 362 by J. Haberle . . . a (r)emarkable piece of imitation of natura(l) . . . ob(je)cts . . . and a most deceptive trompe l'oil* [sic]." This paraphrases an 1887 review of Haberle's *Imitation* (1887, Private Collection) published in the *New York Evening Post*.[19] Although the magnifying glass is available and alludes to a process of close inspection, and thus confirmation of information, its crack playfully undermines this function and exaggerates the difficulty of determining the difference between reality and illusion. This ineffectuality is emphasized by the relation between the magnifying glass and the newspaper clipping: while the glass partially blocks our visual access to parts of the clipping, the clipping is readable enough, with its praise for Haberle's success as a painter of illusion. Indeed, deception wins out, for what is the magnifying glass but a *painted* object?

The painted frame supports simulated carved wooden medallions with portraits of the American presidents through Benjamin Harrison, along with the dates of their administrations. Since the painting was completed a few months before Harrison's inauguration in 1889, a U.S. Navy Button covers the end of his term.[20] The chronology begins at the top with George Washington in the center and then alternates between the left and the right sides until we come to the portrait of Rutherford Hayes on the left. Thereafter, the portraits proceed in a direct line on the right, although the four medallions in the lower right-hand corner remain empty. Directly below George Washington is a medallion that carries the title of the painting on a coin. The peculiar shift in chronology seems to declare that changes of time, or history, are less than linear or predictable, and the four empty medallions leave a place for history yet to be made. Coupled with the overall deceptive qualities of the painting, this historical analysis indicates an awareness of the considerable transformations and instability that characterized the period.

Finally, through epistolary communication and photographic representation, Haberle has signed his painting indirectly,[21] including an envelope addressed to himself in New Haven, where he was born and spent most of his life. It is postmarked New York, with the date '88. A corner of the letter protrudes from the envelope, and the contents are barely visible through the sheer paper.[22] Thus, in writing his name and address, Haberle claims the painting as his own. At the bottom of the painting, on top of the letter, is a tintype photograph of Haberle.[23] A photograph of a woman is located in the upper left-hand corner and tacked onto the illusionistic frame. This was a type of photograph frequently found on cigarette packets as an incentive to purchase a certain brand.[24] Since representations of people generally do not work successfully in trompe l'oeil, Haberle's choice of photography to represent himself and the woman, combined with his use of wood carving to represent the presidents, is a clever solution to this dilemma. It also acknowledges the contemporary industrial and conceptual developments in photography and their relationship to painting. Lastly, by placing his photographed self-portrait next to one of the empty medallions, Haberle seems to have included himself in the honorable chronology of the presidents and history.[25] Within the confines of the logic of trompe l'oeil, in which things are not what they appear to be, Haberle's oblique assertion of himself as a historical figure is consistent: for, although *The Changes of Time* is a masterpiece of deception, Haberle's skill as an artist is, undoubtedly, real.

BETH A. HANDLER

1 For a discussion of the difference between the reproduction and the presentation of objects, see Johanna Drucker, "Harnett, Haberle and Peto: Visuality and Artifice among the Proto-Modern Americans," *The Art Bulletin* 74 (March 1992): 37–50.

2 Quoted in Alfred Frankenstein, *After the Hunt: William Harnett and Other American Still Life Painters, 1870–1900* (Berkeley and Los Angeles: University of California Press, 1953), 117.

3 Ibid. Eventually, the critic of the *Inter-Ocean* apologized for his accusation.

4 For a discussion of the roles played by abundance, consumption, and imitation during the nineteenth century, see Miles Orvell, *The Real Thing: Imitation and Authenticity in American Culture, 1880–1940* (Chapel Hill and London: University of North Carolina Press, 1989).

5 For a discussion of the historiography of trompe l'oeil, see Elizabeth Johns, "Harnett Enters Art History," in Bolger et al., 101–12.

6 William H. Gerdts, *Painters of the Humble Truth: Masterpieces of American Still Life 1801–1939* (Tulsa, Okla.: Philbrook Art Center/Columbia and London: University of Missouri Press, 1981), 21–22. See also William Gerdts and Russell Burke, *American Still-Life Painting* (New York, Washington, London: Praeger Publishers, 1971). For a discussion of artistic, social, and ideological marginalization of trompe l'oeil, see Nicolai Cikovsky, Jr., "'Sordid Mechanics' and 'Monkey Talents': The Illusionistic Tradition," in Doreen Bolger, Marc Simpson, and John Wilmerding, eds., *William M. Harnett* (Fort Worth, Tex.: Amon Carter Museum/New York: Metropolitan Museum of Art, 1992), 19–29. Bryson also has discussed the status of trompe l'oeil within painting hierarchies. See Norman Bryson, *Looking at the Overlooked: Four Essays on Still Life Painting* (Cambridge, Mass.: Harvard University Press, 1990).

7 See Gerdts, 47–65.

8 Jules David Prown, *American Painting: From Its Beginnings to the Armory Show* (New York: Rizzoli International Publications, 1969).

9 Gertrude Grace Sill, *John Haberle: Master of Illusion* (Springfield, Mass.: Museum of fine Arts, 1985), 10.

10 Frankenstein, 118.

11 Bruce Chambers, *Old Money: American Trompe l'Oeil Images of Currency* (New York: Berry-Hill Galleries, 1988), 14. See also Edward J. Nygren, "The Almighty Dollar: Money as a Theme in American Painting," *Winterthur Portfolio* 23 (Summer/Autumn 1988): 129–50.

12 Chambers, 13; Nygren, 129.

13 Frankenstein has stated that money was used for pictorial reasons only (43). Chambers and Nygren, however, locate this interest in contemporary monetary debates.

14 Haberle painted *Imitation* and *Reproduction* in 1887.

15 Harnett generally included paper currency as just one element in his tabletop still lifes. In 1886, however, he stopped painting money after *Five Dollar Bill* was seized by the Secret Service for possibly violating laws against counterfeiting. Interestingly, while Harnett obeyed these restrictions, other painters exploited the notoriety of the case for their own advancement, and paintings of currency flourished. Linda Ayres, "John Haberle, *The Changes of Time*," in *American Paintings from the Manoogian Collection*, exh.

cat. (Washington, D.C.: National Gallery of Art/Detroit: Detroit Institute of Arts, 1989), 110.

16 These include *Imitation* (1887), *Reproduction* (1887), *Can You Break a Five?* (1888), *The Changes of Time* (1888), *U.S.A.* (1889), *Twenty Dollar Bill* (1890), *One Dollar Bill* (1890), and *The Bachelor's Drawer* (1890–94). The most thorough analysis of Haberle's and Harnett's painting of currency is that of Bruce Chambers. See also Frankenstein, 117.

17 Eighteen eighty-six is also the year in which Harnett was warned against painting money (Ayres, 110).

18 I am indebted to Bruce Chambers's identification of the various types of currency in this painting.

19 The original text reads: "'Imitation', No. 362, by J. Haberle, a small canvas which, without being in any sense a work of art, is a remarkable piece of imitation of natural objects and almost deceptive trompe l'oil [*sic*]" (Chambers, 35).

20 Ayres, 110.

21 Frankenstein makes this assertion in regard to the tintype photograph of Haberle in his *Reproduction*, 1888 (ibid., 116).

22 From our perspective, we can see two sheets of paper. On one, the writing is darker and backwards; this would be the top sheet. On the lower sheet, the writing is fainter but right-side-up (ibid., 118).

23 Tintype photographs were first manufactured in 1865. This inexpensive process used tin instead of paper to support the image, on which several images of the sitter could be secured at once.

24 For a discussion of the history of cigarette-pack art, see Chris Mullen, *Cigarette Pack Art* (New York: St. Martin's Press, 1979).

25 Sill, 14.

Otis Kaye

1885–1974

Time Is Money

c. 1929
Oil on wood panel
9 x 12 ³/4 in. (22.9 x 32.4 cm.)

General references to money and the American preoccupation with profit-making appeared repeatedly in the popular press, cartoons, and other money paintings in the late nineteenth and early twentieth centuries. In *Time Is Money*, Kaye has added a personal, wry commentary on an established American genre.

Called "the last of the great trompe l'oeil money painters,"[1] Otis Kaye was a largely self-taught artist. An engineer and businessman by profession, he began painting around 1917 and continued it as a hobby until the 1950s. During the early part of the twentieth century, when interest in Harnett, Haberle, and Peto had generally declined, Kaye remained fascinated by trompe l'oeil painting.[2] His still lifes, many of which paid homage to his predecessors, are precise, witty, ironic, and very personal.[3]

In *Time Is Money*, Kaye used an actual oak-veneered wood panel on which he painted a broken-faced watch suspended by a string over three bank notes of obsolete nineteenth-century currency. Simulating the illusionistic precision of the rack pictures of previous trompe l'oeil masters, Kaye portrayed these objects as existing in a very shallow, almost two-dimensional space. In the lower right, above the tiny, torn newspaper clipping, he signed the painting "N. A. Brooks."

Kaye had met the trompe l'oeil artist Nicholas A. Brooks in New York in 1904, the same year he acquired two of Brooks's paintings. When he began to paint a dozen years later, Kaye taught himself by copying Brooks's work.[4] He signed at least one other painting with Brooks's signature, *Trompe l'Oeil for Bessie Hoffman* (after 1922; Private Collection). It contained a trompe l'oeil newspaper clipping in which Kaye as painter wrote: "To the critic the artist replied, 'Imitation is the highest form of compliment to art, man, or nature.' One critic rose to complain of mere deception; however, he quickly sat down when the painter offered him a brush." Kaye's retort to the critic's charge of "mere deception" in this imaginary exchange not only shows his sense of humor; it comments on the skill involved in creating convincing trompe l'oeil paintings.

In *Time Is Money*, Kaye portrays a twenty-five-cent note at the upper left, a ten-cent note in the center, and an old one-dollar bill underneath. All three are painted with extraordinary detail. Copying the design on the bills with the accuracy of an engraver (or a counterfeiter), Kaye has matched the colors and reproduced the intricate draftsmanship of the

lettering, seal, and signatures with clarity. Unlike other trompe l'oeil money painters, who often made caricatures of the faces on the bills, Kaye reproduces the portrait images with fidelity to the originals. The ten-cent note portrays William Merith, Secretary of the Treasury, 1849–50, and the twenty-five-cent note, Robert Walker, Secretary of the Treasury, 1845–49.

All bank notes valued at less than a dollar, for example the ten- and twenty-five cent notes in *Time Is Money*, are considered "fractional." Fractional currency originated to replace metal coins in the United States in 1862. At the onset of the Civil War, the price of metal rose rapidly; and as the intrinsic value of coins exceeded their face value, people began to hoard them or melt them down for metal. A substantial reduction in the circulation of coins constricted commerce, so the federal government first responded by authorizing postage stamps as currency. In 1863 it began printing notes of 3, 5, 10, 15, 25, and 50 cent denominations. Between 1862 and 1876, five issues of these notes were printed. After 1876, coins slowly returned to circulation, and fractional currency could be redeemed for coinage.[5]

The particular ten-cent and twenty-five-cent notes that Kaye has depicted were issued between 1874 and 1876, and both bills are of the final (fifth) issue. The outdated dollar bill was issued between 1874 and 1917, and here Kaye has painted an 1890 note. The same currency appears in other Kaye paintings, such as *Money to Burn* (1927; Private Collection), *Breakout* (1930; Private Collection), and *Trompe l'Oeil for Bessie Hoffman* (after 1922; Private Collection). Kaye's choice of obsolete bills can be attributed to the fact that by the time he was painting, it was illegal to paint contemporary money. Harnett and Haberle had already had dealings with the authorities because of potential counterfeiting, and the attention actually increased the public's interest in their work.[6] After 1909, a federal law allowed an artist to be prosecuted as a criminal for painting currency, and their work could be confiscated and even destroyed.

Time Is Money plays on the idea of fractions as incomplete parts of a larger whole. Not only are two of the notes fractional, the one-dollar bill itself is also literally "fractional," in that a third of it is missing. The face of the watch is similarly incomplete; the glass is cracked and most of it is missing. A pocket watch—time—is hanging (or suspended) over pocket change—money. The money is obsolete; the watch is most likely stopped; both of them are suspended in a state of inactivity.

Time Is Money was probably painted during the Great Depression (between 1929 and 1940), when the entire U.S. economy was similarly constricted by inactivity.[7] Like millions of other Americans during the depression, Kaye had lost his job. He had also invested heavily in the stock market during the 1920s, and when the market crashed in 1929 lost his savings. The fact that this painting was probably done when Kaye was unemployed and without funds adds to its poignancy: he had plenty of time and little or no money. If "Time is money," then the composition is an ironic comment on the frustrations of the times: the money here is useless, and time has come to a standstill. Kaye saved money by making small paintings and using the minimal amount of materials. Instead of painting a simulation of wood, as a number of other trompe l'oeil artists did, in *Time Is Money*, Kaye used the actual varnished wood veneer of the panel as background for the composition, as he did in a number of other paintings executed during the same period.

Most of Kaye's paintings were created in honor of family and friends. They often contained humorous references to people for whom gifts were made. In *Time Is Money*, Kaye has painted a small piece of a fictitous newspaper clipping that reads: "ZEIT IST GELD! Noted lecturer, Miss G. Szymanski was c[. . .] relate her point of view freely to the pu[blic . . .] "Time is M[oney . . .] and lit[tle . . .]" Kaye has left parts of the text missing, but gives just enough information to pique our curiosity. Miss G. Szymanski was a neighbor who lived in the same apartment building as Kaye. She had no family of her own and was known as the local busybody. Never hesitating to tell others how to conduct their lives, Miss Szymanski has been immortalized here as a "noted lecturer."[8]

"Zeit ist Geld" is German for "Time is money." Benjamin Franklin had coined the aphorism in the mid-eighteenth century,[9] and by the early twentieth century it had become a standard business phrase that was mocked by the press and numerous artists.[10] The term evoked the concept of "Taylorism," or "scientific management," which was deemed a particularly effective business practice by the 1890s. Stressing efficiency, Frederick Winslow Taylor's "time and motion" studies had aspired to make workers more productive by breaking jobs down into short, repetitive tasks. The procedure gave rise to the assembly line, increased production, and made higher profits for factory owners. For the worker it meant greater pressure to perform under ever-increasing time constraints.[11] By the 1930s, the apho-rism "Time is money," rang hollow, as efficiency and scientific management had not ensured the economic stability it seemed to have promised.

ALISON TILGHMAN

1 Bruce Chambers, *Old Money: American Trompe l'Oeil Images of Currency* (New York: Berry-Hill Galleries, 1988), 85.

2 In 1929, Edith Halpert had an important show at the Downtown Gallery in New York that revived an interest in the American trompe l'oeil masters. From the late nineteenth century until the time of this show, precise, illusionistic still lifes were largely unappreciated.

3 Edward J. Nygren has pointed out that painted images of money constituted a major theme in American painting in the last quarter of the nineteenth century that has no parallel in European painting. Nygren, "The Almighty Dollar: Money as a Theme in American Painting," *Winterthur Portfolio* 23 (Autumn 1988): 129–50.

4 My thanks to Bruce Chambers and Paul Banks, both of whom affirmed that Kaye had indeed painted *Time Is Money*. Chambers pointed out that the typesetting in the newspaper clipping is a twentieth-century rather than a nineteenth-century style. Also, Brooks never painted fractional currency, whereas Kaye often did. Kaye also used German in this painting, which Brooks never would have done.

5 See Gene Hessler, *The Comprehensive Catalog of U.S. Paper Money* (Chicago: Henry Regnery Company, 1974), 309.

6 See Chambers; Nygren; and Alfred Frankenstein, *After the Hunt: William Harnett and Other American Still Life Painters, 1870–1900* (Berkeley and Los Angeles: University of California Press, 1953; rev. ed., 1969).

7 I am dating the painting by the reference to Miss G. Szymanski in the clipping. Kaye knew her in Chicago when he, his wife, and two children lived there with his first cousin, Paul Banks, and his wife, Bess Hoffman, during the depression. Kaye painted this picture as a birthday present for his neighbor, Miss Szymanski. It was purchased from her years later by Paul Banks.

8 I am indebted to Paul Banks, Jr., who kindly identified Miss G. Szymanski and offered other information about Kaye's painting and his life.

9 See Chambers, 84; Nygren, 140.

10 Other trompe l'oeil money painters who used the term "Time is money" in their paintings are Ferdinand Danton, Jr., Victor Dubreuil, A. Duran, and Gayle Blair Tate.

11 See Frederick Winslow Taylor, *The Principles of Scientific Management* (New York: Norton, 1967 [1911]). For a discussion of Taylorism and trompe l'oeil money painting, see Chambers, 82–84.

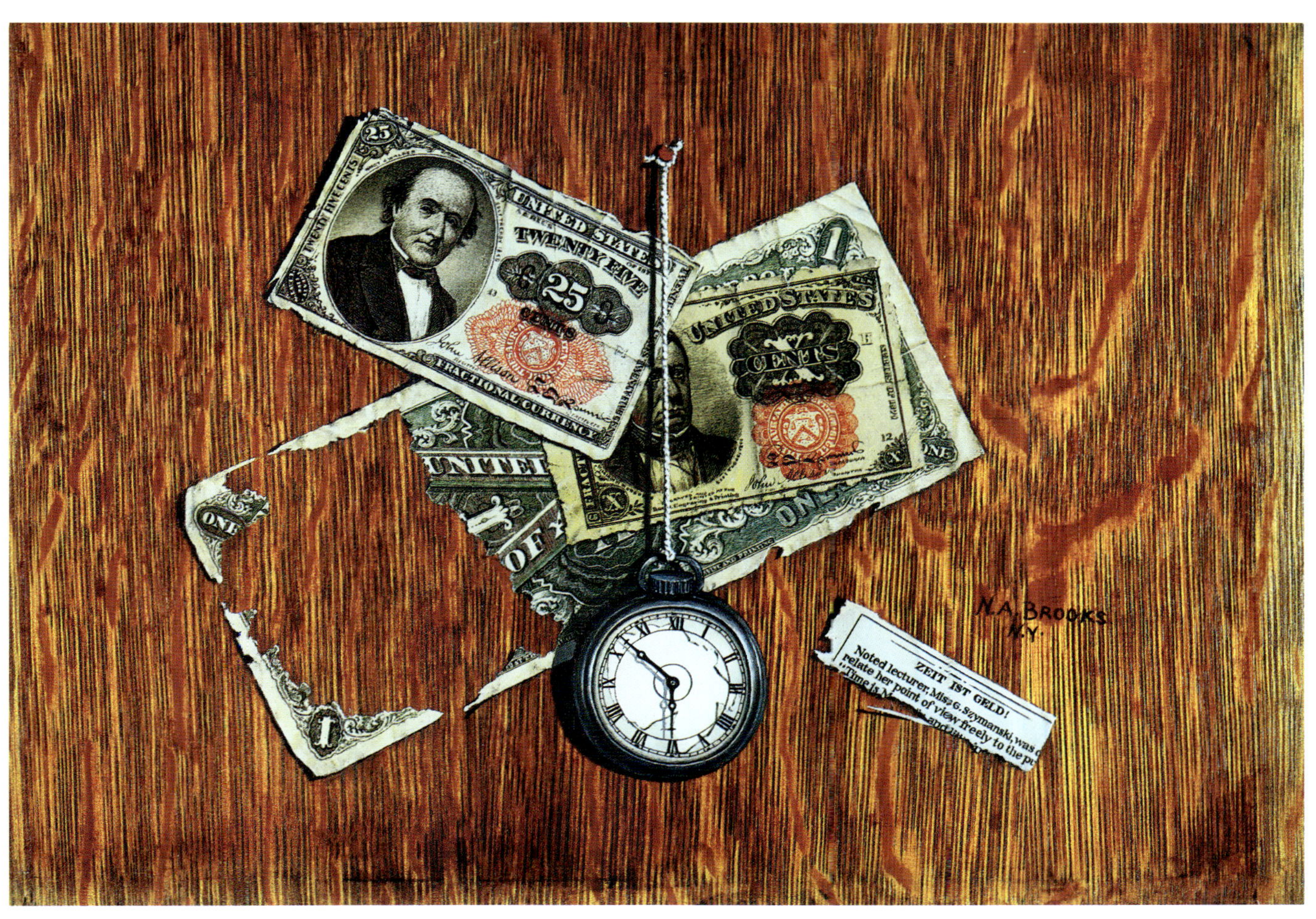

UNITED STATES
TWENTY FIVE
25
FRACTIONAL CURRENCY
UNITED STATES
CENTS
ONE
N.A. BROOKS
N.Y.
ZEIT IST GELD!
Noted lecturer, Miss G. Szymanski, was
relate her point of view freely to the pe
"Time is M

William Michael Harnett

1848–1892

Still Life with Violin

1883
Oil on panel
8 ³/₄ x 7 in. (22.2 x 17.8 cm)

With its intense focus and smooth finish, *Still Life with Violin* creates an almost palpable experience of an intimate setting. The picture tells a story that suggests both a reverence for a time-honored cultural past and the aspiration to enjoy a life enriched by elements of high culture and classical learning. It is a symbolic portrait of a man who has the leisure time and the opportunity to indulge his spirit with music, his intellect with reading, and his palette with a tankard of ale.

This tabletop arrangement was painted by Harnett during a transitional period in his career. Having successfully practiced drawing, engraving, and painting for fifteen years in Philadelphia and New York, in 1880 the artist went to Europe to pursue his studies. He took a studio in Munich for four years; there he made numerous trips to galleries, studios, and museums while creating a prodigious body of work. Harnett had been working in a precisionist style back in the United States, but his trompe l'oeil technique improved during his residence in Germany, where he scrutinized the pictorial methods of the old masters and local artists. The carefully articulated realism of this piece was very much in vogue among still-life painters in Munich at the time.

A sense of intimacy is created in this image by a number of compositional devices. Along with the small scale of the painting, the informal clutter of the arrangement increases the feeling of a closed-in space. The objects are pushed toward the front of the picture plane, parts of the assemblage even sliding off the edge of the table, so that the scene feels engagingly crowded. The deftly painted violin, bow, and tankard are protruding out toward the viewer as if to invite one to lean in and pick them up.

Despite an apparently haphazard arrangement, the composition is surprisingly well balanced. Harnett's placement of each piece contributes to a comforting sense of ease. The horizontal edge of the table lends stable support to a pyramid of objects looming above it. The verticality of the beer stein and the diagonal tilt of the candlestick offset the flatness of the table and some of the books. Other texts lean upward in such a way as to mimic the triangulated corner of the paper in the foreground. To counteract a potentially gridlike effect of straight lines, Harnett has ingeniously included a series of graceful curves in the handle of the tankard, the body of the violin, the shaft of the candlestick, and the bronze bust in the rear. This shrewdly constructed design

brings energy to a scene that might otherwise evoke a static moment in time.

Harnett's dramatic use of chiaroscuro, commonly associated with the Dutch masters, accentuates the painting's feeling of enclosure and immediacy. Resonant shadows in the dark background, a wood-paneled cabinet with antiqued bronze hinges, contrast strongly with the illuminated sheet of music and the mellowed glint of highlighting on the edges of the props. The meticulous rendition of light and shadow makes the display of artifacts stand out with a jewel-like preciousness.

Harnett has in fact chosen items that are meant to signify value and rarity. Emblems of culture and learning, these articles elicit a reverential appreciation for well-crafted and enduring products of Western culture. The volumes piled askew on the tabletop look old, and some remnants of gilding on the covers suggest elegance. The violin, while chosen for its graceful curves, is also an expensive and scrupulously crafted symbol of high culture. Harnett did not play the violin himself, but he read music and played the flute. His choice of a stringed instrument as centerpiece to this still life has intentional implications. Along with signifying an appreciation for classical music and superb craftsmanship, it is meant to exude an aura of sophistication and connoisseurship.

This display of Old World bric-a-brac and antique collectibles would have held an appeal for potential patrons whose personal belongings expressed a veneration for the Western humanist tradition.[1] The items depicted here were all created before the era of mass production, so that, as art historian David Lubin has pointed out, Harnett seems to express a resistance to the conspicuous materialism of the Gilded Age in which he was painting.[2]

Harnett repeatedly used the same props and similar compositions throughout his career; but in his Munich period the artist switched from depicting mundane objects of everyday life, such as the pipes and matchsticks in *The Social Club* (1879) (p. 90), to the more rarefied commodities of *Still Life with Violin*. The latter work by no means suggests pretentiousness or luxury. The pewter tankard might well have been replaced by a silver chalice if Harnett had intended to signify wealth. The well-worn books might have given way to newer volumes. Instead, a dented beer stein and slightly

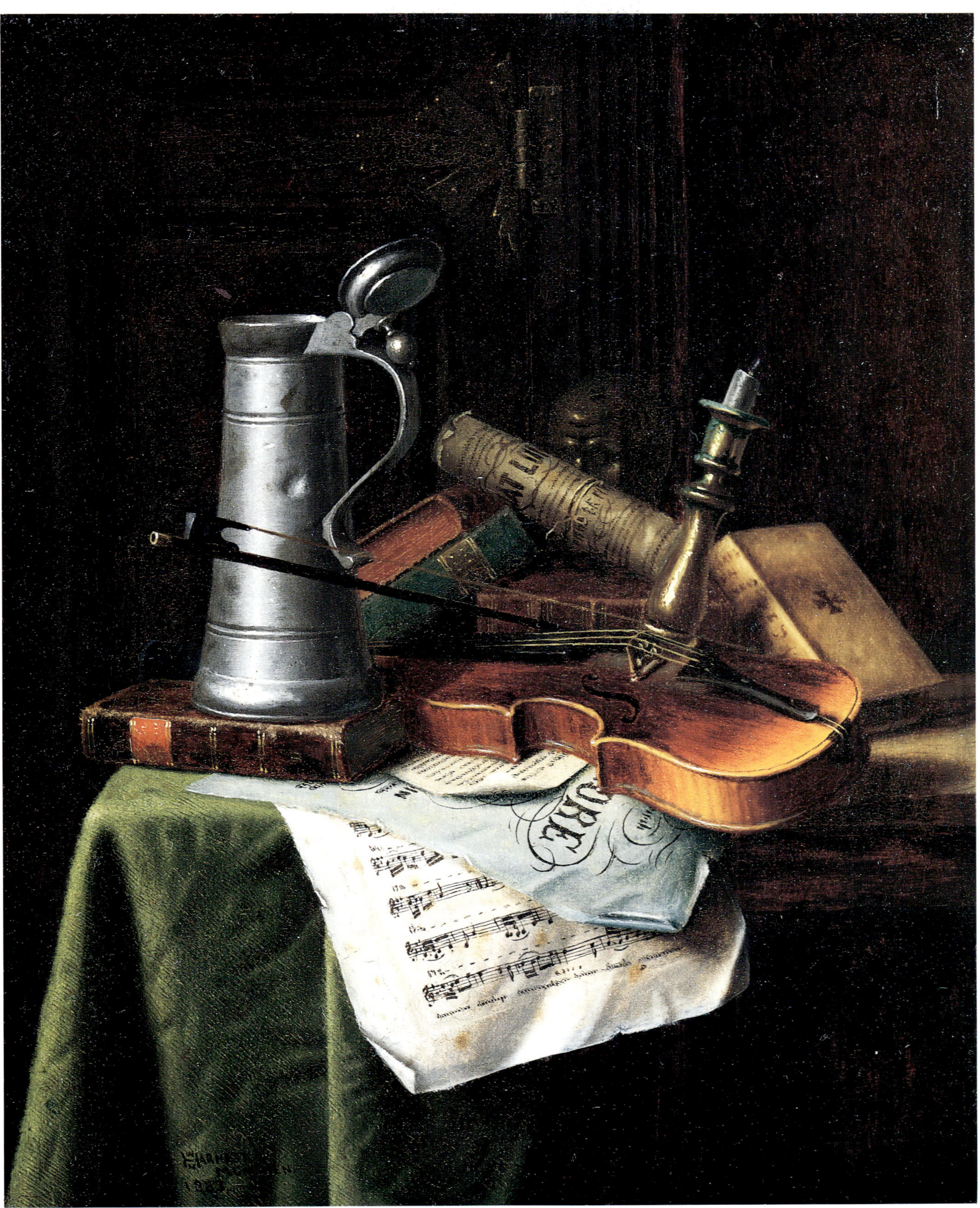

tarnished and skewed brass candlestick symbolize a humble, if cultured, existance—literate and contemplative.

Like the pile of recently handled texts, the bronze bust, probably a portrait of Shakespeare, in the center rear of the composition alludes to the enduring quality of literature.[3] Although Harnett has chosen not to depict the exact titles of the books, the volumes closely resemble ones appearing in other of his paintings from the same period. When he revealed the names of books in his still lifes, they were most often texts from classical literature—works by Dante, Cervantes, Petrarch, and Shakespeare.[4]

We cannot see the title of the musical score in *Still Life with Violin* either, but the notes so painstakingly rendered by the artist are from a violin composition, a variation on the aria "Parigi, o cara" from Verdi's *La traviata*.[5] The same bit of music from this opera also appears in Harnett's *A Study Table* (1882, Philadelphia Museum of Art) and *Munich Still Life* (1884, Newark Museum). The libretto revolves around a beautiful courtesan who relinquishes her lover to protect his family's honor. The aria featured by Harnett comes from the final scene of the opera, in which the lovers sing a tragic song of hope and reconciliation in the face of the heroine's imminent death from consumption. Harnett's repeated use of this Verdi aria, with its focus on self-sacrificing romantic love, suggests an attraction, perhaps reflecting his devout Roman Catholicism, to a past where honor, commitment, and spiritual redemption were paramount.

If *Still Life with Violin* were a traditional *vanitas* painting, Harnett would be employing the music, books, and candles to allude to the transience of worldly existence. But here the artist seems to be pointing to the endurance of the human spirit through the depiction of objects that signify lasting value. The violin, works of literature, music, candlestick, and tankard may have been crafted decades—even centuries—ago, yet they all show evidence of continued use.

A light dusting of rosin under the strings of the violin, the open and dented beer stein, the wrinkled sheet music, and tattered books strewn about at random all imply recent use and an immediate tangibility. Human life may be transitory, but some creations of the human imagination, as Harnett's painting attests, survive to inspire future generations.

ALISON TILGHMAN

1   While Harnett did numerous still lifes for specific patrons, often using artifacts from the patrons' personal collections, this work was most likely executed as an exercise in small-scale composition, since the particular items rendered here appear in a number of other works by Harnett made around the same time. This painting shares identical objects or is closely related by composition to a number of his other works.

2   David M. Lubin, "Permanent Objects in a Changing World: Harnett's Still Lifes as a Hold on the Past," in Doreen Bolger, Marc Simpson, and John Wilmerding, eds., *William M. Harnett* (Fort Worth, Tex.: Amon Carter Museum/New York: Metropolitan Museum of Art and Harry N. Abrams, Inc., 1992), 49–59.

3   Although the bust is obscured, the baldness and deeply creased forehead closely resemble those in a painting of a marble bust done by Harnett in 1878 called *The Bard of Avon* (Hirschl and Adler Galleries, New York). The same bronze bust appears in Harnett's *Munich Still Life* (Newark Museum) of 1884. Harnett also did a number of still lifes in which a bust of Dante is a central feature.

4   Judy L. Larson. "Literary References in Harnett's Still-Life Paintings," in Bolger et al., 265–75.

5   Alfred Frankenstein first identified this music, rendered in Harnett's 1882 *A Study Table* (Philadelphia Museum of Art), in *After the Hunt: William Harnett and Other American Still Life Painters, 1870–1900* (Berkeley and Los Angeles: University of California Press, 1953; rev. ed., 1969). For more in-depth coverage of Harnett's musical references, see Marc Simpson, "Harnett and Music: Many a Touching Melody," in Bolger et al., 289–307 (see 291 and 303, n. 23).

William McGregor Paxton

1869–1941

The Listener

1907
Oil on canvas
20 x 16 in. (50.8 x 40.6 cm)

Paxton began his artistic studies early in life at the Cowles Art School in Boston with the painter Dennis Miller Bunker, a former pupil of the nineteenth-century French academic painter Jean-Léon Gérôme. With Bunker's encouragement, Paxton himself spent several years in Paris under Gérôme's tutelage. Such training encouraged and promoted the exacting illusionism and uncompromising attention to detail characteristic of his mature painting style. Returning to Boston in 1893, Paxton became one of the most prominent members of a group of painters collectively known as the Boston School, artists united by a shared interest in the seventeenth-century Dutch genre painting of Vermeer.[1] Throughout much of his career, he enjoyed popular and academic success for his depictions of upper-class women in interior settings of wealth and refinement.

The Listener is an ambitiously conceived and impressively illusionistic rendering of two women, one seated in the background playing a guitar and another standing in the right foreground ostensibly listening intently to the music being produced. Recent and discerning readings have taken Paxton to task for painting delicately proportioned and elegantly attired women engaged in unproductive occupations while abiding in sumptuous settings indicative of a misspent wealth.[2] They assert that his representations of women were produced for the pleasure and satisfaction of men, accommodating and sustaining sexist stereotypes of women as objects for men to possess, as helpless and infantile creatures unable to function outside the protection of the home, and as treacherous in their desire or even demand for a pampered and insulated life-style. But a close reading of *The Listener* intimates that such characterizations may be invoked, not to confirm the existence or endorse the proliferation of such stereotypes, but to question their validity—or at least challenge assumptions of their naturalness, practicality, or possibility.

From left to right and increasing in scale, the architectural setting in *The Listener* is dominated by three rectangles created by a mirror, a window, and a doorway—paradigmatic symbols, at least since the Renaissance, for realism and verisimilitude in painting.[3] Not incidentally, the mirror, window, and doorway are all, in their own ways, obscured, closed off, or darkened. The conventional meanings and attributes of mirror, window, and doorway are thereby inverted in Paxton's image, giving the space presented, not a sense of the ceaseless and ongoing quality of tangible space, but an oppressive atmosphere of dimness, enclosure,

confinement, and entrapment. This inversion suggests that realism possesses not only the ability to clarify, to represent, or to illustrate in a straightforward and honest fashion, but also the power to obscure reality behind a facade of precise illusionism. In this sense, Paxton's imagery itself acts as a coded message alluding to a content not readily apparent.

The appearance in *The Listener* of a woman playing an instrument, of a woman dressed in a sumptuous and loose-fitting jacket trimmed in ermine, and of a woman holding a letter whose contents remain mysterious to the viewer are all evocations of female figures in Vermeer's art. Paxton's painting has the appearance of updating, redesigning, and reappointing a scene by Vermeer within the milieu of late-nineteenth-century Boston society. However, the semblance of a seamless reality is unraveled by such overt inclusion of art historical reference. The adoption of Vermeer's form and content to depict a scene of relatively contemporary life implies that current lived experience is pervasively determined by past conventions and imbued with constricting tradition.

Through comparable formal shape, brilliant color, and upright position, the woman standing in the foreground is linked to or paired with the lamp placed on the table, suggesting an analogy between the two. Like the lamp, the woman seems to exist as a shimmering surface upon which to gaze, as little more than an object of decoration and visual pleasure. Just as the lamp is snuffed out, so the woman's prisonlike existence can, figuratively speaking, be said to extinguish any flame of her mind or spirit. Such a reading would suggest that what is visually captured in the woman's inward gaze and poised stance is a moment of devastating self-consciousness, an instant in which she recognizes herself in the form of the lamp—as object, as decorative, and as somehow smothered. In marked contrast to the young woman in the background whose face is thrown into shadow, the fully lit facial features of the woman in the foreground signify a consonant illumination of consciousness.

Dressed as she is in a gleaming white gown trimmed in black fur, the standing woman is a reinterpretation, only in a higher key, of the room's stark cream-colored walls and dark wood trim. Pictorially made up of a vocabulary of similarly curved forms, women and objects in the image are presented as categorically similar and interchangeable. This congruence of women and objects is only heightened by the contrast of their shared curvilinear contours compared to the predominantly rectilinear format of the architectural setting.

There is something amiss and discomforting about this scene of supposedly complacent domestic repose. Just as the equation of figures and objects envisions the process by which women are reified or treated as objects in an obsessively consumerist culture, so the rigid and inescapable structure of the room can be interpreted as symbolic of the pervasive and controlling environment of patriarchy itself. Paxton's paintings are usually interpreted as sanctioning and advocating the opulent domesticity to which they give visual form. But the layered symbolism and highly structured composition of his realism reveals assumptions about the various ways in which material abundance and economic wealth imply specific forms of human relations and social institutions. Through both form and content, *The Listener* visually catalogues the status of affluent women within both industrialized economies and patriarchal systems.

KARL EMIL WILLERS

1   For a more extensive consideration of the importance of Vermeer for Paxton and other painters of the Boston School, see Bernice Kramer Leader, "The Boston School and Vermeer," *Arts Magazine* 55 (November 1980): 172–76.
2   For the most insightful feminist critique of Paxton's work, see Bernice Kramer Leader, "Antifeminism in the Paintings of the Boston School," *Arts Magazine* 56 (January 1982): 112–19.
3   For a discussion of Paxton's realism and illusionism, see the essay by Ellen Wardell Lee and biographical sketch by R. H. Ives Gammell in *William McGregor Paxton 1869–1941*, exh. cat. (Indianapolis: Indianapolis Museum of Art, 1979). For reviews of this exhibition and publication, see Mario Amaya, "William McGregor Paxton: Painter of Brahmin Boston," *The Connoisseur* 202 (October 1979): 90–95; and Mahonri Sharp Young, "Letter from the U.S.A.: A Boston Painter," *Apollo* 108 (November 1978): 344–45. Paxton mastered his technical veracity in the atelier of Jean-Léon Gérôme, where he studied between 1890 and 1893. For a consideration of Paxton's formative years in Paris, as well as his earlier studies at the Cowles Art School in Boston under Gérôme's former pupil Dennis Miller Bunker, see H. Barbara Weinberg, *The American Pupils of Jean-Léon Gérôme* (Fort Worth, Tex.: Amon Carter Museum, 1984), 1–3 and 83–99.

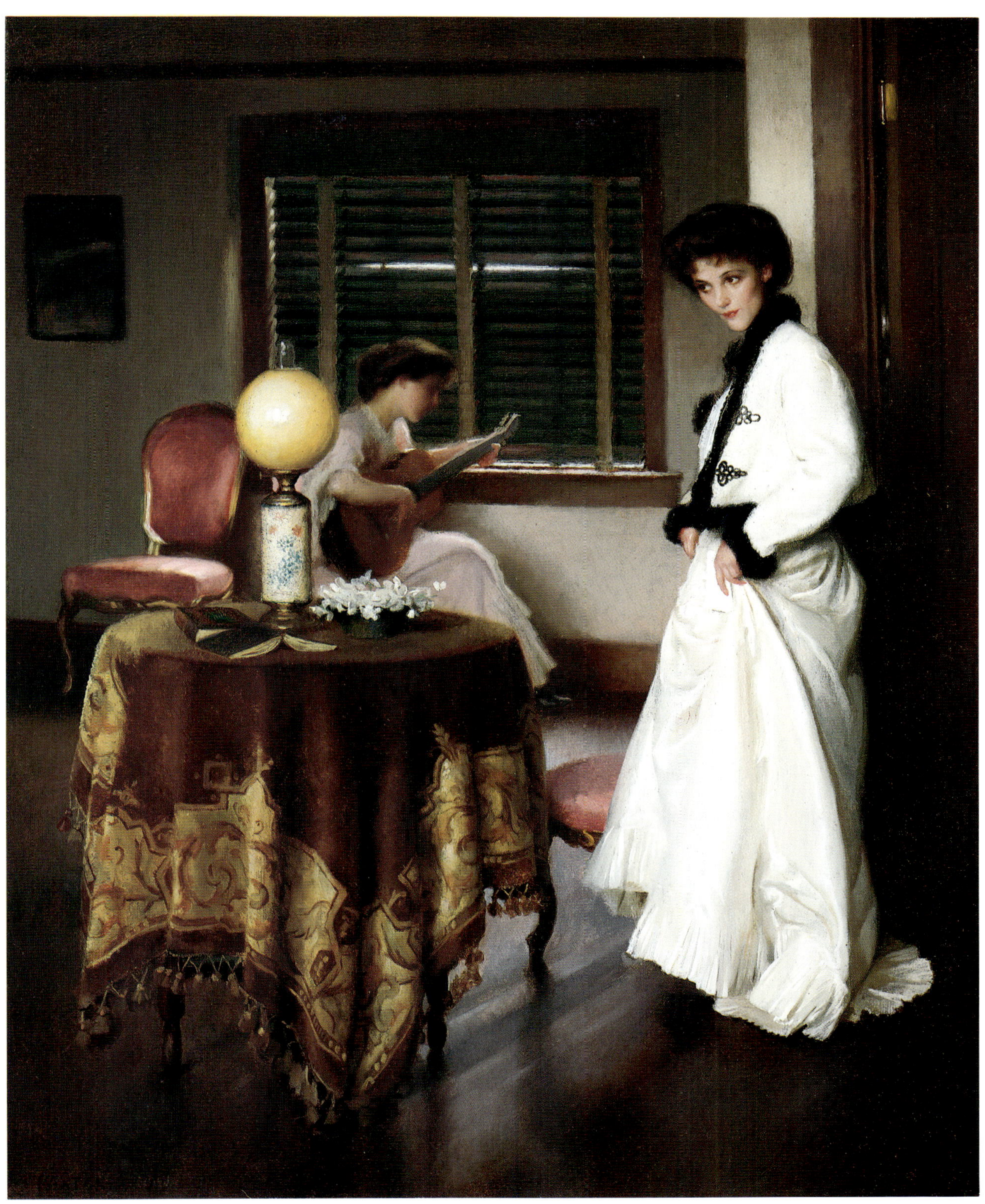

Edward Lamson Henry

1841–1919

Parlor on Brooklyn Heights of Mr. and Mrs. John Bullard

1872
Oil on panel
15 3/8 x 17 5/8 in. (39.1 x 44.8 cm)

In 1872 Henry painted Mr. and Mrs. John Bullard[1] in the ornate parlor of their three-story brownstone at 220 Columbia Heights, an elegant neighborhood of stately dwellings in Brooklyn Heights overlooking the East River and New York City.[2] Bullard and his brothers, William and Isaac, moved from Dedham, Massachusetts, to New York, where they formed the firm of Bullard and Company, a leather and tanning business. Well-known in society circles and charitable organizations, Bullard was a member of the prominent New England Society of New York. In 1881, at seventy-four, he died childless, leaving only his wife, Jane.[3] Nine years before his death, Bullard commissioned Henry to paint his family in their home. Henry accomplished his task—to present the Bullards as a prosperous, well-educated, and cultivated family—by depicting the husband and wife sitting in their richly appointed parlor surrounded by a multitude of books and lavish possessions. This type of small, informal portrait representing people conversing with one another or engaging in a domestic activity, a portrait usually replete with details about the people and their surroundings, is known as a conversation piece.[4]

It is midday in the Bullard parlor; the hands of the mantel-shelf clock are approaching twelve-thirty in the afternoon and the bright sun pours through the parlor windows from the east. The focal point of the room, the river view and the New York City skyline, is framed by an elaborate window treatment of several layers: the richly figured upholstery of the tasseled lambrequins and floor-length curtains cover lace undercurtains and shades.[5] Beyond the windows, the pale-blue cloudless sky, the busy network of sailboats and ferries on the river, the bright sun, and, indoors, the small bouquet of flowers on the table by the window and the red-and-white-striped silk slip-covered armchairs all suggest that the weather is warm and the house set up for the summer months.[6] The fire in the hearth and the iron fireplace tools, however, seem to contradict the warm-weather cues, and perhaps Henry included them to add visual interest.

Henry has portrayed both Mr. and Mrs. Bullard wearing typical daytime clothing. But, while Mr. Bullard is dressed in an elegant suit, Mrs. Bullard is more simply clad in a plain black dress with a white ruffled collar.[7] Appropriately, Henry has depicted the couple in clothing symbolic of their roles— Mr. Bullard, a merchant, looks as if he is ready for work. His newspaper connects him to the outside world and indicates his business interests. Mrs. Bullard, on the other hand, is gracefully posed next to her husband with a white hand-

kerchief in her hand, her full skirt enveloping her, spreading out onto the carpet, and anchoring her to her seat. She looks out into the room, overseeing her domain: the home. They are seated around a center drop-leaf table, an icon of the Victorian parlor; for it is at the center table that the Victorian family gathered for reading, writing, sewing, or other activities that required good lighting. The center table in the Bullard parlor is covered with a thick, red cloth to protect its surface from this type of wear and tear. Like other wealthy families, the Bullards most likely had two parlors in their home, the more elaborate one reserved for formal occasions or entertaining guests, the more informal room, for general family use.[8] The room in which the Bullards are shown here is probably the most decorated one in their home, a room intended to display luxurious furniture, paintings, sculpture, and fine bric-a-brac, and not used on a daily basis.[9]

The parlor is decorated in the most up-to-date fashion of the time. Typically Victorian, it combines an eclectic mix of various revival styles—the Renaissance, the rococo, the Elizabethan, and the Gothic.[10] Predominant and setting the tone for the entire room is the Renaissance revival style. Characterized by stately grandeur expressed through imposing geometric and architectural ornament, black ebonized or gilt incised lines, and classical motifs, this style was popular decoration for the high-ceilinged parlors of the time. The Bullard's parlor features a Renaissance revival mantelpiece with two Ionic columns and a large mirror, topped by a half-round pediment. This unit is flanked by built-in bookcases with glass doors and shelves for the display of collectables. Also in the Renaissance revival style are the upholstered sofa with its carved pediment and throw pillows, the ebonized and gilt center drop-leaf table with reeded legs, the pedestals in the shape of columns with gilt trim, the geometric wall-to-wall carpet and matching footstools with medallions of red, blue, and gold, and the ornate painted and gilt compartmentalized ceiling centered with a sculptural plaster and gilt ornament.

Apart from the sophistication of its decorative scheme, on another level the Renaissance revival style and its associations with classical art and architecture were expressive of the homeowners' knowledge and refinement. Not only Victorian furniture makers but also producers of sculpture and ceramics marketed items that evoked images of the classical past. Thus, the bronze male nude by the window, the ceramic Venus to the right of the mirror, and the large

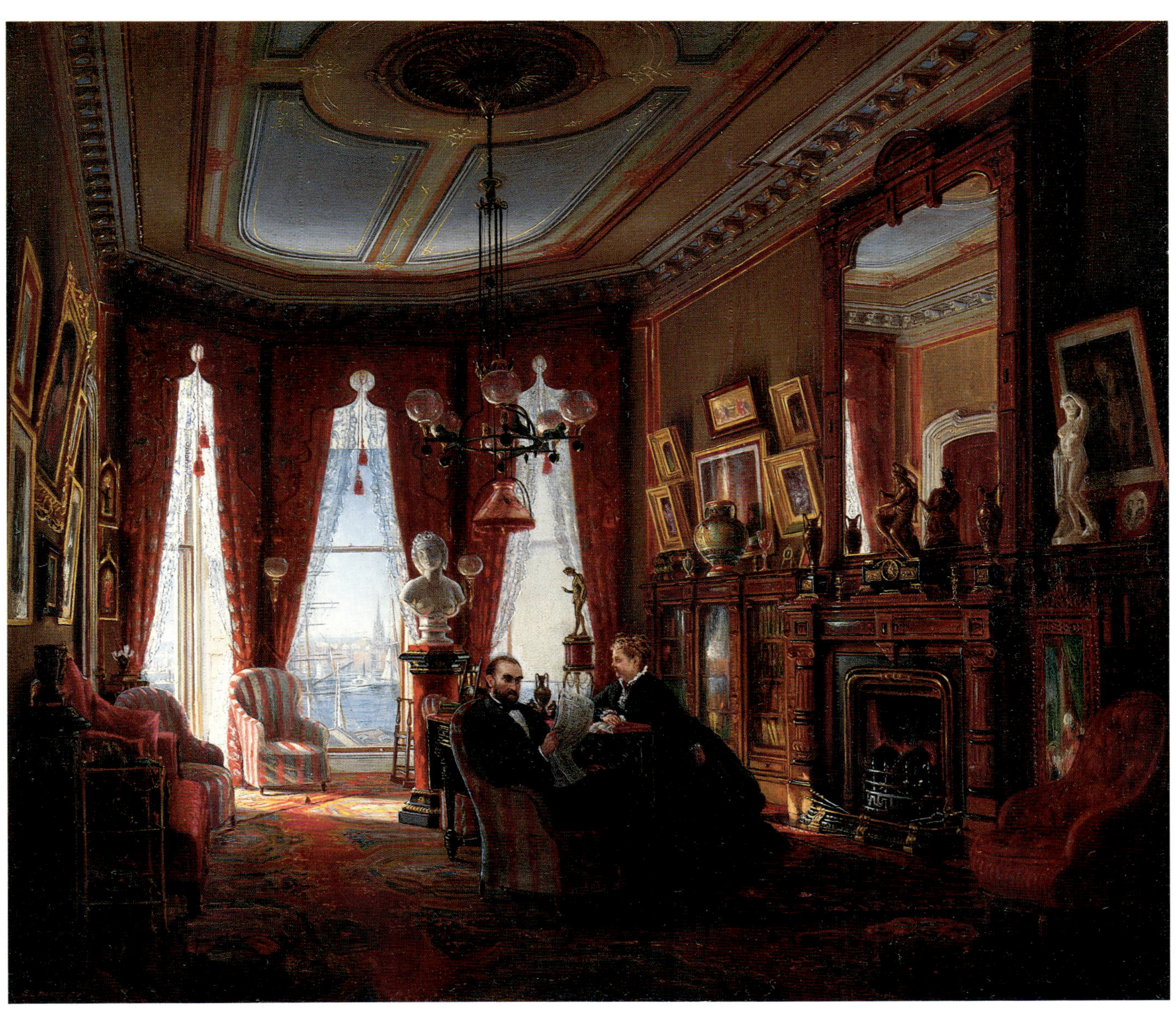

Parlor on Brooklyn Heights of Mr. and Mrs. John Bullard   69

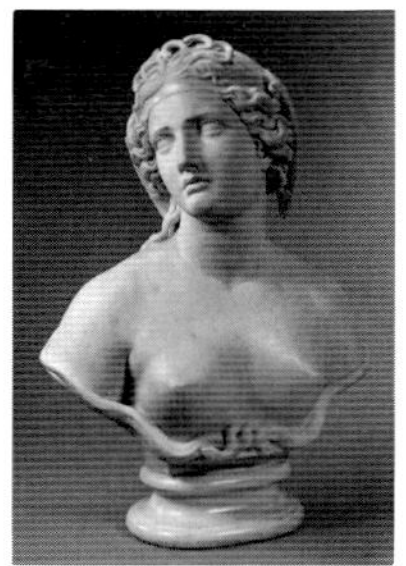

Fig. 1. Harriet Goodhue Hosmer, *Medusa*, 1854, marble bust, height 27 in. (68.6 cm), The Detroit Institute of Arts, Founders Society Purchase, Robert H. Tannahill Foundation Fund

Greek vase on the shelf are probably contemporary pieces. Similarly, the sculptural black marble and gilt mantel-shelf clock, the amphora-shaped vases, and the marble bust of a female nude are also classically inspired.[11] The marble bust near the center of the painting has been identified as *Medusa* (fig. 1), a work by Harriet Hosmer (1830–1908), an expatriate neoclassical sculptor who worked in Rome in the mid-nineteenth century. Hosmer produced at least two replicas of her highly acclaimed bust of *Medusa*. How the Bullards acquired theirs, and whether they traveled to Hosmer's studio in Rome to commission the work directly from the sculptor, unfortunately is not known.[12] The large number of paintings in gilt frames, the collection of books, and the variety of bric-a-brac, such as brass candlesticks and small ceramic and glass items, although not necessarily in the Renaissance style, also tell the viewer something about the Bullards' education and good taste. In a similar way, by depicting a prominent church spire outside the windows, Henry suggests that the Bullards were active participants in the religious life of their community as members of the Church of the Pilgrims. The parlor, then, becomes a world in miniature, a microcosm, where classical learning, hard work, and religion come together as symbols for the Bullards' refinement, as well as a moral lesson for others.[13]

The somewhat ponderous Renaissance revival decoration is softened in the parlor by the presence of decorative art objects in other Victorian styles. For example, the striped slip-covered armchairs and the chair with red tufted upholstery by the fireplace have gently arched balloon backs in the French taste; these rococo curves starkly contrast with the straight lines of the Renaissance revival style. The carved spindles on the fireplace screen, on the other hand, may be identified with the Elizabethan revival, while the pointed arches on the two gold-leaf frames on the left wall are associated with the Gothic. In front of the broad expanse of windows, a wooden ladder-back rocking chair is tucked away by the river view; it is probably a treasured antique, a survival, and lends warmth, comfort, and informality to the otherwise stiffly formal room.[14]

This antique ladder-back rocking chair, the simplest and most outdated object in the Bullard parlor, links this painting to Henry's best-known works—genre paintings that capture scenes of an earlier day. An avid antique collector and preservationist, Henry was an early colonial revivalist, and most of his paintings were historical reconstructions of events from late-eighteenth and early-nineteenth-century

America. Using antique props, authentic costumes, old prints, and books, he meticulously documented his nostalgic subjects. He was particularly fascinated by changing modes of transportation and painted early trains, as well as horses, buggies, automobiles, and bicycles. The principal founder of the Cragsmoor Art Colony in Cragsmoor, New York, near Ellenville, Henry and other American artists who summered there, including Charles Courtney Curran, Eliza Pratt Greatorex, John G. Brown, and Arthur I. Keller, appreciated the simple life in this rural agricultural community away from the city. It was here that Henry found the homely characters for his historical paintings and scenes of contemporary rural life. Although Henry's genre paintings, with their smooth finish and minute detail, were considered out-of-date by the end of his career, they were admired and avidly collected by a public who, like him, appreciated history and sought to preserve a cultural heritage that was quickly disappearing in the wake of urbanization.[15]

Unlike Henry's paintings that recreated scenes from the early period just after the Revolution, *The Parlor on Brooklyn Heights of Mr. and Mrs. John Bullard* is a fascinating and important work because it accurately documents an early 1870s interior contemporary with the artist's own time. His historical paintings are appreciated today more for their embodiment of colonial revivalist ideals, so prominent in Henry's day, than for their historical verity.

BETHANY ASTRACHAN

1   A photograph of a painting by Henry titled *A Parlor on Brooklyn Heights* and inscribed, "This was painted 'from nature' for Mr. and Mrs. John Bullard," has been reproduced in Elizabeth McCausland, *The Life and Work of Edward Lamson Henry, N.A., 1841–1919* (Albany, N.Y.: New York State Museum Bulletin No. 339, 1945), 127, 165. Unlike the Manoogian painting, in this parlor scene, Mr. Bullard is reading a book, Mrs. Bullard is facing the viewer, and a larger portion of the right wall is shown. For information on Henry, see *American Genre Painting in the Victorian Era,* exh. cat. (New York: Hirschl and Adler Galleries, 1978), 25; *American Paintings from the Manoogian Collection,* exh. cat. (Washington D.C.: National Gallery of Art/Detroit: Detroit Institute of Arts, 1989), 76–77.

2   For information on Brooklyn Heights and the Bullard's Columbia Heights neighborhood in the late nineteenth century, see Clay Lancaster, *Old Brooklyn Heights: New York's First Suburb,* 2d ed. (New York: Dover Publications, 1979), 54, 71, and James H. Callender, *Yesterdays on Brooklyn Heights* (New York: Dorland Press, 1927), 103–6.

3   William Gerdts has identified John Bullard's wife as Jane E. Bullard

in "The Medusa of Harriet Hosmer," *Bulletin of the Detroit Institute of Arts* 56 (1978): 107, n. 7. My appreciation to Claire Lamers, Brooklyn Historical Society.

4 For a discussion of conversation pieces and their history, see Louis Auchincloss, *Three Hundred Years of New York City Families: A Loan Exhibition of Conversation Pieces for the Benefit of The Museum of the City of New York,* exh. cat. (New York: Wildenstein, 1966), passim; Mario Praz, *Conversation Pieces: A Survey of the Informal Group Portrait in Europe and America* (University Park and London: Pennsylvania State University Press, 1971), 33.

5 For late-nineteenth-century window treatments, see Edgar de N. Mayhew and Minor Myers, Jr., *A Documentary History of American Interiors: From the Colonial Era to 1915* (New York: Charles Scribner's Sons, 1980), 206. In her thesis, Katherine C. Grier, in *Culture and Comfort: People, Parlors, and Upholstery, 1850–1930* (Rochester, N.Y.: The Strong Museum, 1988), aptly sums up the importance of textiles in the Victorian home as a symbol for progress. She states: "Textile furnishings softened the world of sensation. They obliterated the edges of hard furniture surfaces and mediated, through structural padding, the contact of the body with seats. Heavy door and window curtains muffled sound, literally softened light, and enhanced domestic quiet. Thus textiles could serve as a metaphor for the softening benefits of civility, which was evidence of the progress of civilization" (89).

6 In the Victorian home, it was a common practice to slip-cover furniture in light colors to brighten up a room during the warm-weather months. Mayhew and Myers, 205.

7 Elizabeth Ann Coleman, *Changing Fashions, 1800–1970* (Brooklyn, N.Y.: Brooklyn Museum, 1972), unpaginated.

8 The Victorian center table and its importance in the parlor is discussed in Elisabeth Donaghy Garrett, *At Home: The American Family, 1750–1870* (New York: Harry N. Abrams, 1990), 51, 55–56, 59–61, 64, 76–77, 144, 151; and Grier, 86–87. For a discussion of the front "best" parlor versus the back parlor, see Garrett, 39–77.

9 In fact, the Bullards are dwarfed by the number of objects in the room, and their possessions, in turn, become the focus of the painting. For a discussion of late-nineteenth-century consumerism and the "commodity aesthetic," see Jean-Christophe Agnew's "A House of Fiction: Domestic Interiors and the Commodity Aesthetic," in *Consuming Visions: Accumulation and Display of Goods in America, 1880–1920,* ed. Simon J. Bronner (New York: W. W. Norton, 1989), 133–55.

10 I am grateful to David Barquist of the Yale University Art Gallery for sharing with me his knowledge of nineteenth-century American interiors and decorative arts.

11 The Renaissance revival style has been widely discussed. For an overview of the style, its furniture and characteristic decoration, see Mayhew and Myers, 193–223.

12 William H. Gerdts discusses Hosmer's *Medusa* and identifies the bust in the Bullard parlor in "The *Medusa* of Harriet Hosmer," 97–107. He records that the original *Medusa* bust was commissioned by Samuel Appleton of Boston. Subsequently, the Duchess of St. Albans and Lady Marian Alford each commissioned a replica. If other replicas were ordered is not known. See also Dolly Sherwood, *Harriet Hosmer: American Sculptor, 1830–1908* (Columbia and London: University of Missouri Press, 1991), 83–88.

13 Clifford Edward Clark, Jr., *The American Family Home, 1800–1960* (Chapel Hill and London: University of North Carolina Press, 1986), 107.

14 For late-nineteenth-century American interiors and revival styles, I have drawn largely upon the following sources: Garrett, *At Home;* Grier, *Culture and Comfort;* John Maass, *The Victorian Home in America* (New York: Hawthorn Books, 1972); William Seale, *The Tasteful Interlude: American Interiors Through the Camera's Eye, 1860–1917,* ed. Graham Hood (New York: Praeger, 1975); *Victoriana, An Exhibition of the Arts of the Victorian Era in America,* exh. cat. (Brooklyn, N. Y.: Brooklyn Museum, 1960); Gail Caskey Winkler and Roger W. Moss, *Victorian Interior Decoration: American Interiors, 1830–1900* (New York: Henry Holt and Company, 1986).

15 See McCausland, passim. For Henry's interest in collecting, see Elizabeth Stillinger, *The Antiquers* (New York: Alfred A. Knopf, 1980), 35–41.

Francis Davis Millet

1846–1912

The Window Seat

1883
Oil on canvas
20 1/8 x 30 1/4 in. (51.1 x 76.8 cm)

In describing the paintings of his colleagues in Broadway, England, Henry James marveled at the American painter Edwin Austin Abbey's ability to conjure up the distant past: "For the peculiar sign of his talent is surely this observation in the remote. It brings the remote near to us. . . . Remote in time (in differing degrees), remote in place, remote in feeling, in habit, and in their ambient air, are the images that spring from his pencil, and yet all so vividly, so minutely, so consistently seen!"[1]

James could have made the same observation about the works of Frank Millet, another American painter and illustrator who, along with his close friend, Abbey, George Henry Boughton, James Abbott McNeill Whistler, and John Singer Sargent, worked in England during the 1870s and 1880s. Whereas most of these artists were drawn to England because of its better educational and financial opportunities, Millet and Abbey saw in England signs of a rich past, to be imaged as reminders of America's own past.[2] Like Abbey, Millet was especially fascinated by the past of the seventeenth and eighteenth centuries, which he consistently evoked in interior scenes with period furnishings and figures in period costume.[3] *The Window Seat*, depicting the sitting room of an English cottage occupied by a woman wearing a late-eighteenth-century muslin dress, certainly exemplifies such works;[4] yet in focusing on the architectural details of the room as well as on the dress and activity of the woman, this work, perhaps more than any other of Millet's period paintings, connotes the "cult of domesticity" that was growing in importance at the end of the nineteenth century. Here, through references to the domestic, Millet not only conjures up the past but elevates it, contrasting it with the ugly industrialized world of the 1880s.

The Window Seat introduces the theme of domesticity through its architectural setting, the interior of a picturesque vernacular cottage. First popularized in England around 1790, the vernacular cottage symbolized domesticity in its style— simple, honest, rustic, hearty, and reminiscent of the past, particularly the Gothic period.[5] While the exterior characteristics of the English vernacular cottage might vary, borrowing, for example, from Swiss, German, and Russian influences,[6] the essential structure of the cottage functioned to emphasize the interior, or the domestic: indeed, the cottage was designed not as a classically symmetrical space but as an irregular one, defined both by the layout of the surrounding landscape and by the differing functions of interior rooms.[7]

Almost serving as an advertisement for one of the several nineteenth-century cottage design manuals, *The Window Seat* depicts a front interior room, most likely the sitting room or combination parlor–dining room.[8] Here Millet includes some of the most common features of such a room: muslin-curtained, expansive casement windows that permit the infiltration of light; functional, simple furniture, such as the turned-backed, rush-seated chair on which the woman's feet rest and the mahogany tea or work table; and handmade decorative objects, such as the glazed clay vase that holds a bunch of wildflowers.[9] Partly visible on the far left wall, a print implies that the cottage most likely belongs to middle-class owners rather than peasants.[10] Although Millet had not yet moved into his own Broadway cottage, Farnham, in 1883 when he painted *The Window Seat*, he purportedly modeled the interior on that of a room at the White Lion Inn in the Oxfordshire village of Bidford-on-Avon.[11]

In emphasizing the interior details of this English cottage, Millet recalled the late-nineteenth-century British Arts and Crafts Movement, which promoted the revival of a simple, wholesome life-style embodied by the arts of the craftsman. The leading theorists of this movement—John Ruskin and the architects William Morris, C. R. Ashbee, and Philip Webb—proclaimed that, as modern industrialization had devalued the individual work of craftsmen, it behooved architects, designers, and painters to work together to produce handcrafted yet affordable everyday objects. Theoretically, such a collaborative effort would serve not only to bring art to the "masses" but to remind society of the "honest" guild-based work of earlier periods.[12] Embodying the goals of Arts and Crafts reformers was the country cottage, which both included simplicity and individuality in its design and provided a space in which the domestic arts—including pottery, stained glass, furniture, and tapestries—could be created and displayed.[13] Philip Webb's Red House, built for William Morris in 1859, was the first Arts and Crafts "cottage" to celebrate the domestic arts, as well as the spirit of collaboration: Webb made its furniture; Morris and Edward Burne-Jones decorated its walls, windows, and furniture; and a craftsmen's group from London designed its metalwork, candlesticks, and pottery.[14] Very likely having spent time with Morris in Kelmscott during the fall of 1882, Millet incorporated into *The Window Seat* the two major features of the Red House—its emphasis on an interior space and handmade, decorative objects.[15] For the painting's audience, in turn, these domestic features

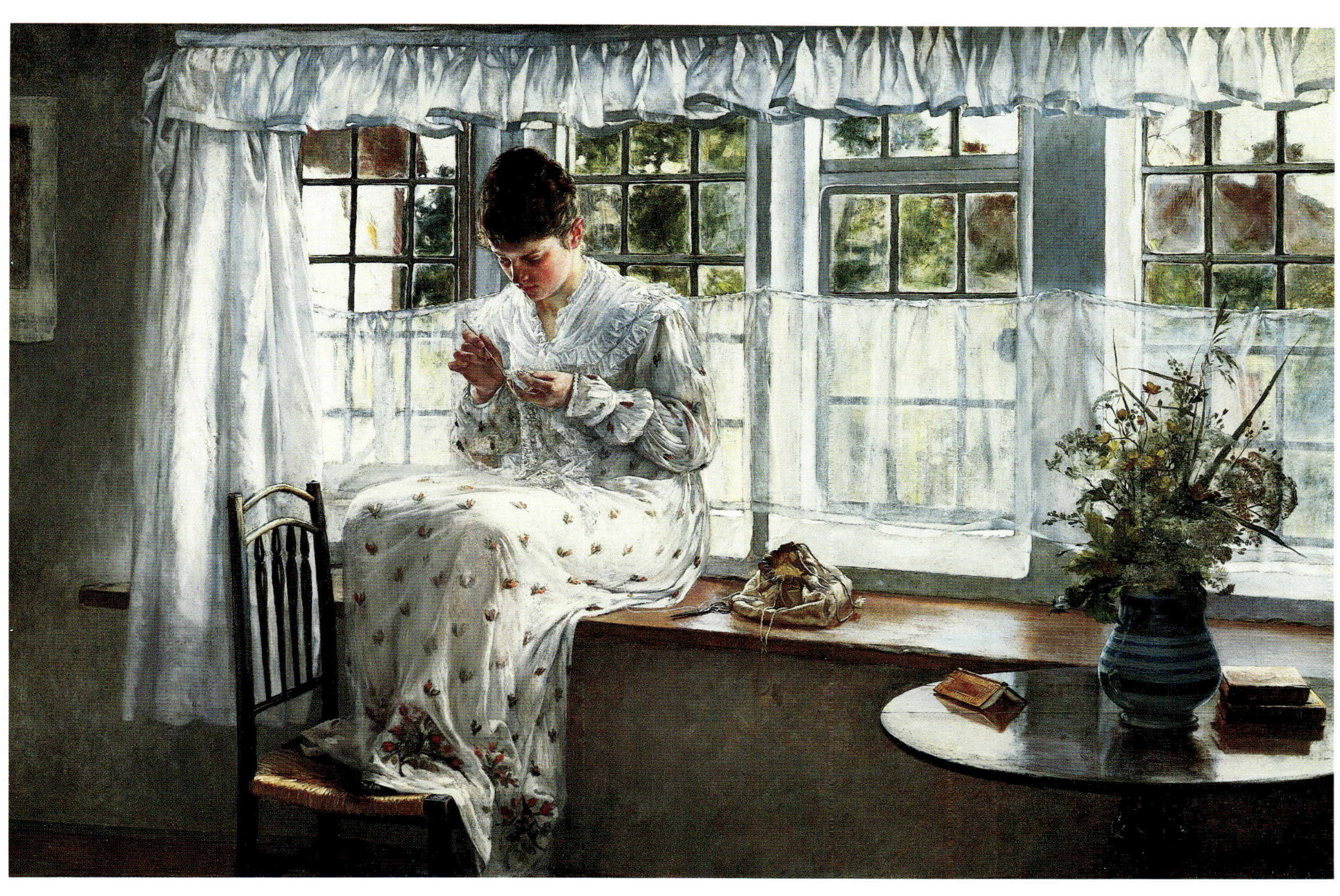

probably functioned as symbolic renunciations of the mass production and alienation of industrialization.

Millet's placement of a woman sewing in *The Window Seat* equally indicates the late-nineteenth-century glorification of the domestic sphere. Not merely sewing, Millet's subject is tatting, or shaping a decorative lacelike fabric by making a series of knots with a hooked needle.[16] On one level, this absorption in "fancy work" alludes to the promotion of women's crafts, particularly needlework, by Arts and Crafts reformers. Even though craftswomen were encouraged to engage only in artistic activities appropriate to their sex— namely, lace-making, spinning, weaving, knitting, and decorating pottery—their handmade products were nonetheless regarded as contributing to the movement's efforts to better society.[17] On another level, needlework symbolized the domestic sphere itself. Indeed, along with cooking and cleaning, sewing was the quintessential domestic task, whether for late-eighteenth- or nineteenth-century women.[18] Here, then, Millet favorably portrays the domestic sphere by presenting tatting as a creative endeavor rather than a chore. By extension, his imaging of this sphere as a light-filled, feminine haven in which serious yet pleasurable activities occur hints at the nineteenth-century "cult of domesticity."

During the early nineteenth century, when England and America shifted from preindustrial to industrial economies, the home came to be regarded as a separate social sphere; the "cult of domesticity" sentimentalized this sphere, deeming it a hallowed refuge from the oppressions of the modern workplace.[19] As the domestic sphere was considered sacred, so too was its guardian, the mistress of the household. Indeed, sentimental literature and evangelical religion propagated the notion that the woman of the household was angelic, saintly—even Marian—in her ability to instill moral values into those around her.[20] Not surprisingly, since a woman's domestic maternal and wifely duties linked her with a form of godliness, a "cult of the Virgin" arose simultaneously with the "cult of domesticity." In late-nineteenth-century American paintings, this virginal woman, who embodied the otherworldly goodness of the domestic sphere, appeared in two forms, either as a "lady in white" or as the Virgin of the Annunciation herself.[21] *The Window Seat* merges these two conventions: resembling Whistler's *White Girl* (1862, National Gallery of Art, Washington, D.C.), the painting is almost a monochromatic study, wherein the central figure's white dress and fichu connote the purity of her domestic surroundings. Likewise, the model's pose recalls that of the

Virgin in fifteenth- and sixteenth-century Annunciation scenes: her slightly spread, massive knees form a "seat" or "throne" that receives the light—in religious terms, the spirit of Christ—traversing the translucent windowpanes behind her.[22] Here it is not simply annunciatory light that signals the healthy, life-giving force of the domestic space, but also several "pregnant" vessels, including the sewing bag and the flower-filled vase.[23]

The domestic emblems in the *Window Seat*—the cottage, the woman in white tatting, and various interior props—most obviously recall a preindustrialized past in all its simplicity and goodness. Stylistically, however, Millet also refers to the past through his use of a sixteenth-century Marian prototype for his model. In so doing, he resembles other late-nineteenth-century "American Renaissance" artists who, in an effort to establish a cultural niche for America within a spectrum of great art, often incorporated classical and Renaissance sources into their work.[24] Two of Millet's paintings, in particular, *Reading the Story of Oenone* (1883, The Detroit Institute of Arts) and *A Handmaiden* (1886, Private Collection), exemplify this trend through their subjects, classically garbed models in period settings. However, since the American Renaissance generally promoted the past as an idealized model for the present, Millet's paintings of American colonial homes or early-nineteenth-century English cottages equally would have worked toward its goals.[25] Like their contemporaries in the Arts and Crafts Movement, American Renaissance artists deemed that the individual and society at large could be reformed through art rooted in the past, whether that past was defined as vernacular or classical.[26] *The Window Seat* combines vernacular-domestic and classical-Renaissance themes and thus, more forcefully than Millet's purely classical subjects, affirms the value of an idealized past over a tainted present.

MARY ADAIR WOODALL

1   Henry James, "Black and White," in his *Picture and Text* (New York: Harper and Brothers, 1893), 15–16.
2   Marc Simpson, "Windows on the Past: Edwin Austin Abbey and Francis Davis Millet in England," *The American Art Journal* (1990), 65–66.
3   *The Quest for Unity: American Art Between World's Fairs, 1876–1893*, exh. cat. (Detroit: Detroit Institute of Arts, 1983), 122; Simpson, 77.
4   Marc Simpson, "Francis Davis Millet, *The Window Seat*," in *American Paintings from the Manoogian Collection* (Washington,

D.C.: National Gallery of Art/ Detroit: Detroit Institute of Arts, 1989), 146. Simpson identifies the dress as muslin and the model as Millet's wife, Lily.

5 Sutherland Lyall, *Dream Cottages: From Cottage Ornée to Stockbroker Tudor, Two Hundred Years of the Cult of the Vernacular* (London: Robert Hale Limited, 1988), 15–16.

6 Ibid., 29–30. Other types included the cottage ornée; the Polish, German, Italian, or Norwegian cottage; and the Old English, Plantagenet, or Rustic cottage.

7 For information concerning the cottage's relationship to nature, see Lyall, 33–36 and 135. For information concerning the structure of the cottage as reflective of its interior function, see Elizabeth Cumming and Wendy Kaplan, *The Arts and Crafts Movement* (New York: Thames and Hudson, 1991), 31.

8 Lyall, 35 and 107. The primary textbook for cottage-in-the-country designers was James Malton's 1798 *British Cottage Architecture*.

9 For discussions about the role of light in the English cottage, see Lyall, 36, and Dean Hawkes, ed., *Modern Country Homes in England: The Arts and Crafts Architecture of Barry Parker* (Cambridge: University Press of Cambridge, 1986), 47–49. In addition to these features, the main room of a cottage typically included a fireplace, wooden bench, corner cupboard, and dinner table. For other examples of cottage interiors, see Lawrence Weaver, *The "Country Life" Book of Cottages* (London: Country Life, 1913), 28, 76, and 107; R. Randal Phillips, *The Book of Bungalows* (New York: Charles Scribner's Sons, 1920), 36, 40, 121, and 136; and Donald J. Berg, ed., *Country Patterns: A Sampler of American Country Homes and Landscape Designs from Original Nineteenth-Century Sources* (Pittstown, N.J.: Main Street Press, 1986), 116, 117, and 121.

10 Phillips, 42.

11 Simpson, 71. Henry James described the Worchestershire region as one that contained "grass-bordered vista[s] of brownish gray cottages, thatched, latticed, mottled, mended, ivied, immemorial. . . . the perfection of the old English rural tradition" (Simpson, 72–73). Millet's interest in the English cottage extended beyond the canvas; in 1892, for example, he appealed to the Society for the Protection of Ancient Buildings to restore Broadway's oldest domestic building, the Grange (Simpson, 78–79).

12 Cumming and Kaplan, 6–14; and Isabelle Anscombe and Charlotte Gere, *Arts and Crafts in Britain and America* (New York: Rizzoli International Publications, 1978), 7–10. For a discussion of the relationship between the Arts and Crafts Movement and the political climate in England during the 1880s, see Peter Stansky, *William Morris, C. R. Ashbee and the Arts and Crafts* (London: The Nine Elms Press, 1984), 1–14.

13 Cumming and Kaplan, 22 and 72–73. For examples of American Arts and Crafts pottery, see *American Art Pottery* (New York: Cooper-Hewitt Museum, 1987), 72–78.

14 For a more detailed description of the Red House in Upton, Kent, see Cumming and Kaplan, 16 and 31.

15 Simpson, 87. In the fall of 1882, Abbey, and thus most likely Millet, visited William Morris in Kelmscott. William Morris and Edward Burne-Jones had also lived in Broadway before the arrival of the American artists (Simpson, 74).

16 Sophia F. A. Caulfield and Blanche C. Saward, *The Dictionary of Needlework: An Encyclopaedia of Artistic, Plain and Fancy Needlework* (New York: Arno Press, 1972), 476–89.

17 Cumming and Kaplan, 18, 28, and 158. By the beginning of the twentieth century, several magazines, including *The Needle* (1903–10), *The Ladies' Fancy Work Magazine* (1907), and *Home Handicrafts* (1907–17) were avidly promoting women's needlework.

18 For accounts of the prominence of sewing in women's lives, see Laurel Thatcher Ulrich, *Good Wives: Image and Reality in the Lives of Women in Northern New England, 1650–1750* (New York: Vintage Books, 1991), 70–71, and Jeanne Boydston, *Home and Work: Housework, Wages, and the Ideology of Labor in the Early Republic* (New York: Oxford University Press, 1990), 78–79, 82.

19 Karen Halttunen, *Confidence Men and Painted Women: A Study of Middle-Class Culture in America, 1830–1870* (New Haven and London: Yale University Press, 1982), 58–59.

20 Michelle Perrot, ed., *A History of Private Life from the Fires of Revolution to the Great War* (Cambridge, Mass.: Harvard University Press, 1990), 58–64 and 190.

21 Charles C. Eldredge, *American Imagination and Symbolist Painting* (New York: Grey Art Gallery and Study Center, 1979), 68–77. Among others, Thomas Dewing, James McNeill Whistler, and Julian Alden Weir painted "ladies in white," while Sarah Dodson and Henry Prellwitz painted modern Annunciation scenes.

22 Carla Gottlieb, *The Window in Art: From the Window of God to the Vanity of Man* (New York: Abaris Books, 1981), 71. "Because Christ manifests Himself through light, the simile of the sun rays which pass through a windowpane without damaging it, as an explanation for the mystery of Mary's virginal motherhood, was particularly appropriate" (67).

23 Contemporary critics praised *The Window Seat* for its demonstration of light "most dextrously managed" (Simpson, "Windows," 71). Gottlieb points out that "the vase is a well-known symbol for Mary's body" (117).

24 *The American Renaissance*, exh. cat. (New York: Brooklyn Museum, 1979), 11–12. Millet was a member of the Tile Club, a group of upper-middle-class artists affiliated with this movement (63).

25 *American Renaissance*, 28. American Renaissance artists imaged both American and English subjects from the recent past (39 and 41–42).

26 Ibid., 29.

John Singer Sargent

1856–1925

Young Girl Wearing a White Muslin Blouse

between 1882 and 1885
Oil on canvas
19 1/2 x 15 in. (49.5 x 38.1 cm)

The most successful international society portraitist of his generation, Sargent recorded the features of the leading personalities of his day, yet he desired to be free from the demands of commissioned portraiture: "No more paughtraits [*sic*] whether refreshed or not. I abhor and abjure them and hope never to do another especially of the Upper Classes."[1] His was a supremely social art, tied to rules of decorum and inevitably compromised by the need to meet his clients' approval. He also painted genre and landscape scenes as well as mural decorations; but it was portraiture that first brought him fame—and scandal.[2] His career epitomizes the problematic nature of portraiture at the end of the nineteenth century—in particular, its conflicted goals. In a world inundated with inexpensive photographic likenesses, even more was expected of the painted likeness, which had to detail sumptuous surfaces, and then suggest something beyond appearances while still shielding the inner self from public scrutiny.

In *Young Girl Wearing a White Muslin Blouse*, Sargent has turned the formula inside out: he reveals the interior character of the child, but less of the costume and bearing evocative of class so often associated with his art. She appears to be distracted, and we are left wondering what has captured her attention, what she sees. Throughout his career, Sargent created many small portraits like this one—usually of friends or family, often noncommissioned—that intentionally emphasize intimacy rather than formality. *Young Girl* exemplifies his commitment to simplicity: he uses color sparingly, depicting his sitter with an economy of means. Here the artist directs his attention to such expressive details as the lips slightly parted, the head gently bent, the evasive gaze avoiding his scrutiny. Most of his informal portraits concentrate on the face, or the single figure alone in an undefined environment. Such portraits have been favored by many critics in the years since Sargent's death: ". . . Sargent is, perhaps, the epitome of the professional in the good nineteenth-century tradition. His best work will charm generations to come just as the masterpieces of the English school have done. But what is most admired today is a smaller, sketchier type of likeness painted as a rule to please himself or some close friend."[3]

Stylistic evidence suggests that *Young Girl* was painted between 1882 and 1885.[4] Sargent's art is an amalgam of stylistic tendencies that reflect the rapid evolution of European and American art in the late nineteenth century. That amalgam was particularly varied during this transitional period, when he was flirting with moderately progressive tendencies in art. He had completed his professional training in Paris in the late 1870s under Carolus-Duran, the most socially prominent portraitist of the Belle Epoque, who emphasized the technique of painting wet paint into wet paint, *au premier coup*—an approach that gives *Young Girl* a strong sense of immediacy. Here Sargent fused the straightforward format of the eighteenth-century British portrait bust with an innovative sketchy technique inspired by masters such as Velázquez, whose works he had studied and copied at the Prado in 1879, and Hals, whose portraits he copied in Holland the following year. During the early eighties, Sargent was living in Paris but traveling constantly—to Tangier, Venice, Haarlem, Rome, and London, among other places. *Young Girl* was made during a time of exploration, when he was enjoying moderate success but before he had fully established himself at the center of London's artistic establishment. It may have been painted as late as 1884–85, when the artist began his experimentation with impressionism in outdoor portraits of children made in England but still refrained from flooding his canvases with color and sunlight. Despite this portrait's minimal color range, it does reveal Sargent's growing awareness of the expressive potential of paint applied with a loaded brush. In its directness, the portrait recalls Manet—whom Sargent admired—especially in the abstractness implicit in the tonal contrasts and the sudden beauty of white paint against dark ground.

As surely as he captured the beauty of this young girl, Sargent also detected her vulnerablity, the outward manifestation of a child coming to terms with an adult world. For boys, doors opened with adulthood; for girls, social constraints meant the closing of doors. The loss of freedom that girls usually experienced at some point between thirteen and sixteen years old was symbolized by the practice of gathering their hair up into a mass spiked with hairpins, called "clubbed-up hair." Here the young girl still wears her hair loose, but she is nearing that trying time described repeatedly in nineteenth-century women's autobiographies and diaries as "fateful." Her head and upper body emerge from a green-brown background, emanating a dreamy, melancholy quality. Although Sargent responded sensitively to the child's sensuality, it is the ambiguity of this stage of life that seems to have attracted him, and that holds us.

Sargent's essentially introverted portrait represents one side of his own personality—not the phenomenally successful careerist, but the shy man who tended to stammer when

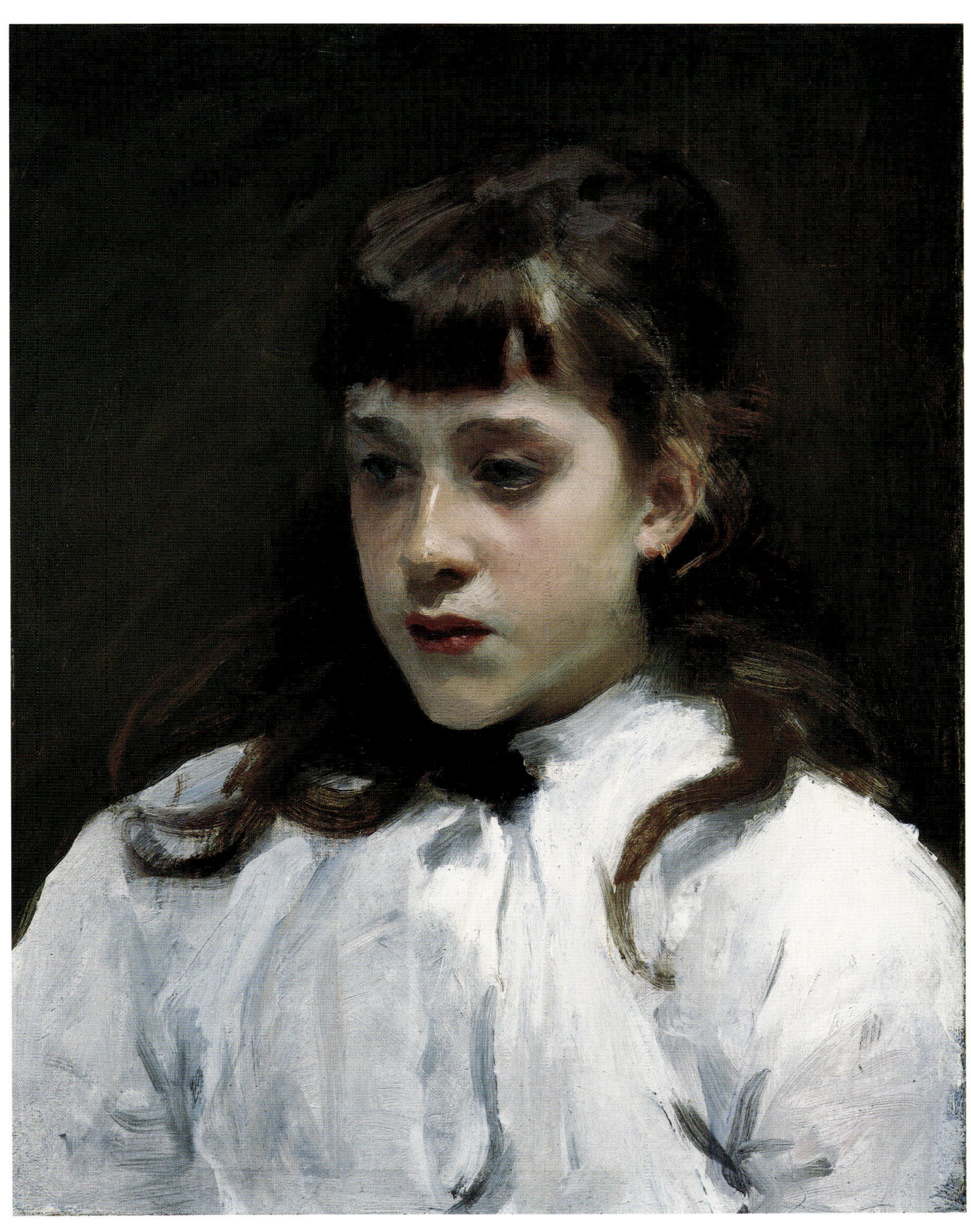

Young Girl Wearing a White Muslin Blouse 77

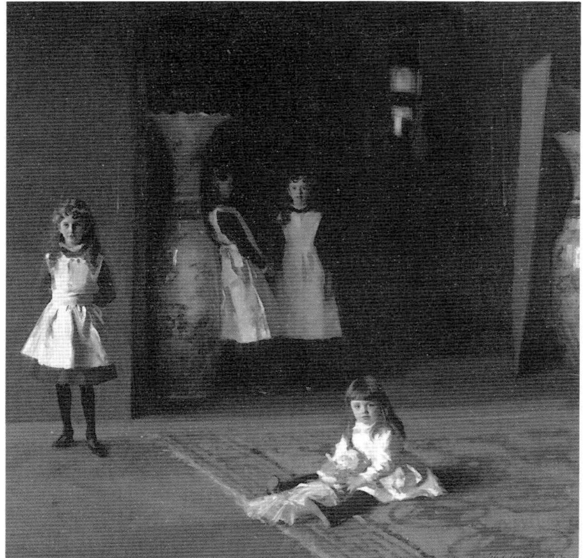

Fig. 1. John Singer Sargent, *The Daughters of Edward D. Boit*, 1882, oil on canvas, 87 x 87 in. (221 x 221 cm), Museum of Fine Arts, Boston, Gift of Mary Louisa Boit, Florence D. Boit, Jane Hubbard Boit, and Julia Overing Boit, in memory of their father, Edward Darley Boit

speaking in public. He made friends with artists and patrons through his portrait commissions in Europe and America, and was a welcome guest in many houses. He felt at ease with children, as is attested to by the tender yet unsentimental portraits he made of them. At his best capturing the fashionable, frankly sexual allure of both men and women of the upper classes, he seldom painted conventionally pretty young girls, scrutinizing them with less mawkishness than most of his peers. Here the particularity of his vision renders the girl tangible on one level, even as her self-absorption distances her from his (and our) intrusion.

The aura of gravity in *Young Girl* is particularly striking given the rosy ideal of childhood that found widespread expression in the image of happy youth during the second half of the nineteenth century.[5] Ubiquitous in literature, popular illustration, and academic painting, portrayals of carefree children invited adults to experience vicariously the joys of youth. Unlike the portrayals of so many of his contemporaries, Sargent's more sober vision is closer to the solemn tone of much popular writing on childrearing. Influenced by the sentimentalized image of the child, middle- and upper-class parents felt pressured to raise perfect children. More and more, psychologists, theologians, educators, and other authorities regarded children as vulnerable beings. Nurturing and protecting their mental and physical health required constant vigilance on the part of parents, especially the mother, who often was blamed for her children's failures.[6] Popular misunderstandings concerning the nature of heredity compounded widespread apprehensions.

Perhaps Sargent's own childhood made him uncommonly sensitive to the deep gap between the ideal and the real. In his commissioned portraits, he masterfully captured the intricacies of his clients' costumes in order to place them securely in their social milieu; but in this private portrait, the young girl's white blouse conveys nothing about her family's social status, country of origin, or even her exact generation. The artist must have deemed such information about the

subject irrelevant to the story he chose to tell: childhood cuts across distinctions of class and time. Indeed, in its generic, schoolgirl simplicity, the blouse resembles the one worn about fifteen years earlier by Sargent's sister Emily at age ten, in a photograph of her with him taken around the time of their sister Minnie's death.[7] Emily suffered from a deformed spine, the result of an injury when she was three, followed by forced immobility, mistakenly prescribed to aid recovery. During Emily's long ordeal, her primary companion was her brother. In format and mood, *Young Girl* resembles numerous close-up portraits of family members painted by Sargent, including one of Emily dated 1875 (Collection of the Ormond Family). No doubt his lifelong closeness to his sisters, Violet and Emily, and his awareness of the less sunny aspects of childhood, account in part for his many images of introspective children, especially girls, painted with close scrutiny yet without the prurient interest often evident in such portrayals from his era.

Although historians have frequently considered Sargent a detached observer, a recent study of his genre paintings finds the subjective imprint of his complex personality on his choice and interpretation of subjects.[8] Like the "private" genre works, *Young Girl* reveals that probing aspect of his vision uncompromised by a client's expectations. Indeed, this portrait shares with many of his genre scenes and small landscape sketches "a mood of sad and quiet longing" at once discovered in and projected upon his subjects by the artist himself.[9] Recent scholarship has also discovered that Sargent's privileged, expatriate youth roaming through Europe with his parents and sisters was in fact "a merciless orbit passing through illness and death and back again."[10] Contrasting views see either his father or his mother as the more difficult parent, but in either case the atmosphere at home—a constantly shifting place—was apparently suffocatingly close, yet lonely. Given that emotional landscape, it is not surprising that the analytic powers of Sargent's mind and eye repeatedly uncovered something other than an idyllic image of childhood.

Throughout his career, Sargent included children in some of his most ambitious paintings, including his great Salon success in 1883, *The Daughters of Edward D. Boit* (fig. 1). Whereas *Young Girl* discloses no reference to place or position, the portrait of the Boit children visually equates the young girls with expensive vases, in accord with frequent portrayals of children as "Household treasures! . . . jewels rich and rare."[11] Sargent felt free to experiment with the composition of this portrait, painted in the Boits' Paris apartment, because the girls' American artist-father was his friend. Although the four sisters are dressed much alike and resemble one another, Sargent's unconventional use of empty space and mysterious shadows isolates them, evoking the uncertainty and aloneness of growing up. They recede, from the youngest with her doll seen in bright light in the foreground, to the oldest, slouching back against a huge vase and half-hidden in shadow in another room.

The melancholic beauty that Sargent saw in his friend's children also found expression in *Young Girl*, painted at around the same time. Indeed, considering stylistic similarity, probable execution date, and the physical resemblance to the eldest Boit daughter, the sitter may be Florence Boit.[12] In the Salon painting, she alone is seen in profile, while her younger sisters solemnly confront the artist; in *Young Girl*, the sitter also evades his gaze. The mood of both the large and the small portrait is surprisingly similar: hushed silence.

Oscar Wilde, a close associate of Sargent, commented on the inaccuracy of our perceptions, the impossibility of responding to a painting of another individual without exposing oneself, in the 1891 preface to his novel, *The Picture of Dorian Gray*: "All art is at once surface and symbol. Those who go beneath the surface do so at their own peril. . . . It is the spectator, and not life, that art really mirrors."[13] As in his best portraits, so in *Young Girl* Sargent allowed underlying uncertainties about our possibilities of knowing one another to add a psychological dimension to his art that can also be found in much of the art and literature of the fin-de-siècle. Despite the intimacy of mood, the undefined setting, generic costume, and fluidity of this young girl's transitory facial expression as recorded by Sargent's brush make it impossible to reduce the meaning of her portrait to a single biography. We cannot help interpreting her story as told by Sargent through our own.

ROBIN JAFFEE FRANK

1 Evan Charteris, *John Sargent* (New York, 1927), 155.
2 The French press was provoked by Sargent's *Madame X (Madame Pierre Gautreau)* (Metropolitan Museum of Art), exhibited at the Salon in 1884.
3 Monroe Wheeler, commenting on the Museum of Modern Art's Twentieth-Century Portrait Show; quoted in *Ten Sargents from Sargent's Own Collection, Now Owned by Mrs. Stevenson Scott*, exh. brochure (New York: Scott and Fowles, 1948), n.p.
4 I am immensely grateful to Richard Ormond, Trevor Fairbrother, and Erica Hirschler for discussing the dating of this portrait with me. Dated 1885 in the exhibition catalogue *Sargent at Broadway: The Impressionist Years* (New York: Coe Kerr Gallery, 1986), plate XVI, stylistic evidence suggests that it was probably painted between 1882 and 1885.
5 For examples, see Sarah Burns, "Barefoot Boys and Other Country Children: Sentiment and Ideology in Nineteenth-Century American Art," *The American Art Journal* 20 (1988): 24–50; Susan P. Casteras, *Victorian Childhood: Paintings Selected from the Forbes Magazine Collection* (New York: Harry N. Abrams, 1986); and Lee M. Edwards, *Domestic Bliss: Family Life in American Painting, 1840–1910*, exh. cat. (Yonkers, N.Y.: The Hudson River Museum, 1986).
6 See Orson S. Fowler, *Creative and Sexual Science* (Philadelphia: The National Publishing Company, 1870), and G. Stanley Hall, *The Contents of Children's Minds* (New York: E. L. Kellog, 1893).
7 Photograph of Sargent with his sister Emily (Collection of the Ormond Family), reproduced in *John Singer Sargent*, exh. cat. (New York: Whitney Museum of American Art, 1987), 14.
8 See Trevor Fairbrother, "Sargent's Genre Paintings and the Issues of Suppression and Privacy," *Studies in the History of Art* 37 (1990): 28–49.
9 Ibid., 31.
10 Stanley Olsen, "On the Question of Sargent's Nationality," *John Singer Sargent*, exh. cat. (New York: Whitney Museum of American Art, 1987), 14.
11 J. E. Carpenter, "Household Treasures"; quoted in Mary Lynn Stevens Heininger, "Children, Childhood, and Change in America, 1820–1920," in *A Century of Childhood*, exh. cat. (Rochester, N.Y.: The Margaret Woodbury Strong Museum, 1984), 25.
12 I am indebted to Cora Lee Gibbs and Kent Ahrens for sharing information on the Boit family and putting me in touch with family members, to whom I extend my gratitude.
13 Oscar Wilde, preface to *The Picture of Dorian Gray* (1891), in *The First Collected Edition of the Works of Oscar Wilde*, ed. Robert Ross, 15 vols. (London: Dawsons of Pall Mall, 1969), 12:ix–xi. For a discussion of the overlapping lives and aesthetic attitudes of Sargent and Wilde, see Albert Boime, "Sargent in Paris and London: A Portrait of the Artist as Dorian Gray," in *John Singer Sargent*, exh. cat. (New York: Whitney Museum of American Art, 1987), 75–109.

William Merritt Chase

1849–1916

Seated Woman in Black Dress

c. 1888
Pastel on canvas
20 x 16 in. (50.8 x 40.6 cm)

Beginning in the 1880s, Chase's approach to portraiture reflected a thorough but personalized understanding of the portraits created by Whistler after 1870. He admired Whistler's art and had observed his working method first-hand during the summer of 1886 in London, where the two artists' clashing egos impeded the continuation of their tense friendship. Already experimenting with formal innovations in his own art, Chase was receptive to Whistler's emphasis on the carefully orchestrated pictorial effect.

Like Whistler, Chase frequently depicted subjects seated in an armchair sihouetted against an austere background in a frontal, frame-filling composition. In *Seated Woman in Black Dress*, the gentle curves of the sitter's body are echoed by the fabric-covered chair and contrasted with the geometric pillow with a self-consciousness that accords with the Whistlerian philosophy of art for art's sake.[1] But when compared to Whistler's nearly monochromatic portraits, Chase's pastel is more richly colored: the pillow and fabric provide areas of pinks and greens with vigorous daubs of red, yellow, and blue crayon that create an alternative to the dramatic charcoal-black gown. And the fan adds Chase's signature red note. The fabric and pillow lend an exotic touch—also found in many of Whistler's portraits—in keeping with the fascination with oriental objects then pervasive in European and American art. Both Chase and Whistler often placed their subjects against a softly modulated color; the flatness is made more apparent here by Chase's large signature in the upper left-hand corner. However, he has retained the attention to detail seen in his early Munich-style portraits, so that he achieves a convincing rendering of the sitter's physical appearance. Although her features are sensitively handled, Chase is more concerned with exploring formal problems of color and design than with individual characterization. As he told a class of students in 1894, "You look at a portrait and you do not care who the person was—the artist alone lives."[2] Indeed, here the identity of the sitter remains unknown, although she may have been one of his female students, for they frequently served as his models.

Chase experimented with a variety of media, most notably pastel. Toward the end of the nineteenth century, drawing in pastel, long considered a pastime for amateurs, experienced a rebirth in Europe and America. As a founder of the Society of Painters in Pastel, which held its first show in 1884 and its last in 1890, Chase was instrumental in elevating the public appreciation of the medium.[3] As in *Seated Woman*, Chase often treated pastels as though they were paintings, bringing them to an equal degree of finish, rather than approaching them as sketches, as Whistler did. Indeed, one of Chase's pupils declared, "It was his delight in pastel that opened our eyes to the medium. Up to then no one handled pastel in so painter-like a manner."[4] He achieves in his pastel portraits, often bathed, like *Seated Woman*, in a soft light, a velvety airiness only possible with this medium. Chase's best pastel portraits convey, above all else, a sense of serenity.

In *Seated Woman*, the model is purposefully posed and the accessories carefully selected from Chase's personal possessions to create an impression of the refinement of the sitter, and by extension the artist.[5] These props appear in many of his works: for example, the fabric is wrapped around the figure in the pastel *Back of a Nude* (Collection of Mr. and Mrs. Raymond J. Horowitz) and draped over the chair in the oil painting *Dorothy and Her Sister* (Private Collection); the pillow is similar to the one behind the visitor in the famous *A Friendly Call* (fig. 1).[6] The latter painting is one of many studio or domestic interiors Chase painted during the 1880s and 1890s in which attractive women in resplendent costume are surrounded by mesmerizing accessories. The objects he collected were part of a larger cultural vogue for acquiring eclectic pieces and bringing them together in interiors that expressed the personality of the owner. Chase's studio paintings not only testify to the importance to the artist of a designed space in which he could live and work gracefully, but also reveal his attitude toward women's role in the environment he shaped. A contemporary critic objected to the way the female figures became part of his display: "They count for almost less than the embroidered cushions and the tall mirror. . . ."[7]

In contrast, the few accessories in *Seated Woman* complement rather than overwhelm the figure. Nonetheless, they do define her, for Chase devoted equal attention to the figure and the objects, and gave no other clues to her personality. He masterfully conveys—through only a few still-life elements—that the subject is at home in a world of opulence. Although we know that the exotic pillow and fabric are artist's props, in the fiction of the image, they serve to suggest the sitter's (or her husband's) economic status and cultured taste.[8]

The elegantly covered—or clothed—chair itself can be seen as an equivalent of the woman's sensual charm and physical anatomy. Chase reveals little flesh, so that the pillow, with its pale-pink coloring and stuffed softness, is comparable to

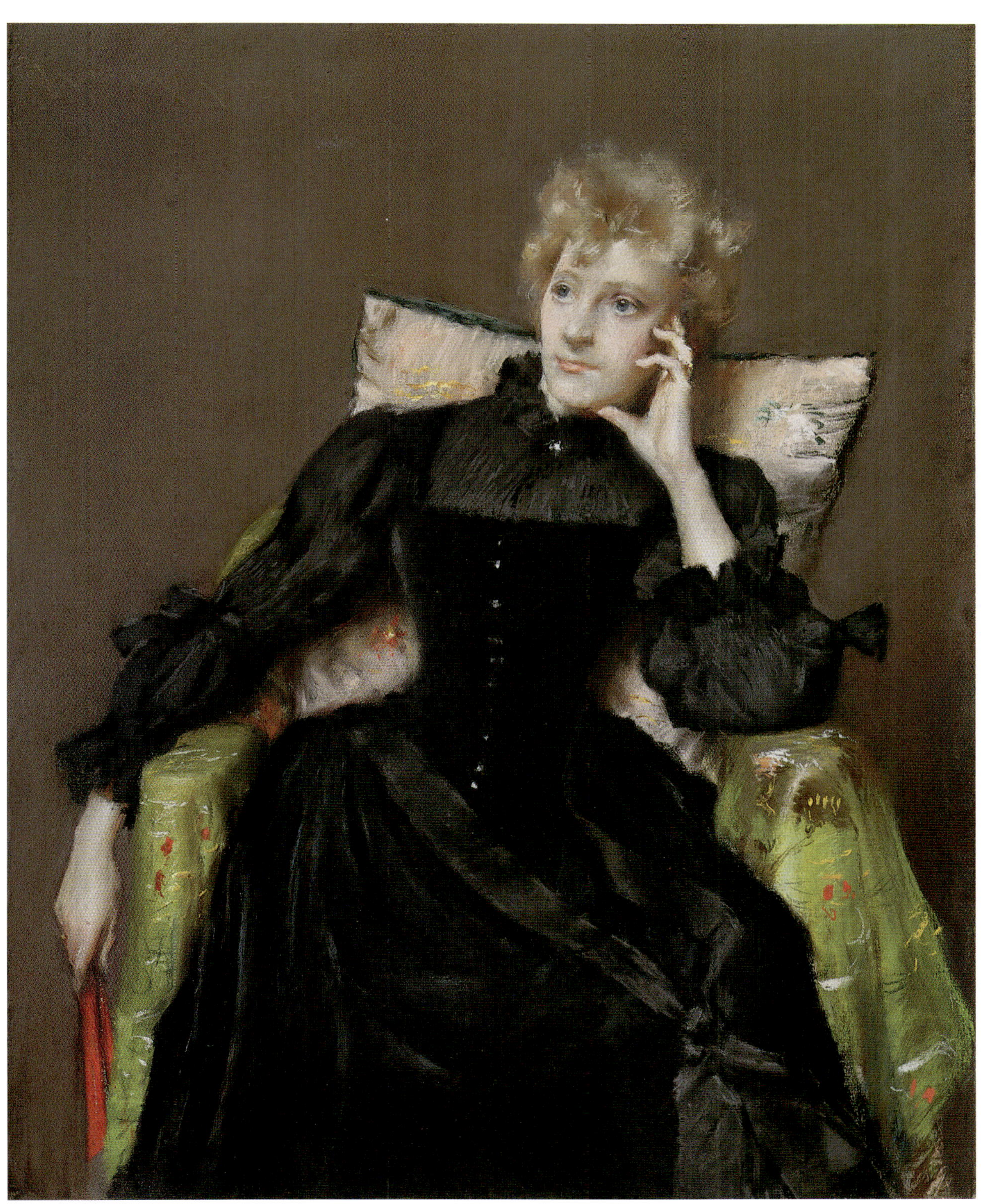

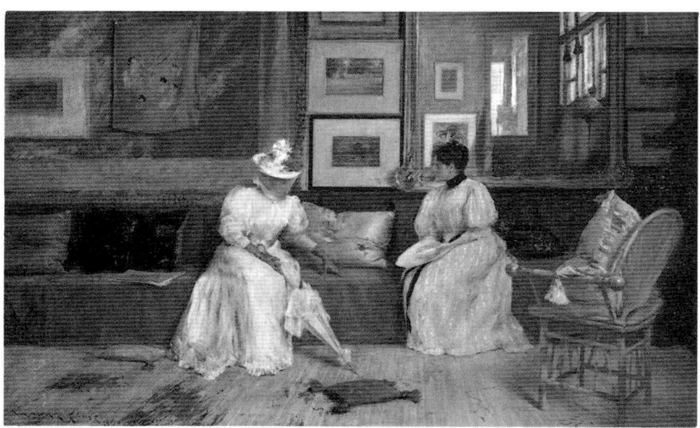

Fig. 1. William Merritt Chase, *A Friendly Call*, 1895, oil on canvas, 30 ⅛ x 48 ¼ in. (76.5 x 122.6 cm), National Gallery of Art, Washington, D.C., Chester Dale Collection

her upper torso, which we can only imagine. The seat, draped with flowing fabric, resembles the shape of her gown. Through his suggestive treatment of still-life elements, Chase enhances the allure of his chastely dressed but appealingly proportioned sitter.

Like so many lissome ladies of American and European late-nineteenth-century paintings, Chase's sitter is posed in an attitude that presupposes an appreciative male gaze. His frontal vantage point emphasizes the well-rounded shape of the sitter, whose mature figure conforms to the Victorian ideal of the nurturing female still valued at the close of the century. The fashionable full sleeves diminish the size of the waist. The woman's elegantly positioned fingers frame one side of her face, while the languid line of her other arm repeats the hourglass shape of her body. Chase's portraits of women were increasingly distinguished by an emphasis on such attitudes of modish ennui, perhaps intended to connote the wealth of the subject.

Here the artist has also devoted great attention to the tactile qualities of the sitter's gown, with its shimmering satin, swelling gathers and ruffles, and glistening buttons. Chase set for himself the then popular painterly challenge of rendering the rich range of blacks in the subject's dress. His first biographer contrasted his distinctive handling of satin to that of his contemporaries: "The texture of satin is ever fascinating to the painter. In the good modern canvas it is often beautifully handled, crisp, clean, sharp, and fine, with all its play of light felt and recorded; yet often, despite that fact, it remains the material of the shop-window, whereas the satin gown in a Chase portrait has the dignity and distinction of an immemorial fabric."9

The female subjects of Chase's late portraits are often dressed in such beautiful gowns and are rarely occupied in any activity. Leisure-class ladies—rather than men or working-class women in mundane garments—were almost exclusively chosen by artists at the turn of the century to evoke a contemplative mood. Women who did not work outside the home represented a cultural ideal, the other pole in the human duality defined by the era in terms of gender and class. Unlike those whose lives were spent in prosaic pursuit of money in the public sphere, middle- and upper-class women were allowed—even encouraged—to indulge their poetic sensibilities in the private female sphere. Doing nothing was a mark of status, according to Thorstein Veblen in his sociological analysis of 1899, *The Theory of the Leisure Class*: "She is

exempted, or debarred, from vulgarly useful employment—
in order to perform leisure vicariously for the good repute
of her natural (pecuniary) guardian."[10] Although these ladies
were sheltered from (or denied full access to) active participation in the capitalist world, most male artists depicted
them as both beneficiaries and objects of acquisitive male
desire—as much a part of the display of wealth as the precious possessions invariably included in depictions of female
idleness. And while she is doing nothing, the viewer is
offered the mildly voyeuristic experience of admiring her
beauty.

The bold confrontation with the viewer by the artist's daughter, Alice, in *Tired* (p. 32) contrasts with the elusive gaze of
this sitter. Here, Chase's subject looks away, avoiding the
immediacy and emotional pitch that often characterize his
more informal portraits. Combined with the empty background, his portrayal in *Seated Woman* of a self-absorbed sitter suggests a quality of personal isolation. Unlike many society portraits, in which the sitters' imperious bearing and
expression accord with their trappings of wealth, Chase's
model seems distracted, distanced from us and her surroundings. Thus, although class is an important aspect of
this portrait, it is not primarily about status but about mood.
And the mood here, as in *Tired*, is one of reverie; yet the
young woman's thoughts are not explicitly connected to
the artist/viewer, and the object of her gaze lies beyond the
picture frame.

Unlike numerous Victorian artists, as well as many of
Chase's contemporaries, such as Alfred Stevens and Thomas
Dewing, who often supplied clues to the subject of the
woman's thoughts—a picture on the wall, music, a letter in
her hand, an empty chair evoking absence—Chase stripped
the portrait to its essentials. A closed fan held languidly in
her fingers, she sits on a chair covered by material from a distant land. Her mind also wanders from the here and now.
Her meditative state, released from ties to a specific source,
encourages the viewer to indulge in free associations of his
or her own.

ROBIN JAFFEE FRANK

1   The title, *Seated Woman in Black Dress*, is descriptive. Two thus far
    unlocated pastels by Chase might relate directly to this work:
    Study—Black Against Pink, exhibited at his first one-man show at
    the Boston Art Club in 1886; and *Waiting*, exhibited at the St.
    Louis Exposition, 1890. I am much indebted to Ronald G. Pisano,
    an American art consultant specializing in Chase's work, for this
    information.
2   David Abraham Milgrome, "The Art of William Merritt Chase"
    (Ph.D. diss., University of Pittsburgh, 1969), 130; quoted in
    Carolyn Kinder Carr, *William Merritt Chase: Portraits*, exh. cat.
    (Akron, Ohio: Akron Art Museum, 1982), 35.
3   For further information on Chase's role in the society, see Ronald
    G. Pisano, *A Leading Spirit in American Art: William Merritt
    Chase, 1849–1916* (Seattle: Henry Art Gallery, University of
    Washington, 1983), 66–71.
4   Quoted in Dianne Pilgrim, *American Impressionist and Realist
    Paintings and Drawings*, exh. cat. (New York: Metropolitan
    Museum of Art), 28. The statement was made by Irving Ramsay
    Wiles, who also exhibited with the Society of Painters in Pastel.
5   In addition, the curve of the arms and back of the chair resembles
    that of the pedestal-based chair Virginia Gerson sits on in a
    c. 1884 pastel by Chase, *In the Studio* (reproduced in Pisano, 1983,
    plate 73).
6   Note that the pillow on the chair in the right foreground of *A
    Friendly Call* may be the same one placed behind Chase's daughter
    in *Tired* (p. 32).
7   *Art Amateur* (May 1895), 157; quoted in Ronald G. Pisano, *William
    Merritt Chase* (New York: Watson-Guptill Publications, 1979), 70.
8   Her marital status is indicated by the ring on her left hand.
9   Katherine Metcalf Roof, "William Merritt Chase: The Man and
    the Artist," *Century Magazine* 93 (April 1917): 834.
10 Thorstein Veblen, *The Theory of the Leisure Class: An Economic
    Study of Institutions*, New American Library ed. (New York, 1953;
    first published 1899), 232.

Martin Johnson Heade

1819–1904

Magnolias on a Blue Velvet Cloth

1885–1895
Oil on canvas
15 1/8 x 24 1/4 in. (38.4 x 61.6 cm)

From his earliest known still life, *Vase of Corn Lilies and Heliotropes*, done in 1863, Heade established himself as both a painter in the mainstream of American flower painting and a beguiling outsider. Until the middle of the nineteenth century, flower painting was largely unknown as an American genre. Beginning in the 1840s, a "language of flowers," an iconography of flower imagery associated with human relationships and characteristics, emerged in the Victorian consciousness. The decorative flower scenes of Severin Roesen, George Cochran Lambdin, and Ellen Robbins belong to this development,[1] and while Heade's might join them, his works participate on very different terms.[2] Heade's flower paintings suggested from the beginning an austerity that asserts itself even in *Apple Blossoms in a Nautilus Shell Vase*, where a most baroque element assumes a strange, almost cryptic restraint. Dramatically lit, normally in simple vases or tumblers set on ledges or merely placed on an undefined surface, Heade's early flowers in particular convey a mysterious, melancholic reserve that recalls the still lifes of the Peales, with which the Philadelphia-trained artist was familiar earlier in the century.

In the early 1880s, Heade, having left New York to live permanently in St. Augustine, Florida, added the reclining flower to his repertoire of flower imagery. Paintings of great visual beauty, these depict roses and varieties of tropical flowers, including water lilies, lotus flowers, and orange blossoms, and, later, in his last great series, the giant magnolia, of which *Magnolias on a Blue Velvet Cloth* is part. Rather than bouquets, Heade's reclining flowers are either single blossoms or, at the most, two or three blossoms or buds, sometimes placed on bare ledges, occasionally on sumptuous red, gold, and later, blue velvet. They are far more assertive than his earlier flower scenes, both as a result of the substantially larger canvases and of the placement of flowers close to the picture plane. The viewer is beckoned to the flower's core and, because of its undulations of petals and leaves, views the flower from every curve and angle. John Baur, writing on another Heade magnolia painting, perceived "the fleshy whiteness of magnolia blossoms startlingly arrayed on sumptuous red velvet like odalisques on a couch."[3] This comparison and sexual connotation are even more arresting in Heade's orchid and passion flower landscapes painted from the 1870s until shortly before his death.

John Baur's analogy might extend to something deeper than frank sexuality. Through the coarse, brown underside of some of the magnolia's leaves and the conspicuously cut stem, the flower is consigned to a fantasy zone lying between life and fresh beauty and death and decay. With its eerie lighting and bare, airless background, and the hard sheen of the magnolia's petals and leaves, the scene further insinuates a discreetly dark vision, akin to a *vanitas*, that belies its surface lushness. That what we see here is a highly personal, expressionistic vision is undeniable, and that it should appear in the epoch of Ryder, Inness, and Blakelock[4] suggests a modernity in the work of Heade which those who associate him only with luminist landscape will find surprising.

The rediscovery of Heade in the 1940s might have been impelled by parallels perceived between *Thunderstorm over Narragansett Bay*, displayed at the Metropolitan Museum of Art for the first time in 1943, and Surrealism,[5] but his reclining magnolias from the 1880s and 1890s also vividly establish his links with our century. Heade, always the underachiever in the game of popular success, was still as familiar with European trends in art as any other painter working in America. The work of this widely traveled artist is characterized by an incorporation of European trends, and perhaps even an anticipation of them. Seen in Heade's seascapes, for instance, is the same inspiration, contemporaneously expressed, of Courbet's crashing waves painted in the 1860s. Scholars have cited the influence of Pre-Raphaelite art beginning in the 1860s on his flower and hummingbird landscapes,[6] which, in their dispersed quality and delicacy also recall Asian art. His palette darkened and his brushstroke became more painterly in the 1880s and 1890s, consonant with the appearance of these new approaches in the art of Americans who studied in Munich and among Hispanophiles in Paris. One movement, Impressionism, never affected Heade's style, for which Church might have congratulated him in 1894.[7]

Magnolias on a Blue Velvet Cloth and many of Heade's late flower scenes show an interest in abstraction of form that is unexpectedly compatible with twentieth-century tastes. His late magnolias are large, dominant, and pure, their forms arranged so we seem to see the flower from multiple angles, while the scene's accessories are subordinated to a central image and idea. In many of the late reclining flower paintings Heade also emphasized the two-dimensionality of the canvas by arranging his flowers close to the frontal plane, the scene's darkly enigmatic backgrounds serving as tonal foils to the sumptuous colors and shapes of the petals and pushing the flower even closer to us. In this way, the painting develops, not strictly as a flower image, but as a design asserting a

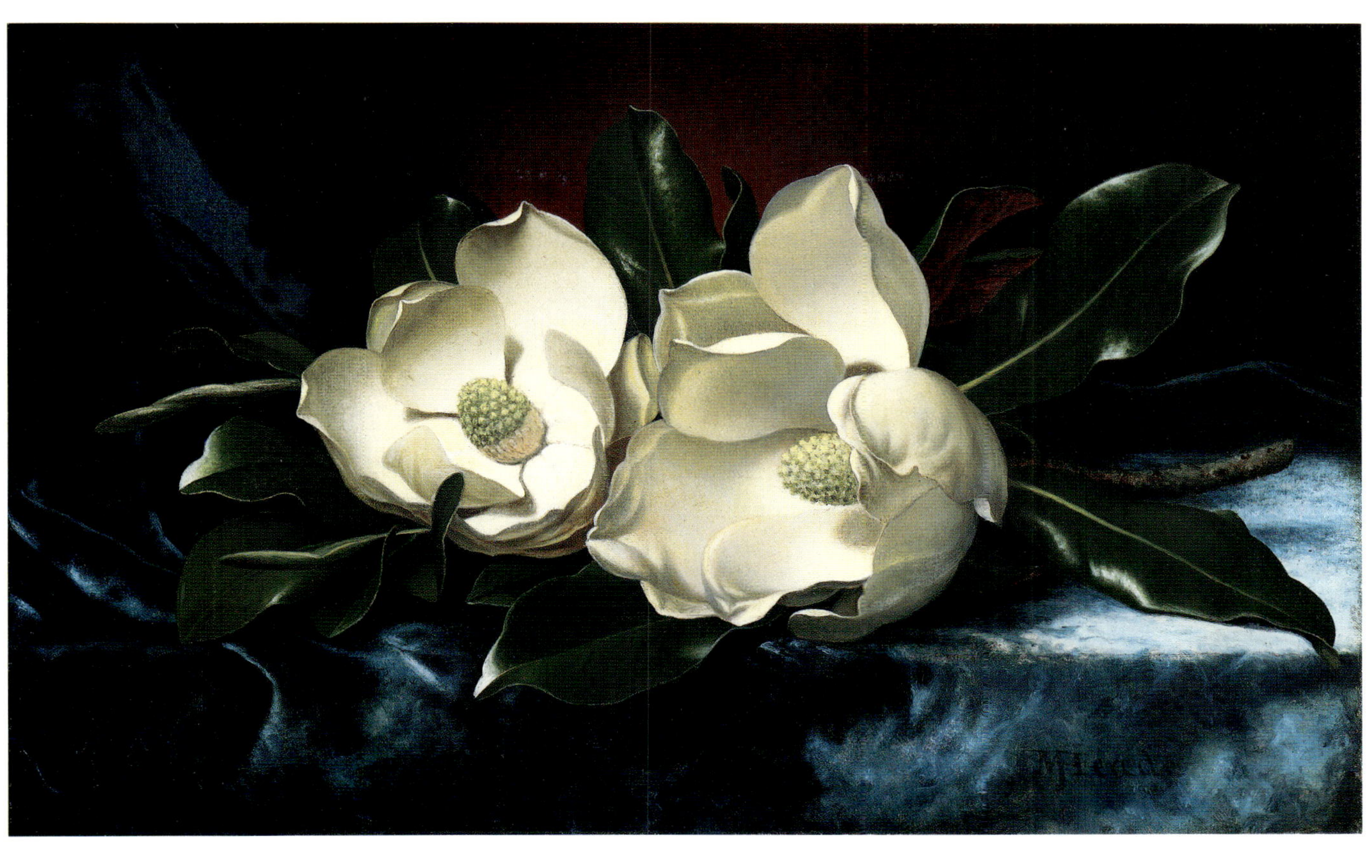

fundamental equilibrium, formal structure, and rhythm. It is
a sensibility that associates Heade with the flower paintings,
not only of Georgia O'Keeffe, but also of Charles Burchfield,
Joseph Stella, Arthur Dove, and Charles Demuth. In this
respect, the painting places its artist, who, after all, lived until
1904, in the context of the new formalism that affected the
spectrum of American painting in the twentieth century.

BRIAN T. ALLEN

1 For a general history of flower painting, see William H. Gerdts and
Russell Burke, *American Still-Life Painting* (New York: Praeger
Publishers, 1971).

2 Heade's participation in the symbolism of American flower painting is reviewed in T. E. Stebbins, Jr., *Martin Johnson Heade* (New
Haven and London: Yale University Press, 1975), 115–21. Although
Heade painted several types of roses, one of the most commonly
painted and iconographically established of flowers, the great
majority of his flower paintings depict flowers seldom treated by
others, such as apple blossoms, heliotrope, laurels, and
cornflowers. Heade might have hoped in this way to free himself
from the pressures of bourgeois flower symbolism and to pursue
new formal challenges.

3 J. I. H. Baur, introduction to *Commemorative Exhibition: Paintings
by Martin J. Heade and F. H. Lane from the Karolik Collections in the
Museum of Fine Arts, Boston* (Boston: Boston Museum of Fine
Arts, 1954).

4 Stebbins, 96.

5 Ibid., 78, notes the seascape's "crystalline surfaces and apparitional
luminosity" as the basis for this possible confluence in taste.

6 W. Gerdts, "The Influence of Ruskin and Pre-Raphaelism on
American Still Life Painting," *American Art Journal* 1
(Fall 1969): 80.

7 Church commended Heade in a letter for having avoided becom-
ing "the slave of baleful foreign influences," a likely reference to
Impressionism, which by the 1890s was becoming a sensation in
America and among a considerable group of American painters.
Quoted in R. G. McIntyre, *Martin Johnson Heade* (New York:
Pantheon, 1948), 24.

John Frederick Peto

1854–1907

The Writer's Table: A Precarious Moment

probably 1890s
Oil on canvas
27 1/8 x 22 in. (63.9 x 55.9 cm)

On the corner of a table, a collection of objects is haphazardly arranged on top of a rumpled blue velvet cloth. Light shines from the left, modeling forms in high relief and casting long shadows. The somber palette is relieved by touches of cool and hot color: the pale sky-blue of the dangling book cover, the deep red of the book's pages, the bright yellow of the inkwell's label. A vellum-bound book stands upright in the middle of the composition, the other objects tilting to the right and left, away from this center point. A soiled book, fanned open, rests upside down on its bent pages; below it, a tattered book with a frayed binding lies on the foreground edge of the table, its cover hanging by a thread and dangling off the table. A rusty, dented beer stein, an old, oxidized candle snuffer, a tarnished candlestick with a guttered candle, and a cylindrical inkwell, marred by drops of ink, are propped on the cloth's folds and lean precipitously, as if at any moment they might topple over.

In *The Writer's Table: A Precarious Moment*, Peto portrays the objects in his composition illusionistically by recording their subtleties with minute precision. The frayed edges of paper, the careless pencil mark on the inside cover of a pamphlet, the interlocking feathers on a quill pen—these fine details heighten the painting's naturalism, deceiving the eye with their realism and inviting the viewer's scrutiny. Another way in which Peto emphasizes the illusionism in his work is by placing the objects at the edge of the table in front of a dark, impenetrable background, thus creating a shallow pictorial space where objects are pushed up against the surface of the picture plane. Moving out toward the viewer, they become even more real and suggest man's presence.[1] The artist's concern seems to have been to capture the moment immediately following human activity: the candle has just been extinguished; the ink is still dripping down the side of the inkwell.[2]

The old book and the guttered candle, along with such ancillary items as the inkwell, the candle snuffer, and the beer stein, are objects associated with a long tradition of illusionistic still-life painting known as the *vanitas* still life, paintings that deal with the subject of life's transience.[3] Popular in seventeenth- and eighteenth-century Europe, these paintings traditionally incorporated objects that related to the themes of earthly existence, temporality, and resurrection.

Traditional *vanitas* still lifes often included a skull in the composition, as a reminder of man's mortality and a warning against materialism or egoism. An old, battered man-made object, a wilted flower, or a piece of rotten fruit might serve as a substitute symbol of decay, underscoring the theme of time's passage.[4] In Peto's composition, all of the objects show the effects of age: the vellum-bound book, its pages softly disintegrating, is hinged with iron straps, recalling antique medieval manuscripts; the fanned book's soiled cover is marred with stains; the old book on the edge of the table is about to lose its cover as it dangles from a single thread; the beer stein and candle snuffer are rusty; the candlestick is tarnished and its candle melted down; the feather on the quill pen is worn with use. The old book is a powerful symbol that represents two diametrically opposed ideas: the uselessness of knowledge in the face of man's mortality and the ability to achieve salvation through wisdom.[5] On another level, the representation of books or writing implements serves as an admonition against excessive pride in one's erudition, just as the beer stein warns against frivolity. The extinguished candle, like the black background, is a reminder of darkness, deepening the symbolism of the inevitability of death and, ultimately, the fugacity of worldly things.[6]

Peto's choice of objects not only reflects memento mori themes but evokes traditional *vanitas* paintings. The "baroque restlessness"[7] of the crowded composition, expressed in the underlying movement of the tilted objects on the rumpled cloth and the torn book cover hanging by a thread, is reminiscent of many *vanitas* works by Dutch, Flemish, and Italian seventeenth- and eighteenth-century painters.[8] The overall feeling is one of instability and imminent chaos—a "precarious moment," in Peto's words, symbolizing the ephemerality of life.[9]

BETHANY ASTRACHAN

1 See William H. Gerdts and Russell Burke, *American Still-Life Painting* (New York: Praeger Publishers, 1971), 134; and Gerdts, *150 Years of American Still-Life Painting*, exh. cat. (New York: Coe Kerr Gallery, 1970), 23.
2 Alberto Veca, *Vanitas: The Symbolism of Time* (Bergamo, Italy: Galleria Lorenzelli, 1981), 164.
3 John Wilmerding, *Important Information Inside: The Art of John F. Peto and the Idea of Still-Life Painting in Nineteenth-Century America*, exh. cat. (Washington, D.C.: National Gallery of Art, 1983), 130–31. Wilmerding links Peto's paintings of old books to traditional *vanitas* images. He writes: "His soiled and chaotic books stand as reminders of our mortality, affecting reformulations of the *memento mori* convention."

4 Charles Sterling, *Still Life Painting: From Antiquity to the Twentieth Century*, 2d rev. ed. (New York: Harper and Row, 1981), 72.

5 Veca, 184.

6 Chad Mandeles discusses the tradition of *vanitas* in the work of William M. Harnett. See: Mandeles, "William Michael Harnett's *The Old Cupboard Door* and the Tradition of *Vanitas*," *American Art Journal* 18, no. 3 (1986): 51–62; and Mandeles, "Grave Counsel: Harnett and *Vanitas*," in *William M. Harnett*, exh. cat. (Fort Worth, Tex.: Amon Carter Museum/New York: Metropolitan Museum of Art, 1992), 253–63. Barbara S. Groseclose also discusses Harnett's work in terms of its associations with traditional *vanitas* images in "Vanity and the Artist: Some Still-Life Paintings by William Michael Harnett," *American Art Journal* 19, no. 1 (1987): 51-59.

7 Alfred Frankenstein, *After the Hunt: William Harnett and Other American Still Life Painters, 1870–1900,* rev. ed. (Berkeley and Los Angeles: University of California Press, 1969), xv.

8 Sterling, 70.

9 See Veca, 189–90; Wilmerding, 108; and Groseclose, 55.

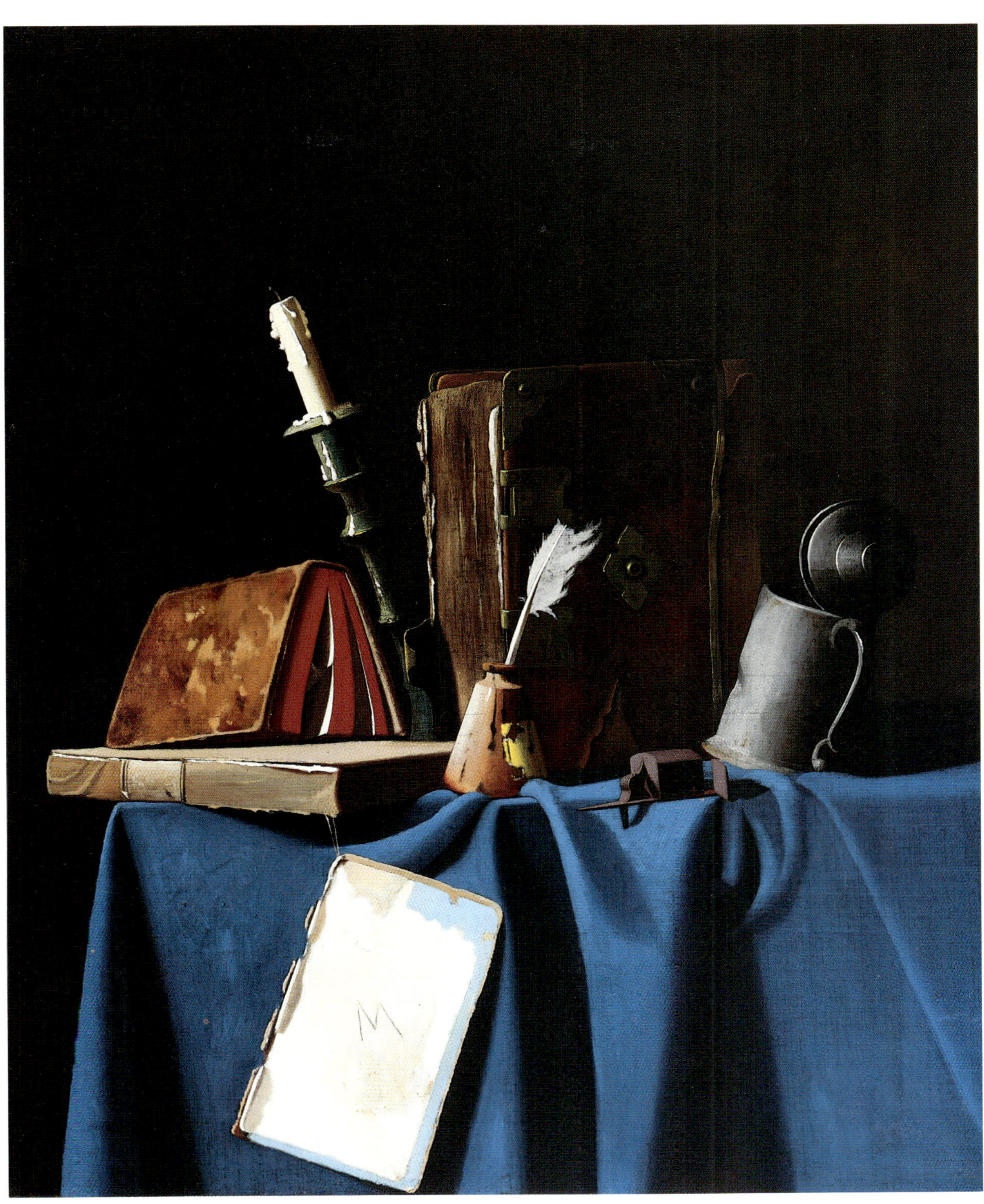

William Michael Harnett

1848–1892

The Social Club

1879
Oil on canvas
13¹/₂ x 20¹/₄ in. (34.3 x 51.4 cm)

Harnett is probably the most famous American painter of still life and trompe l'oeil in the last quarter of the nineteenth century. In this genre, he depicted a wide variety of items ranging from simple compositions of paper currency to elaborate renderings of books, musical instruments, bric-a-brac, and hunting paraphernalia. *The Social Club* was painted in 1879 in Philadelphia, one year before Harnett's departure for Europe, where he lived for six years. During his stay, notably in Munich, his paintings became increasingly more sophisticated in terms of content, composition, and symbolic meaning. As one of his earlier and simplest pieces, *The Social Club* is remarkable for converging complex meanings by means of a striking economy of objects.

The painting depicts eight pipes and an open box of tobacco, with "Colorado Ma[d] . . . ro" written across the front, in which four of the pipes rest, a cup of matches, and several used matches scattered across a marble tabletop. The two pipes in the foreground are, respectively, a meerschaum with a cherrywood stem and a briar pipe with a gold collar and band. These pipes were among Harnett's favorite still-life objects during the first part of his career, especially in his mug-and-pipe paintings, an invention that art historian Alfred Frankenstein attributes to Harnett. After *The Social Club*, these two types of pipes fail to reappear in his work, while the other clay meerschaum pipes, quite popular during the period, do.[1]

With its fine display of a group of pipes, *The Social Club* alludes to the contemporary American penchant for collecting bric-a-brac, which included original craftwork as well as reproductions of artistic objects. The popularity of such collecting was due in part to the development of mass production and the influence of Aestheticism, a decorative arts movement (mid-1870s to mid-1880s) that introduced artistic elements into the manufacture of furniture, metalwork, ceramics, stained glass, textiles, wallpapers, and books.[2] Although only the wealthy could afford to purchase authentic antiques and original works of art, reproductions of such objects allowed the middle class to imitate upper-class tastes without the expense. In this sense, the attraction toward bric-a-brac was indicative of class identity and a rise in materialism and consumerism. Concurrent with collecting was the displaying of these objects in one's home, a cultural phenomenon in which Harnett participated: not only did he paint bric-a-brac, in 1874 he began to use it as studio props, and from 1880 to 1882 was an avid collector on a more personal level.[3]

Harnett's oeuvre was distinguished by an emphasis on distinctly masculine objects and activities. During the Victorian era, masculinity was associated with business, financial matters, and monetary exchange; femininity, with the home, family, and leisure activities. In *The Social Club*, the slight variation in pipe styles and their diverse positions suggest that each pipe might belong to and even represent an individual person, most certainly a man.[4] Yet, as the title suggests, this is a painting about a group activity. Pipe smoking, considered inferior to cigar smoking,[5] was a middle-class male activity that occurred in public places of leisure, such as saloons, or in the business arena. Nothing in *The Social Club* suggests domesticity or the feminine as it was then defined. (Compare, for example, *The Social Club* with Francis Millet's *The Window Seat* or William Paxton's *The Listener* (pp. 72 and 65, in which the subject matter reflects more traditionally feminine activities).[6]

Harnett was popular with the public long before he was appreciated by the critics. When *The Social Club* was first exhibited at the National Academy of Design in New York in 1879, it was reviewed by an anonymous critic for the *New York Tribune*. This extensive review provides a superlative example of the depreciated status of the imitative arts. Harnett's artistic skills and the subject matter of his paintings were seen as resembling more closely the products of a machine than an artist, a quality that placed *The Social Club* in disfavor with art critics. As the *Tribune* critic wrote:

Only a very few artists of merit have ever condescended to apply their skill to the sole purpose of imitation, making so-called pictures out of dead objects painted to deceive the eye as far as possible. . . . The real fact is that this charge of inferiority is justified by the consideration that this imitative work is not really so difficult as it seems to the layman . . . it is evident that only time and industry are necessary to the indefinite multiplication of them.[7]

It is not surprising, then, that Harnett's paintings were often commissioned by businessmen and exhibited in places of public and private commerce.[8] Nonetheless, his works were also purchased by some of the country's foremost collectors of American art.[9]

Considering its close ties to social life, *The Social Club* might seem far removed from the traditional theme of *vanitas*, which utilizes still-life motifs to address the ephemeral nature of human life and achievement.[10] Yet, while Harnett's early memento mori paintings clearly employed the theme in

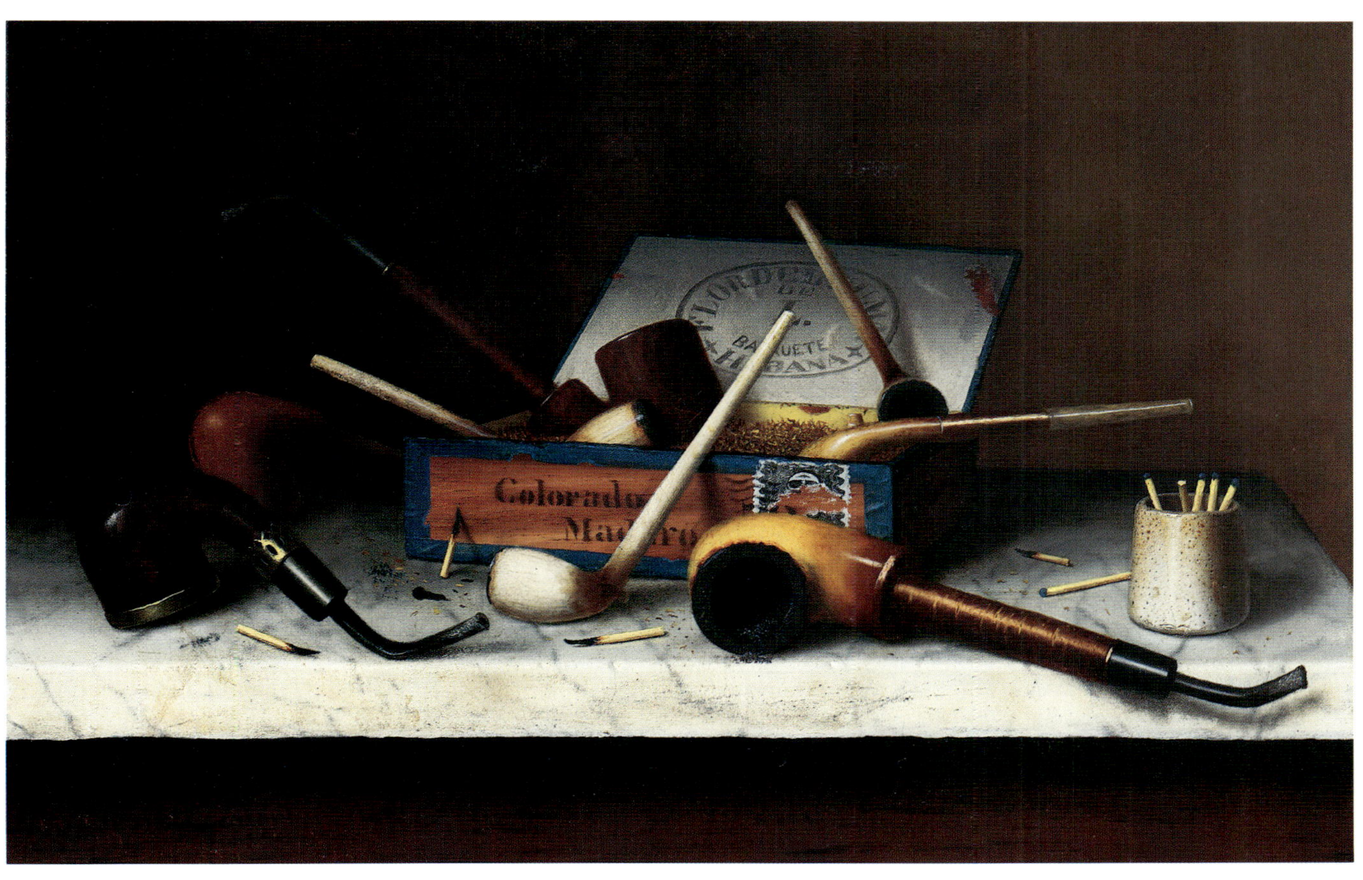

which a skull and a worn or broken object are meant to articulate time's power over man and matter (for example, *Mortality and Immortality*, 1876, Wichita Art Museum, and *Memento Mori—"To This Favour,"* 1879, The Cleveland Museum of Art), his paintings of everyday objects lend themselves to a similar interpretation.[11] The static quality of the objects, coupled with their air of having been abandoned by their users, carries a "moralizing message . . . that hints at the transience of human existence and the ephemeral nature of earthly pleasure."[12] Furthermore, the label on the inside of the lid of the tobacco box reeks of allusions to the vanity of life. It reads "FLORDEL[FUMAR] DE L. BA[. . .]UETE H[A]BANA." *Flordel* is Spanish for "flower of," and *fumar* for "smoke"—both symbols of the impermanence of earthly existence.[13]

Harnett possessed an uncanny ability to merge objects containing clues to contemporary American social life, art, and ideas with the more traditional themes of still life. His pioneering work in a highly realistic style inspired a generation of American still-life painters.

BETH A. HANDLER

1   Alfred Frankenstein, *The Reality of Appearance: The Trompe l'Oeil Tradition in American Painting* (New York: New York Graphic Society, 1970), 60, 64. As Roxana Robinson notes, clay meerschaums were available inexpensively or in more ornate versions and were enthusiastically collected. Roxana Robinson, "Common Objects of Everyday Life," in Doreen Bolger, Marc Simpson, and John Wilmerding, eds., *William M. Harnett* (Fort Worth, Tex.: Amon Carter Museum/New York: Metropolitan Museum of Art, 1992), 166.

2   Doreen Bolger Burke et al., *In Pursuit of Beauty: Americans and the Aesthetic Movement* (New York: The Metropolitan Museum of Art, 1986), 19.

3   Sylvia Yount, "Commodified Displays: The Bric-a-Brac Still Lifes," in Bolger et al., 243–51. With their emphasis on contemporary objects, Harnett's paintings are splendid sources for material culture studies, in which artifacts are examined in order to understand the particular belief structure of a given community at a specific historical time. See Jules David Prown, "Mind in Matter: An Introduction to Material Culture Theory and Method," *Winterthur Portfolio* 17 (Spring 1982): 1.

4   See also Johanna Drucker's similar evaluation. Johanna Drucker, "Harnett, Haberle and Peto: Visuality and Artifice among the Proto-Modern Americans," *The Art Bulletin* 74 (March 1992): 40.

5   Robinson, 166.

6   Henry Adams, "A Study in Contrasts: The Work of Harnett and La Farge," in Bolger et al., 61–69. For another analysis of still life and gender, see Norman Bryson, *Looking at the Overlooked: Four Essays on Still Life Painting* (Cambridge, Mass.: Harvard University Press, 1990), 136–78.

7   Quoted in Alfred Frankenstein, *After the Hunt: William Harnett and Other American Still Life Painters, 1870–1900* (Berkeley and Los Angeles: University of California Press, 1953), 50.

8   For example, Theodore Stewart hung several paintings in his New York saloons, including the famous *After the Hunt* (1885; The Fine Arts Museums of San Francisco), whose visual trickery attracted a large audience and received extensive publicity. Ibid., 78–82.

9   These included William Barnes Bement, Thomas Benedict Clarke, George Arnold Hearn, George Ingraham Seney, Thomas Barlow Walker, and Henry Clay Frick. Doreen Bolger, "The Patrons of the Artist," in Bolger et al., 73–74.

10 Chad Mandeles, "Grave Counsel: Harnett and *Vanitas*," in Bolger et al., 253; Barbara S. Groseclose, "Vanity and the Artist: Some Still-Life Paintings by William Harnett," *The American Art Journal* 19 (1987): 53.

11 See Groseclose; Mandeles, "Grave Counsel"; and Chad Mandeles, "William Michael Harnett's *The Old Cupboard Door* and the Tradition of *Vanitas*," *The American Art Journal* 18 (1986): 51–62.

12 Mandeles, "Grave Counsel," 258.

13 Ibid., 258–59.

Raphaelle Peale

1774–1825

Fruit in a Silver Basket

1814
Oil on panel
12 ¹/₂ x 19 ¹/₂ in. (31.8 x 49.5 cm)

On a narrow, painted shelf, Peale proffers us a silver cake basket filled with yellow apples, topped by a cluster of dark-red grapes. To the left of the basket he places a pair of green peppers; to the right, half a melon; and toward the center of the painting, in front of the shallow dish, a ripe red pepper. The brightly illuminated fruit, shelf, and polished basket contrast strongly with the black background. Light streams in from the left of the canvas, creating highlights on both the fruit and the raised portions of the cake basket. At the bottom right of the composition, on the edge of the shelf, Peale signed his work *Raphaelle Peale Oct'. 8 1814*.

The painting exhibits a clear cyclical progression of ripening fruit, moving from the green, unripe peppers on the left through the reddening pepper, to the lush melon, and up to the ripe apples, with their increasingly large spots of decay. Noting this progression of growth and rot, one scholar has suggested that the work comments abstractly on the cycle of life.[1]

The painting, in fact, may be seen as a link in the long tradition of *nature morte* still lifes begun in Netherlandish painting in the sixteenth century. Peale, however, has particularized this image, as he did with many of his still lifes, by inscribing it not only with the year but also with the month and day of the painting's completion. In this way he parsed out time, not in years, as was more common with American paintings of the period, but rather in months and days.

This practice seems fitting, given that Peale's own years were divided into sick and healthy months—months when he was so stricken by gout that he could not paint and productive months during which he produced the still lifes from which he earned his livelihood. From a letter he wrote in 1816 to a prospective buyer, we learn that Peale's yearly gout attacks descended upon him with regularity every November.[2] This painting, then, finished in early October, must have been among the last canvases Peale completed before the winter of 1814.

It is perhaps not surprising that only fruits with *peels* show signs of decay, as the peel was a commonly used trope with which the Peale family emblematically signed their canvases (fig. 1). The blighted apples may allude generally to the passage of time, while making a specific reference to the artist's yearly cycles of sickness and health.

It has been noted that Peale's still lifes "are overwhelmingly [of] food . . . rather than flowers or dead animals," and that they exhibit a certain "stringency and austerity."[3] His choice of objects and their arrangement differ markedly from the northern European still-life tradition, whose works tend to be crowded, overstuffed canvases frequently displaying dead animals as well as a wide variety of opulent foods (fig. 2). Aside from fish, Peale's paintings rarely depicted animal products, and never animals themselves. What they did show was fruit, vegetables, fish, nuts, raisins, cakes, and an occasional glass of wine. In choosing to present largely vegetarian fare, Peale displayed many foods that were recommended in the last century for the treatment of gout. An 1822 medical text lists a number of factors, such as "fermented liquors, and animal food, [that] are the principal causes which give rise to the gout." The author suggests that "those who live upon vegetable[s] . . . are seldom affected with the gout," and he finally "recommends fish in preference to other animal food," along with a moderate consumption of madeira wine.[4]

Peale's austere canvases never appear lavish, but rather display a few simple, carefully chosen objects, resembling the Spanish tradition of quiet, ordered still-life scenes (fig. 3).[5] This pictorial restraint corresponds very closely to his father's recommended practice of dietary control. In an 1820 letter to Raphaelle, Charles Willson Peale advised his son about how to best avoid gout. His admonishments included the suggestion that one eat only enough to "nourish the body, for a single particle more becomes a clog and a burden to the digestive powers, [and] therefore, produces disease more or less in due proportion to excess." "*Taste*," the elder Peale continued, "shall not be *superior to reason*."[6]

Peale's art, like his father's diet, is all about reason; it can, in fact, be interpreted as an intellectual commentary on the act of painting. Trompe l'oeil painting is a genre which tries to "fool the eye" into believing that a two-dimensional surface (like canvas or plaster) is actually a three-dimensional object (such as fruit or architecture). In other words, the painter creates a pictorial illusion to convince viewers that an object is something it is not. The genre is one that both denies and affirms the presence of the artist: artists are negated by their own precise and careful brushstrokes, which attempt to replicate the "real" as if it were unmediated by the artist's craft. But most trompe l'oeil works, especially those which are

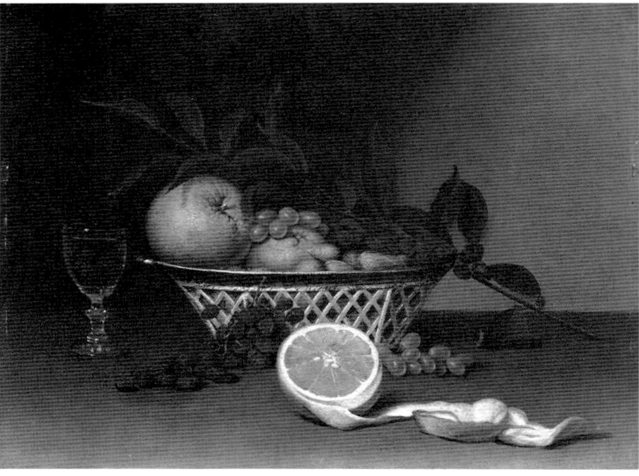

Fig. 1. Raphaelle Peale, *Still Life with Oranges*, c. 1818, oil on wood panel, 18 5/8 x 22 15/16 in. (47.4 x 58.3 cm), The Toledo Museum of Art, Purchased with funds from the Florence Scott Libbey Bequest in Memory of her Father, Maurice A. Scott

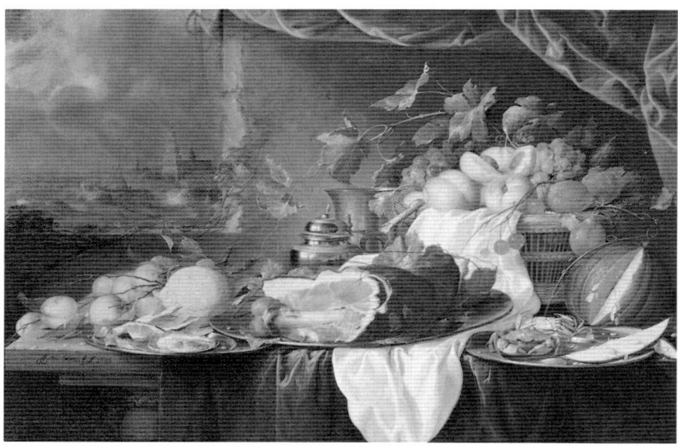

Fig. 2. Jan de Heem, *Still Life with a View of the Sea*, 1646, oil on canvas, 23 3/8 x 36 1/2 in. (59.4 x 92.7 cm), The Toledo Museum of Art, Purchased with funds from the Libbey Endowment, Gift of Edward Drummond Libbey

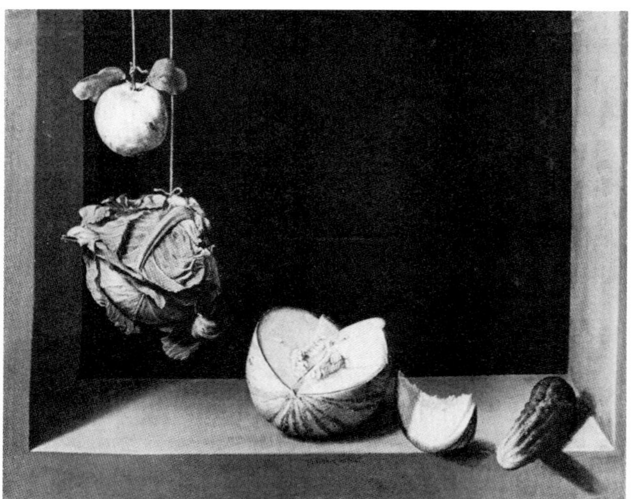

Fig. 3. Juan Sánchez Cotán, *Quince, Cabbage, Melon, and Cucumber*, c. 1602, oil on canvas, 27 1/4 x 33 1/2 in. (69.2 x 85 cm), San Diego Museum of Art, Purchased for the Museum by the Misses Anne R. and Amy Putnam

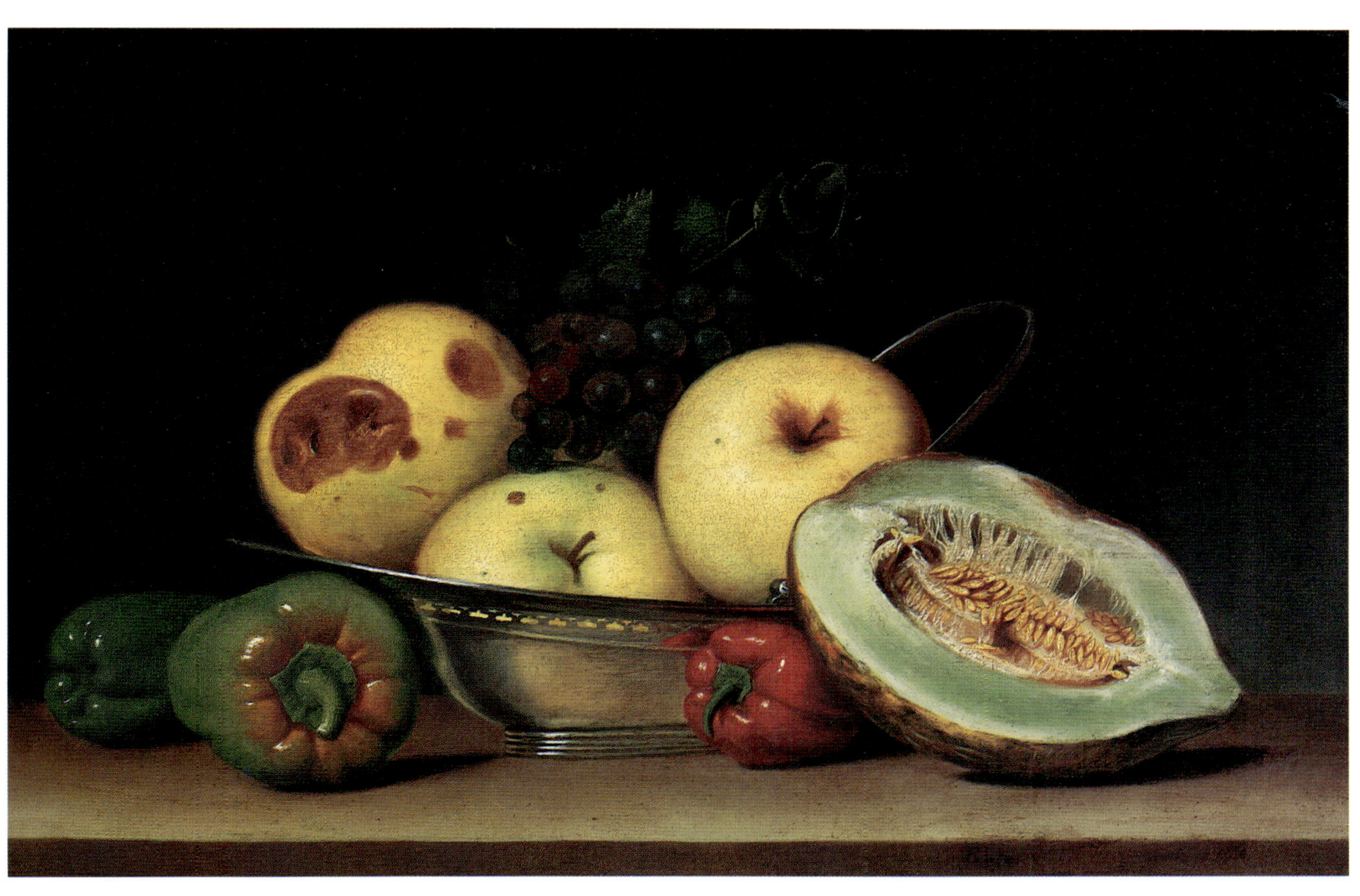

signed or framed, are more concerned to impress the viewer with the artists' technical skills than actually to fool him. Thus, in an odd way, these images affirm the artists by pointing to their facility in making works from which they are ostensibly absent.

In *Fruit in a Silver Basket*, the artist's accomplishments are given even further stress. Like a number of Peale's still lifes, this one is painted not on canvas but on a piece of wooden board, similar, in fact, to the shallow shelf pictured in the composition. The shelf is approximately "two feet wide and shallower in depth," which makes it very close to the size of the actual painting.[7] Peale must have been aware of the ironic nature of his creation; for, in painting the work, he effaced the wooden board with primer only to recreate it again in paint. His trompe l'oeil is not merely an effort to convince viewers that the wooden board is fruit, or even shiny metal; it is also an attempt to "fool" the viewer into accepting the fact that a wooden board is simply itself. By enabling the board to look like wood only through the artist's intervention, Peale created a subtle parody of the trompe l'oeil genre.

This work that initially appears to negate the artist is in fact a highly personal painting that makes reference both to the artist and to his creative endeavor. While *Fruit in a Silver Basket* must be seen as relating to the political and cultural milieu of its day, the start of any analysis should acknowledge the highly personal and intellectual nature of the work for its creator.

MARTIN A. BERGER

1   Jules David Prown, "Raphaelle Peale, *Fruit in a Silver Basket*,"in *American Paintings from the Manoogian Collection*, exh. cat. (Washington, D.C.: National Gallery of Art/Detroit: Detroit Institute of Arts, 1989), 98–100.

2   Letter of Raphaelle Peale to Charles Graff, Sept. 6, 1816, in *The Selected Papers of Charles Willson Peale and His Family: The Belfield Farm Years, 1810–1820*, ed. Lillian B. Miller (New Haven and London: Yale University Press, 1991), 3:447.

3   Nicolai Cikovsky, Jr., *Raphaelle Peale Still Lifes*, exh. cat. (Washington, D.C.: National Gallery of Art, 1988), 48, 50.

4   Robert Hooper, *Lexicon-Medicum; or Medical Dictionary* (New York: J & J Harper Printers, 1822), 83–84.

5   Cikovsky, 50.

6   Letter of Charles Willson Peale to Raphaelle Peale, July 4, 1820, in Miller, 833.

7   Prown, 98.

De Scott Evans

1847–1898

Free Sample, Take One

n.d.
Oil on canvas
12 x 10 1/4 in. (30.48 x 26.04 cm)

Free Sample, Take One is one of about twenty trompe l'oeil still-life paintings by Evans that incorporate the motif of the edible nut.[1] Paradigmatic in form and content, the painting is a depiction of eleven peanuts set inside a shallow rectangular niche cut into a wooden plank. A broken glass panel, held in place by six nails, partially covers the niche's opening. In the upper right corner, a card is inserted with the handwritten message "Free Sample, Take One." With meticulous detail, Evans has captured the subtle qualities of his subject matter: the raw, blond wood, splintered and peeling; the rough surface of the rustic container; the back panel of the niche stained in a darker tone and streaked in the areas where the wood has split. In contrast to the rough-hewn quality of the wood, the green-tinged glass cover is smooth and slick, the sharp and jagged edges shining in the reflected light. Evans's other nut paintings are similar to this one—depictions of peanuts or almonds in a shallow wooden niche covered by a broken glass panel. These works are signed with a variety of pseudonyms, and most are undated; two recorded examples that do bear dates are marked 1890 and 1891, when Evans was working in New York.

For centuries, trompe l'oeil painters have depicted objects displayed in shallow recessed spaces that might serve as cupboards or shelves. By limiting the illusion of depth, the painter can portray objects parallel to the picture plane, and the subject matter, in turn, appears to be part of reality, projecting forward into the viewer's space. In *Free Sample, Take One*, the flat, vertical wooden panel and its cut-out rectangular niche create the same shallow pictorial depth. One peanut is foreshortened and dangles beyond its narrow shelf, challenging the viewer to nudge it back into place. The broken glass and the card with its witty invitation is another way in which Evans tempts the viewer, yet the entire configuration makes him uneasy. The viewer assumes that at one time the niche was filled with peanuts, but when the glass was broken most of the nuts slipped out. Now the jagged edges of the broken glass and the possibility that the rest of the peanuts, too, will fall out of their container give the composition an unsettling but dynamic quality.[2]

The edible nut, and particularly the peanut, was a popular subject for trompe l'oeil painters working in the New York vicinity during the late nineteenth century. For example, John Frederick Peto's *Peanuts—Fresh Roasted, Well Toasted* (Private Collection), probably from the early 1900s, is a painting of a vertical wooden panel with a rectangular opening. Inside, a wooden shelf is filled with a generous supply of peanuts, a tin measuring cup, and a yellow apple. Joseph Decker, too, portrayed nuts in a trompe l'oeil manner during these years: in *A Hard Lot* (1866; destroyed by fire, 1955) he showed a large wooden grocer's box filled with a variety of nuts, a tin cup, a weighing pan, and a nutcracker. And, in 1887, John Haberle painted *Fresh Roasted* (Yale University Art Gallery, New Haven, Connecticut), showing a container of peanuts with a hinged glass lid. Like Evans, Haberle depicted the lid with a broken glass cover.[3]

The large number of peanut paintings produced during these years reflects the growing popularity of the nut, now a common food in the United States. During the Civil War, Northerners acquired a taste for roasted peanuts, which had been harvested in the South in limited quantities. After 1865, there was rapid growth in the industry, and a variety of nuts were imported throughout the country, as various Southern organizations promoted the crop. And by 1890 the popularity of the peanut led to the development of a new product—peanut butter.[4] In fact, the peanut was so popular during these years that in 1885 a music publisher, Oliver Ditson Company, even copyrighted a college tune entitled *Peanut Song*.[5]

Unlike the nut paintings by Peto, Decker, and Haberle that include familiar commercial props—the tin measuring cup, the wooden bin, the weighing pan, or the nutcracker—Evans's paintings display the peanuts in an uncommon container; the peanuts' inaccessibility may be the clue to its identity. If the glass were intact, it would be impossible to reach the peanuts, which would be stacked neatly behind their protective glass covering. This peanut receptacle, therefore, was probably just a display case, a visual sign identifying the product as available for purchase and consumption elsewhere.[6] Although no firm evidence verifies the container's original use, where it was hung, and whether it was part of a larger unit, it is interesting that during the 1880s vending machines had become popular in the United States, the first commercial peanut-vending machine being developed in the late 1890s. Some early machines that marketed a variety of products utilized a shallow, glass-fronted area where the vended item could be tantalizingly displayed.[7] In *Free Sample, Take One*, someone has succumbed to temptation. By including the sign stuck casually behind the broken glass, Evans slyly suggests a narrative: at one time the peanut display case was obviously filled; but someone broke into it and, after eating most of the nuts, left a note inviting others to do likewise. Inviting images and titles such as *Free Sample,*

Take One were not exclusive to Evans. Peto's 1881 painting, *Help Yourself* (Private Collection), which shows a bag of hard candy torn open, its contents spilling out onto a wooden tabletop, also tempts the viewer to indulge. Perhaps both artists were responding to the plethora of new consumer goods now available in the late-nineteenth-century market-place.[8]

Evans's trompe l'oeil paintings are only part of his oeuvre; he also produced portraits, genre, and more traditional tabletop still lifes. He was best known in his day, however, for his genre paintings of elegant Victorian women engaged in leisure activities.[9] Applying some of the precise recording techniques of his trompe l'oeil paintings to his figural works, Evans was interested in rendering different textures and was praised for his ability to paint "with something better than photographic accuracy."[10] It has been speculated that the painter used various pseudonyms for his trompe l'oeil still lifes because he wanted to conceal his identity, preferring to be associated with his genre works. For, although trompe l'oeil paintings were popular with the late-nineteenth-century art-buying public, they were frequently lambasted by the critics for their slavish imitation.[11] The irony is that today we value Evans's trompe l'oeil pictures more than his genre paintings.

BETHANY ASTRACHAN

1   For material on Evans, I have drawn largely upon Nannette V. Maciejunes, *A New Variety, Try One: De Scott Evans or S. S. David,* exh. cat. (Columbus, Ohio: Columbus Museum of Art, 1985). The earlier study of Evans's body of work was conducted by Nancy Troy in "From the Peanut Gallery: The Rediscovery of De Scott Evans," *Yale University Art Gallery Bulletin* 36 (Spring 1977): 36–43. Along with nuts, Evans also produced vertical trompe l'oeil paintings of objects hanging from string or nails against a wooden backdrop. Some of the suspended objects he depicted included fruit, hatchets, paper, or shoes.

2   Maciejunes, 7, 10.

3   *Peanuts—Fresh Roasted, Well Toasted,* reproduced in John Wilmerding, *Important Information Inside: The Art of John F. Peto and The Idea of Still-Life Painting in Nineteenth-Century America,* exh. cat. (Washington, D.C.: National Gallery of Art, 1983), 91. *A Hard Lot,* reproduced in Helen A. Cooper, "The Rediscovery of Joseph Decker," *The American Art Journal* 10 (May 1978): 56. *Fresh Roasted,* reproduced in Gertrude Grace Sill, *John Haberle: Master of Illusion,* exh. cat. (Springfield, Mass.: Museum of Fine Arts, 1985), 9.

4   For the history of the peanut in the United States, see Jasper Guy Woodroof, *Peanuts: Production, Processing, Products* (Westport, Conn.: AVI Publishing Company, 1966), 1, 9–10, 127, and F. N. Howes, *Nuts: Their Production and Everyday Uses* (London: Faber and Faber, 1948), 81.

5   Troy, 40. See also William Arms Fisher, *One Hundred and Fifty Years of Music Publishing in the United States* (Boston: Oliver Ditson Company, 1933). For the lyrics of *Peanut Song,* see Henry Randall Waite, ed., *College Songs: A Collection of New and Popular Songs of the American Colleges* (Boston: Oliver Ditson Company, 1887), 51.

6   The conclusion that the peanut container may be a display case is supported by the composition of another trompe l'oeil painting by Evans, titled *Homage to a Parrot* (Fresno Metropolitan Museum, Fresno, Calif.; reproduced in Maciejunes, 9), a painting of a stuffed parrot displayed in a shallow wooden niche with a broken glass cover.

7   For the history of vending machines in the United States, see G. R. Schreiber, *A Concise History of Vending in the U.S.A.* (Chicago: published by *Vend,* 1961). An illustration of an envelope-and-paper-vending machine from New York in 1896 shows in the upper section of the machine a shallow, glass-fronted case where the variety of paper goods could be displayed (16).

8   *Help Yourself,* reproduced in Wilmerding, 95. For a discussion of late-nineteenth-century consumerism and the resultant growth of commercial industry, see Simon J. Bronner, ed., *Consuming Visions: Accumulation and Display of Goods in America, 1880–1920* (New York and London: W. W. Norton and Company, 1989).

9   Evans's genre paintings are discussed by Cromwell Childe in "A Painter of Pretty Women," *The Quarterly Illustrator* 1 (October-December 1893): 279–82. Childe refers to Evans's landscapes and animal paintings (282). Wilbur D. Peat, in *Pioneer Painters of Indiana* (Indianapolis: Art Association of Indianapolis, 1954), refers to his portraits (118–19).

10 Childe, 280.

11 See William H. Gerdts and Russell Burke, *American Still-Life Painting* (New York: Praeger Publishers, 1971), 167–68; and Gerdts, *Painters of the Humble Truth: Masterpieces of American Still Life, 1801–1939,* exh. cat. (Tulsa, Okla.: Philbrook Art Center, 1981), 200–204.

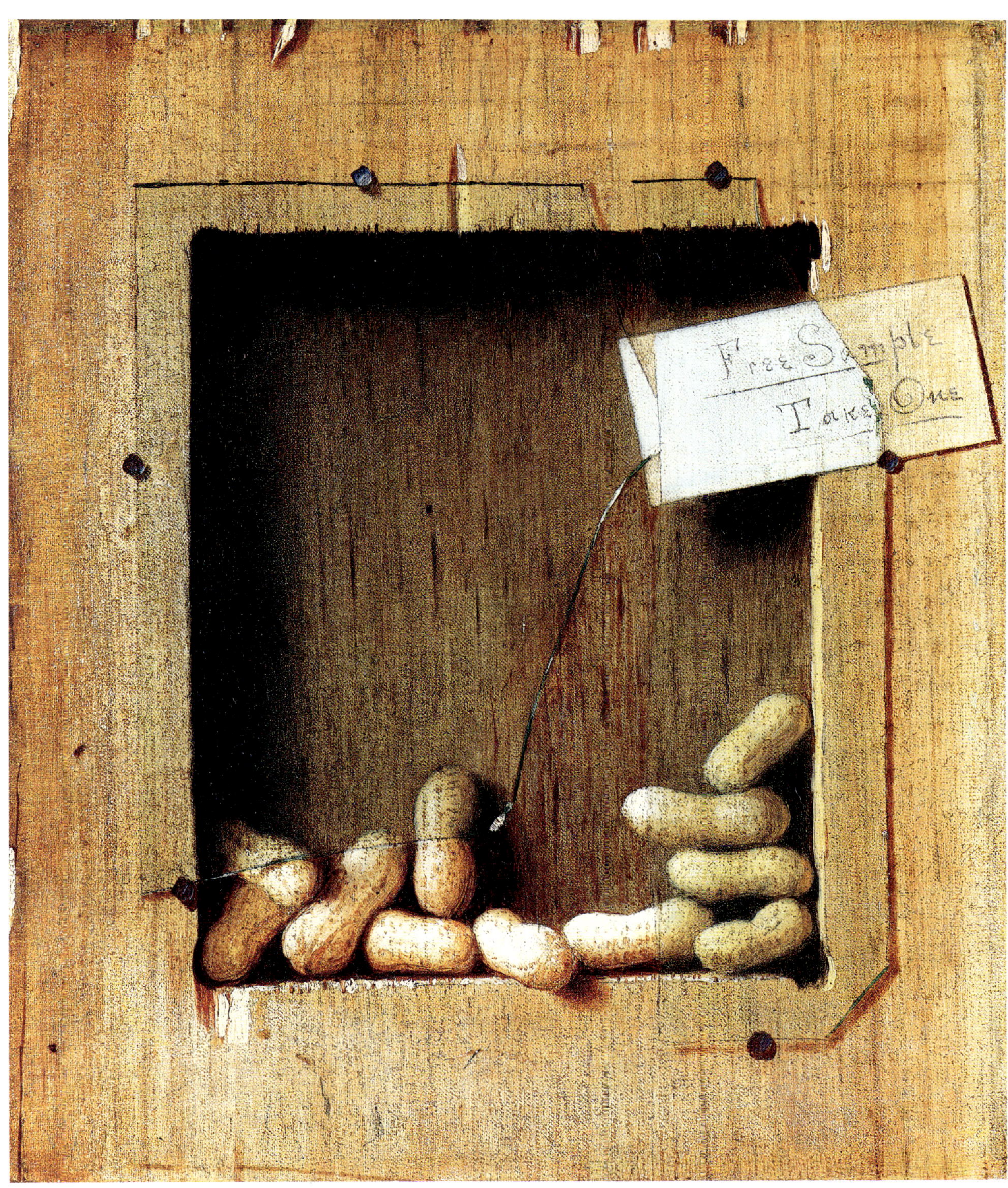

Free Sample
Take One

John Frederic Peto

1854–1907

Oranges Wrapped

probably 1890s
Oil on academy board
6 x 9 in. (15.2 x 22.9 cm)

Peto's *Oranges Wrapped* celebrates the orange.[1] By the late nineteenth century, semitropical citrus fruits such as the orange and lemon had become an important product of the burgeoning farming industry and a new subject for the still-life painters of this time. Prior to the 1880s, oranges and lemons were not widely available in the northeastern United States or the country's interior. Because of its rarity, citrus was associated with the exotic, and it was represented in still-life paintings from the early part of the century less frequently than produce that was grown locally, such as berries, peaches, apples, or grapes.[2] With the completion of the Second Transcontinental Railroad in the 1880s and the invention of the ventilated refrigerator railroad car in the 1890s, California citrus was shipped in large quantities to a broad marketplace throughout the country. With these developments in transportation and refrigeration, the artist had a variety of fruits, both tropical and local, at his disposal for his still-life arrangements during different times of the year.[3]

Citrus was packed with care for shipment to distant markets. Because oranges and lemons are picked ripe, the fruit is prone to bruising during shipping and, in both Europe and America, thin tissue paper was used to wrap the individual fruits to prevent puncturing of the rind and the possible spread of mold.[4] Fruit wrappings probably had aesthetic appeal for the marketer as well: the tissue paper in white or a pastel color protected the citrus, suggesting its preciousness. The paper also attracted the late-nineteenth-century trompe l'oeil painter because of its hard and soft qualities: its crisp outlines and rough texture contrasted with its fragility and transparency. Peto was not the only artist interested in the illusionistic effects of fruit wrapped in tissue paper. One of the most prolific was William John McCloskey, a still-life painter and one of Peto's contemporaries, who earned himself the sobriquet "Master of the Wrapped Citrus" because he continually exploited this subject throughout his career, depicting in his paintings oranges in white tissue and lemons in colored tissue.[5]

Here, Peto has made an intimate arrangement of two wrapped oranges and a section of the fruit nestled in its rind. The fruit rests on a shallow stone table in front of a dark, indistinct background. This neutral and impenetrable space creates a flat backdrop, an ideal foil for the oranges, which stand out in high relief on their shallow stage. To increase the prominence of the oranges further, he abandoned the traditional view from above, placing the table at eye level and

parallel to the picture plane. A diffused light falls from the upper left-hand corner of the composition, illuminating the oranges on their left side, leaving their right side in shadow. By modeling the oranges in this way, the artist could focus on the large, bulbous shape of the fruit and its flawless roundness.

Peto's use of a limited palette of orange, brown, black, and white also draws attention to the monumental oranges and complements the spare composition. Space is compressed, and the composition is cropped, the twisted tissue paper reaching to the boundaries of the picture plane in the upper left and the lower right and accentuating the diagonal line of light. The openness of the sides of the painting suggests movement, as if the round forms could roll out of the picture; even the section of fruit seems to be caught in motion, rocking slowly on its softly curved base. The marked horizontality of the composition, echoed in the strong line of the table's edge, the section of orange on its side, and the twisted paper wrapping that runs parallel to the table, arrests the underlying movement and fills the space with an overall calm. The tissue paper's crushed folds create abstract shapes for Peto, who reduced the wrapped oranges to the basic geometries of circles and lines, horizontals and verticals, light and shadow. His emphasis on design and the simplification of forms point to a highly sophisticated and modern vision.[6]

Alfred Frankenstein refers to these small still lifes on academy board by Peto as his "little summer-boarder pictures" because they were produced and sold as souvenirs for neighbors or visitors to his Island Heights, New Jersey, home. He sold them for as little as three to four dollars apiece, and *Oranges Wrapped* is probably an example of one of these souvenir works.[7] In 1889, Peto had moved from Philadelphia to Island Heights, where he spent his time painting and playing the cornet at Methodist camp meetings.[8] In Philadelphia, he occasionally submitted works to the annual exhibitions at the Pennsylvania Academy of the Fine Arts, where he had enrolled as a student in 1877, but he achieved little artistic acclaim in this city.[9] The move to the small resort community of Island Heights isolated him even more from the mainstream, and by the time of his death in 1907 Peto was virtually unknown as a painter.[10]

What further obscured Peto's reputation was the fact that many of his still lifes had been confused with the work of his contemporary, William Michael Harnett. Frankenstein salvaged Peto's name in the 1950s when he published the

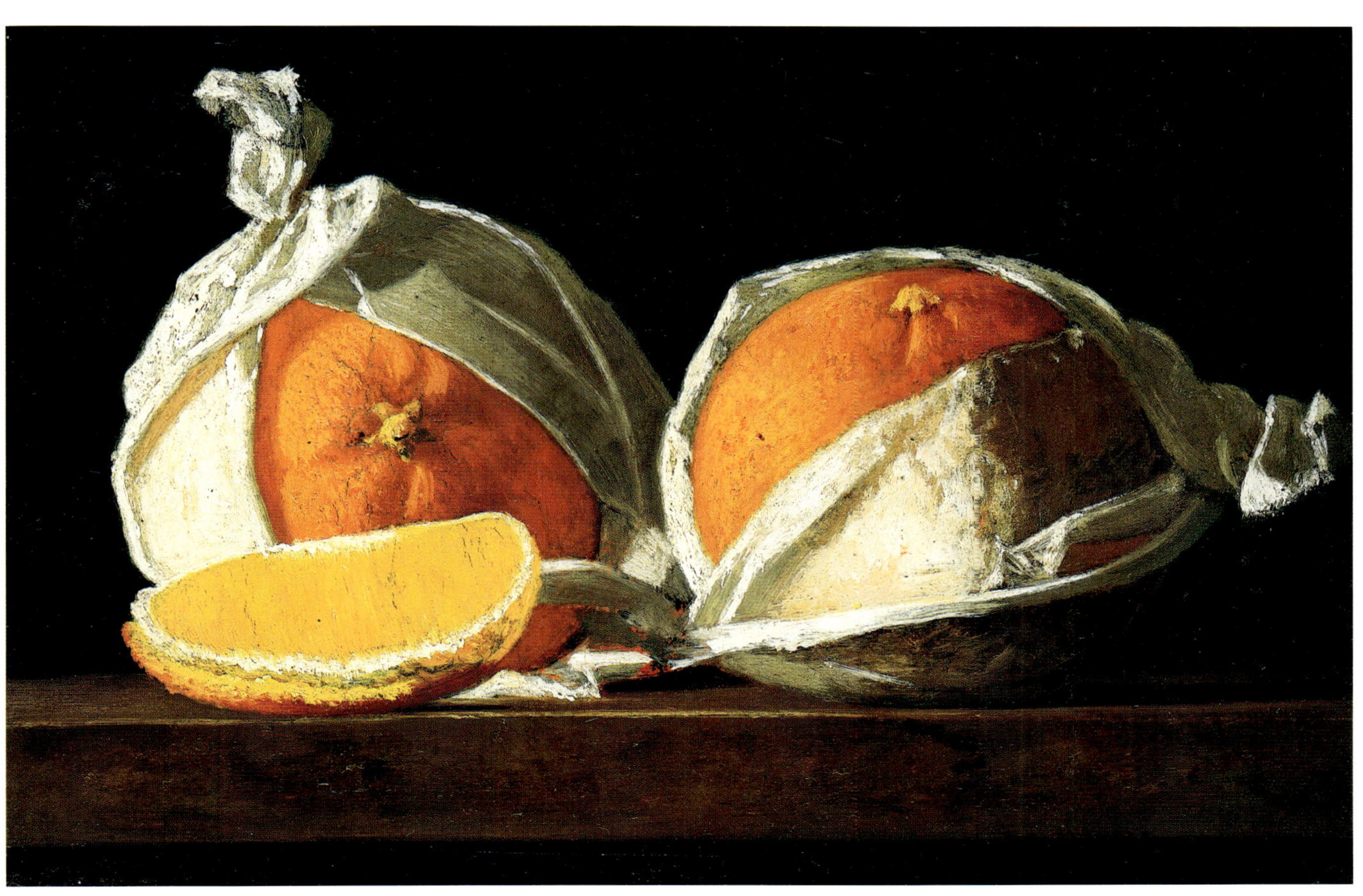

findings of his seminal research on Harnett, Peto, and other late-nineteenth-century American still-life painters in his book *After the Hunt: William Harnett and Other American Still-Life Painters, 1870–1900*. He defined Peto's style as inherently "soft," with smooth edges, diffused lighting, powdery textures, and an impressionistic touch.[11] This nascent impressionism is evident in *Oranges Wrapped*, in which the paint handling is spontaneous and loose, producing an overall velvety surface and rich coloration. Peto has successfully rendered the "smooth bumpiness"[12] of the oranges and used this same texture in depicting the coarse surface of the tissue paper. In this way, he united the fruit with its wrapping, simplifying extraneous details in favor of bold design.

Peto's fruit still lifes have often been overlooked, probably because of their small size and because they have rarely been reproduced.[13] But the monumentality of the oranges in this work belies their actual size. The starkness and unrelenting simplicity of the composition, as well as the plain and humble subject matter of the fruit, directly confront the viewer and invite reflection. The oranges, whole or partly eaten, mark time and remind us of transience.[14] Even the pristine white wrapping cannot protect the fruit from the inevitable process of decay.

BETHANY ASTRACHAN

1 The dating of this work is based on its similarity to other dated still lifes of food subjects reproduced in John Wilmerding, *Important Information Inside: The Art of John F. Peto and the Idea of Still-Life Painting in Nineteenth-Century America*, exh. cat. (Washington, D.C.: National Gallery of Art, 1983), 82–90.

2 See, for example, works by the American still-life painters Raphaelle Peale or Severin Roesen. These painters were active in the first half of the nineteenth century and produced tabletop arrangements of a variety of fruits, including citrus.

3 See William H. Gerdts and Russell Burke, *American Still-Life Painting* (New York: Praeger Publishers, 1971), 166–67; and Richard J. Hooker, *Food and Drink in America: A History* (Indianapolis and New York: Bobbs-Merrill, 1981), 233. For a history of California and its citrus culture, see Ralph J. Roske, *Everyman's Eden: A History of California* (New York: Macmillan, 1968), 399; and N. P. Chipman, *Report upon the Fruit Industry of California* (California State Board of Trade, 1889), 10–16; and Oscar Edward Anderson, Jr., *Refrigeration in America* (Port Washington, N.Y., and London: Kennikat Press, 1972), 120.

4 See J. F. Madden, *The Newcastle Fruit District* (Newcastle, Calif.: n.p., 1887), 54–57; and Gillian Saunders, *Oranges and Lemons: Fruit Wrappers from the Victoria and Albert Museum*, exh. cat. (London: Victoria and Albert Museum, 1985), unpaginated. Orange wrappers are not used with much frequency today; instead, fungicides and wax are used to prevent the spread of mold. See also Gordon T. McClelland and Jay T. Last, *California Orange Box Labels* (Beverly Hills, Calif.: Hillcrest Press, 1985), 128. Beginning in 1917, a wrapped orange logo was used on orange-box labels as the Sunkist trademark.

5 William H. Gerdts, *American Cornucopia: Nineteenth-Century Still Lifes and Studies*, exh. cat. (Pittsburgh, Pa.: The Hunt Institute, Carnegie-Mellon University, 1976), 11.

6 For a discussion of Peto's still lifes in terms of their inherent modernism, see Wilmerding (68–72, 82) and Alfred Frankenstein, *After the Hunt: William Harnett and Other American Still Life Painters, 1870–1900*, rev. ed. (Berkeley and Los Angeles: University of California Press, 1969), 103.

7 Referring to another still life on academy board of the same size as Peto's *Oranges Wrapped*, Frankenstein describes it as typical of the many pictures Peto produced as souvenirs for summer boarders. See Alfred Frankenstein, *The Reality of Appearance: The Trompe L'Oeil Tradition in American Painting*, exh. cat. (Berkeley and Los Angeles: University Art Museum, 1970), 94, 102; and *After the Hunt*, 104–6.

8 Frankenstein, *After the Hunt*, 104.

9 See Peter Hastings Falk, ed., *The Annual Exhibition Record of the Pennsylvania Academy of the Fine Arts*, 3 vols. (Madison, Conn.: Sound View Press, 1988), 2:380; and Wilmerding, 15–18.

10 William H. Gerdts, *Painters of the Humble Truth: Masterpieces of American Still Life 1801–1939*, exh. cat. (Tulsa, Okla.: Philbrook Art Center, 1981), 185.

11 For a discussion of the differences between Peto's style and the style of his colleague, William M. Harnett, see Frankenstein, *After the Hunt*, 9–10. See also John I. H. Baur, "Peto and the American Trompe L'Oeil Tradition," *Magazine of Art* 43 (May 1950): 182–85; and Lloyd Goodrich, "Harnett and Peto: A Note on Style," *The Art Bulletin* 31 (March 1949): 57–59.

12 A. J. H. Way, "Fruit Painting in Oils: II–Treatment of Pineapples, Oranges, Lemons, Bananas, and Apples," *The Art Amateur* 16 (January 1887): 32.

13 Wilmerding, 32.

14 Alberto Veca, *Vanitas: The Symbolism of Time* (Bergamo, Italy: Galleria Lorenzelli, 1981), 204.

John Frederick Peto

1854–1907

Still Life with Orange and Banana

probably 1890s
Oil on academy board
6 x 9 in. (15.2 x 22.9 cm)

Peto incorporated ordinary items of everyday life into his still lifes throughout his career, utilizing the tabletop or the flat surface of a wall or vertical board as the support for his objects. His earliest still lifes from the 1870s, for example, are tabletop arrangements of simple foods or commonplace, man-made objects, such as mugs, pipes, newspapers, or books. In his illusionistically rendered rack paintings, he combined a variety of familiar ephemera in his compositions, such as renderings of photographs, letters, currency, sheet music, postcards, ticket stubs, newspaper clippings, and envelopes, tacked directly to a wall or board or stuck haphazardly into mounted crossed tapes (p. 50). In *Still Life with Orange and Banana*,[1] Peto portrayed his characteristically humble subject matter—two pieces of fruit in an intimate tabletop grouping. It was painted during the latter half of his career when he was living in the small resort community of Island Heights, New Jersey, where he painted many works similar to this one, small still lifes on academy board that he sold as souvenirs to friends or visitors to his home.[2]

Peto's interest in still life was undoubtedly fostered by his training at the Pennsylvania Academy of the Fine Arts. He enrolled there in 1877 and, for the next eleven years, periodically submitted works to the school's annual exhibitions.[3] Since the early part of the nineteenth century, Philadelphia had been known as a center for still life, and the Academy encouraged the study of this genre. During the 1870s, the curriculum was expanded to include still-life classes, and Christian Schussele and his successor, Thomas Eakins, taught these classes for the first time. Peto's concentration on still-life subjects also reflects his friendship with William Michael Harnett, a fellow student. Harnett's tabletop still lifes of food, mundane objects of everyday life, and Victorian objets d'art probably inspired Peto's arrangements (see pp. 62, 90).

This focus on still life as a viable subject for the artist sparked a new appreciation of the works in the Academy's own collection, which included examples by Dutch and Flemish seventeenth-century painters and by the early-nineteenth-century Philadelphia painter Raphaelle Peale, eldest son of the artist Charles Willson Peale, and one of the first American painters to concentrate on still-life subjects for most of his career.[4] Peale's refined style and typical format of a small group of fruits placed in an elegant bowl on a wooden table may have served as a model for Peto, whose small tabletop fruit still lifes are tempered by a similar restraint and are characterized by their bold design, lack of unnecessary detail, and

shallow pictorial space.[5] Peto and his peers inherited and drew upon a long tradition of still-life painting—a tradition that became part of the vocabulary of the late-nineteenth-century painter and served as his model.

It is difficult to establish, however, whether Peto and other American artists intended their still lifes to suggest the same subtle meanings and moral lessons as their European counterparts. Seventeenth-century European fruit and flower still-life painters utilized symbolic motifs traditionally associated with the futility of materialism and vanity and served as reminders of life's transitoriness. The objects in these still lifes suggested two opposed meanings: the fruit and flowers alluded both to vital abundance and to its antithesis, decay—the ripe fruit will rot and become inedible; the fully bloomed flower will wilt and lose its beautiful form. Exotic fruit and flowers combined with other expensive items, such as jewels, oriental carpets, precious glass, metalwork, sugar, and wine, were symbols of wealth, yet, on another level, warned against extravagance.[6]

In contrast to this group of sumptuous European still lifes that recorded rare and costly items, Peto's simple tabletop composition, with its partially peeled orange and banana on a shelf, is aptly described as a celebration of commonplace, everyday items.[7] By the 1880s, oranges and bananas were readily available in local markets. Within a few years of the completion of the Second Transcontinental Railroad in 1881, large quantities of citrus fruits were being shipped to the east from California.[8] Bananas, like citrus, had been sold only in limited quantities before the Civil War; but by the time of the Philadelphia Centennial Exposition in 1876, they were a usual commodity in coastal cities. And, probably because of the greater variety of fruit now easily attainable, it was becoming a healthy breakfast food. Peto's still-life arrangement may represent the foods of this new breakfast custom.[9]

Here, Peto placed the orange and banana in front of an impenetrable, dark background, the banana's crusty top extending over the shelf's edge. The smooth, curving line of the banana's shape is echoed by the striations on its peel and starkly contrasts with the orange's jagged silhouette of peeled rind. A piece of rind has been placed next to the banana, reminding the viewer that the still-life painter has control over his choice of subject matter and its arrangement. Probably peeled for several days, the orange is beginning to rot; a soft green mold creeps over its white skin. The rind, too, shows the effects of age: separated from the moist fruit, it has dried and hardened. The banana is also overripe. Covered with brown spots, it has begun the inevitable process of decomposition; but, like the part of the orange not yet attacked by mold, the one green spot on the banana implies the unripe—the one area that has not yet fully matured.

Still Life with Orange and Banana suggests the whole life cycle from youth to maturity, from perfection to imperfection, reflecting the stages of our own lives. Just as the fruit has its moment of ripeness, so man has his moment, no matter how fleeting. The fruit ultimately reminds us that our control over our destinies is limited, and that, like the ripened orange and banana, life is indeed transient.[10]

BETHANY ASTRACHAN

1 *Still Life with Orange and Banana* is reproduced as *Banana and Orange* and dated "probably 1890s," in John Wilmerding, *Important Information Inside: The Art of John F. Peto and the Idea of Still-Life Painting in Nineteenth-Century America*, exh. cat. (Washington D.C.: National Gallery of Art, 1983), 86.

2 Referring to another still life on academy board of the same size as Peto's *Still Life with Orange and Banana*, Alfred Frankenstein describes this work as typical of the many paintings Peto produced as souvenirs for visitors to his Island Heights home. See Alfred Frankenstein, *The Reality of Appearance: The Trompe L'Oeil Tradition in American Painting*, exh. cat. (Berkeley and Los Angeles: University Art Museum, 1970), 94, 102; and *After the Hunt: William Harnett and Other American Still Life Painters, 1870–1900*, rev. ed. (Berkeley and Los Angeles: University of California Press, 1969), 104–6.

3 The following works by Peto are listed in *The Annual Exhibition Record of the Pennsylvania Academy of the Fine Arts*: 1879–*Any Ornaments for Your Mantelpiece?*; 1880–*Still Life and Poor Man's Store*; 1881–*Still Life*; 1885–*Your Choice*; 1887–*Fish-House Door*; 1888–*For a Leisure Moment: Still Life*. See Peter Hastings Falk, ed., *The Annual Exhibition Record of the Pennsylvania Academy of the Fine Arts*, 3 vols. (Madison, Conn.: Sound View Press, 1988), 2: 380.

4 See Wilmerding, *Important Information Inside*, 57–58; and Doreen Bolger, "The Education of the American Artist," in *In This Academy: The Pennsylvania Academy of the Fine Arts, 1805–1976*, exh. cat. (Philadelphia: The Pennsylvania Academy of the Fine Arts, 1976), 66.

5 See *Temporary Catalogue of the Permanent Collection of the Pennsylvania Academy of the Fine Arts*, 2d ed. (Philadelphia, 1879), 3-6; and *Descriptive Catalogue of the Permanent Collections of Works of Art*, 2d ed. (Philadelphia: Pennsylvania Academy of the Fine Arts, 1894), 26. Both Wilmerding, in *Important Information Inside* (57), and Frankenstein, in *The Reality of Appearance* (8), discuss the similarities and possible influence of the still-life paintings of Raphaelle Peale on the works of Peto and Harnett.

6 See Charles Sterling, *Still Life Painting: From Antiquity to the Twentieth Century*, 2d rev. ed. (New York: Harper and Row, 1981), 71; and Sam Segal, *A Prosperous Past: The Sumptuous Still Life in the Netherlands 1600–1700*, ed. William B. Jordan (The Hague: SDU Publishers, 1988), 15–16; 35.

7 John Wilmerding, "The American Object: Still-Life Paintings," in *An American Perspective: Nineteenth-Century Art from the Collection of JoAnn and Julian Ganz, Jr.*, exh. cat. (Washington, D.C.: National Gallery of Art, 1981), 86.

8 William H. Gerdts and Russell Burke, *American Still-Life Painting* (New York: Praeger Publishers, 1971), 166–67.

9 Richard J. Hooker, *Food and Drink in America: A History* (Indianapolis and New York: Bobbs-Merrill, 1981), 232–33; 317.

10 For a discussion of the spiritual aspects of still-life painting and the symbolism of the life cycle, see Jules David Prown's analysis of Raphaelle Peale's *Fruit in a Silver Basket* in *American Paintings from the Manoogian Collection*, exh. cat. (Washington, D.C.: National Gallery of Art/ Detroit: Detroit Institute of Arts, 1989), cat. no. 37, pp. 98–101.

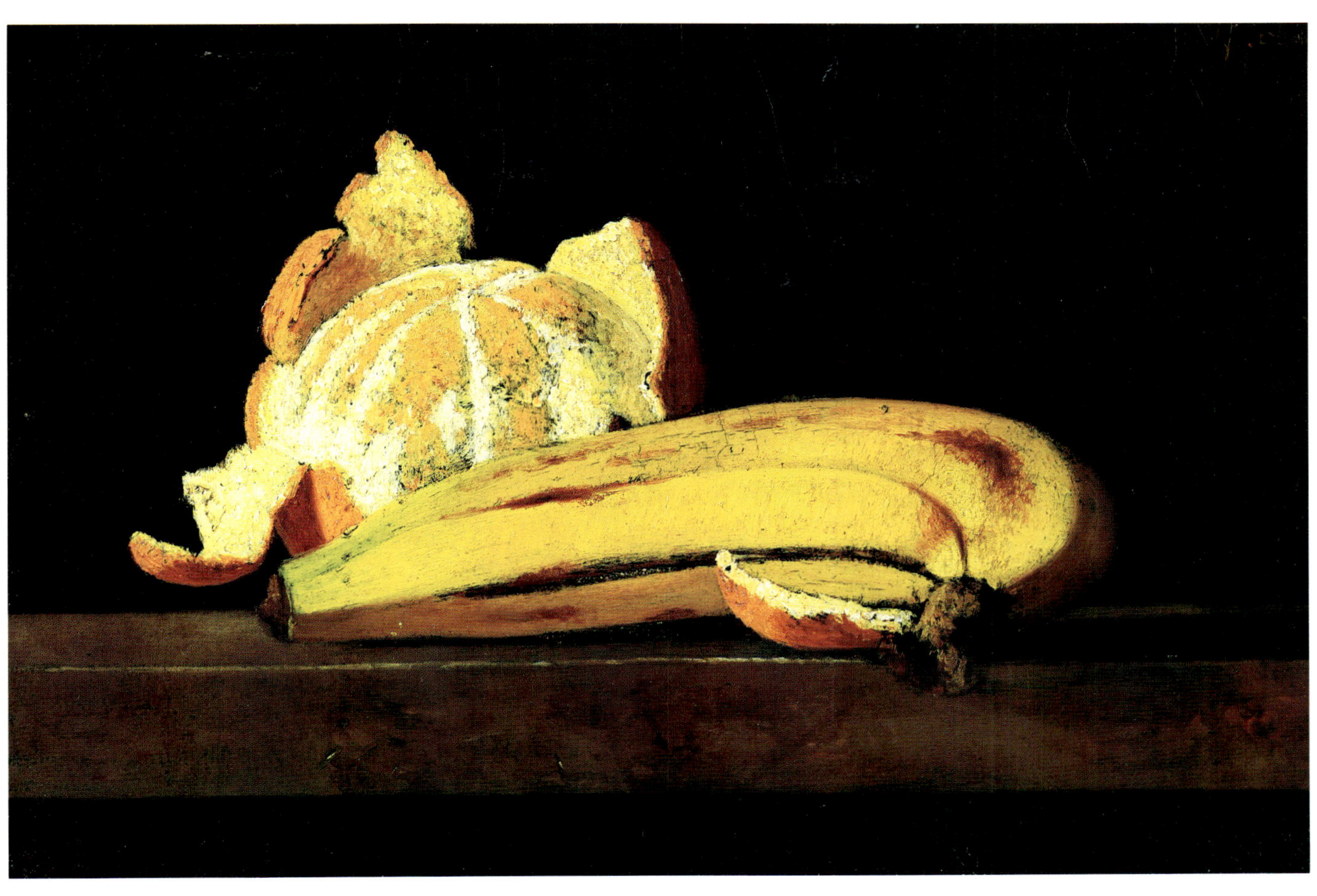

William Mason Brown

1828–1898

The Monarch
with Pansies and Fruit

n.d.
Oil on canvas
16 x 24 in. (40.6 x 61 cm)

Brown's first exhibited works were romantic landscapes in the style of the Hudson River School, but in 1865 he also began to exhibit still lifes. In fact, except for a few landscapes he continued to show at the Brooklyn Art Association into the 1870s and early 1880s, he exhibited exclusively still lifes until the early 1890s.[1] *The Monarch with Pansies and Fruit* is an example of a still life in a natural setting, a format fostered by the English critic and aesthetician John Ruskin, who attacked painting that idealized nature, espousing a "moral" art that sought to be true to nature and capture God's immanence through the depiction of humble natural subjects. An anonymous writer for *The Crayon*, a journal promulgating Ruskin's teachings in America, described the artist's task: "But this one thing ever remember, that before Nature you are to lose sight of yourself, and seek reverently for truth. . . . You will find, in after times, that the rudest effort to tell a fact in Nature will have a value, which will shame your studied prettinesses into the obscurity of rubbish portfolios."[2] In the 1850s and early 1860s, the height of Ruskin's popularity, his closest followers were the American Pre-Raphaelites, who worked out of doors and made informal but minutely detailed studies of nature.[3]

However, by the 1870s and 1880s, when Brown probably painted the *The Monarch with Pansies and Fruit*, Ruskin's popularity had declined. His focus on art true to nature was criticized for preventing the painter from making artistic choices and for producing unimaginative works.[4] As one critic aptly put it: "While it may readily be granted that truth is indispensable, yet a picture which has nothing else to recommend it will be very uninteresting, for it will betray a lack of knowledge in composition—of beauty of form and color."[5] Nevertheless, Ruskin's aesthetic ideas continued to exert an influence on the subject matter of still-life painters to such an extent that there even seems to have been a revival of some of his aesthetic concepts, which shaped the style of many artists during these years; their focus on depicting scrupulously detailed and highly finished objects in natural settings probably reflects the impact of his teachings.[6]

In *The Monarch with Pansies and Fruit*, the fruits and flowers lie on the forest floor among rocks, weeds, and a large, split hemlock log. On top of the log is a bunch of strawberries, a bountiful display pouring forth from the upper part of the composition. In the foreground, Brown has rendered an assortment of ornamental flowers, including yellow and purple pansies, honeysuckles, and fully bloomed yellow and red roses—flowers that could have been picked from any gar-den.[7] Capturing an instantaneous moment, Brown added a monarch butterfly perched in the foreground of the composition. The soft bumps on the surface of the strawberries, the folding petals on the rose, the threadlike veins on the surface of the leaves—these minute details are portrayed with an exacting technique. Characteristic of Brown's still lifes, the painting is sharply focused and possesses vivid color and a high degree of finish.[8]

Despite its adherence to the ideal of bringing the still life out into nature, Brown's painting is, on the whole, very un-Ruskinian. Unlike his Pre-Raphaelite predecessors, Brown has not captured a true corner of nature; rather, he has made an arrangement of fruits and flowers that could not have occurred in the natural order of things. The fully bloomed ornamentals and ripe strawberries have been plucked from the plants; the log has been rolled into place. It is likely that the artist worked from sketches for some of his flowers because they would not have been in bloom at the same time, as pansies usually bloom in the spring, while roses and honeysuckles prefer the summer heat. Probably a studio arrangement with strong, controlled lighting, Brown's still life could not be further from Ruskinian ideals. Indeed, a substantial number of his still lifes are tabletop arrangements of fruit and elegant glass or metalware placed on top of a cloth—works that Ruskin would have criticized for their artificiality.[9]

BETHANY ASTRACHAN

1 In 1865, Brown exhibited two still-life paintings at the National Academy of Design's annual exhibition. For Brown's exhibition records, see Mary Bartlett Cowdrey, ed., *The National Academy of Design Exhibition Record, 1826–1860*, 2 vols. (New York: New York Historical Society, 1943), 1:57; Maria Naylor, ed., *The National Academy of Design Exhibition Record, 1861–1900*, 2 vols. (New York: Kennedy Galleries, 1973), 1:112–13; Clark S. Marlor, ed., *A History of the Brooklyn Art Association with an Index of Exhibitions* (New York: James F. Carr, 1970), 137; Peter Hastings Falk, *The Annual Exhibition Record of the Pennsylvania Academy of the Fine Arts, 1807–1870*, 3 vols. (Madison, Conn.: Sound View Press, 1988), 1:39; Falk, *The Annual Exhibition Record of the Pennsylvania Academy of the Fine Arts, 1876–1913*, 3 vols. (Madison, Conn.: Sound View Press, 1989), 2:110.

2 "Studying from Nature," *The Crayon* 1 (June 6, 1855): 354.

3 For information on Ruskin, his aesthetic theories, and his influence on American still-life painting, see William H. Gerdts, "The Influence of Ruskin and Pre-Raphaelitism on American Still-Life Painting," *The American Art Journal* 1 (Fall 1969): 80–97; Gerdts,

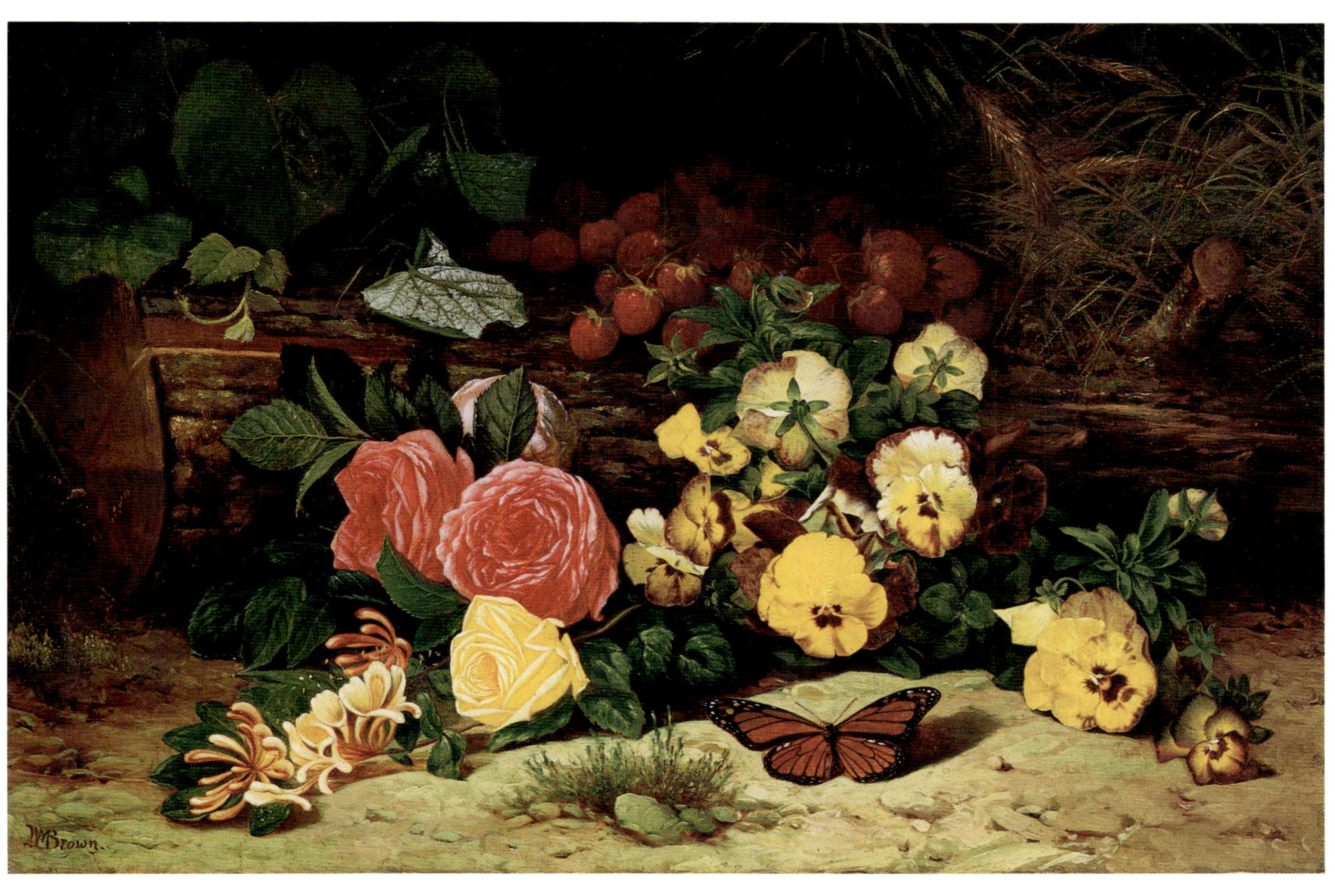

"Through a Glass Brightly: The American Pre-Raphaelites and
Their Still Lifes and Nature Studies," in William H. Gerdts and
Linda S. Ferber, *The New Path: Ruskin and the American Pre-
Raphaelites*, exh. cat. (Brooklyn, N.Y.: Brooklyn Museum, 1985),
39–77; William H. Gerdts and Russell Burke, *American Still-Life
Painting* (New York: Praeger Publishers, 1971), 93–97; 113–20;
Roger B. Stein, *John Ruskin and Aesthetic Thought in America,
1840–1900* (Cambridge, Mass.: Harvard University Press, 1967),
passim; Susan P. Casteras, *English Pre-Raphaelitism and Its
Reception in America in the Nineteenth Century* (London and
Toronto: Associated University Presses, 1990), passim.

4 See Gerdts and Ferber, 54, and Stein, 194–95.

5 A. J. H. Way, "Fruit-Painting in Oils: IV—Small Fruit—Cherries
   —Apricots—Wild Fruits," *The Art Amateur* 16 (April 1887): 102.

6 I wish gratefully to acknowledge William H. Gerdts for his kind
   guidance and generosity in sharing his knowledge about the pervasive Ruskinian influence on American still-life painting throughout
   the middle to late years of the nineteenth century.

7 Plant identification and information on seasonal flowering times
   are courtesy of The Brooklyn Botanical Gardens, Brooklyn, New
   York, and Thomas Siccama, lecturer, School of Forestry and
   Environmental Studies, Yale University, New Haven,
   Connecticut.

8 The strong clarity, pure, unblended colors, and crisp outlines of
   Brown's still lifes made them ideally suited for the chromolitho-
   graphic process, and his profusion of detail appealed to the masses
   who would purchase inexpensive prints. His most celebrated chro-
   molithograph, and one that brought him wide acclaim, was *A
   Basket of Peaches Upset*. This work was based on a painting by
   Brown that was purchased for two thousand dollars by William
   Schaus, a New York art dealer and distributor who financed the
   production of chromolithographs. (See "W. M. Brown's Death,"
   The Brooklyn Daily Eagle, Sept. 6, 1898, 14.) For further informa-
   tion on Brown's chromolithographs, see Gerdts and Burke, 68–69;
   Harry T. Peters, *America on Stone* (New York: Doubleday, Doran
   and Co., 1931), 357–58; Peter C. Marzio, *The Democratic Art:
   Chromolithography 1840–1900, Pictures for a 19th-Century America*
   (Boston: David R. Godine, in association with the Amon Carter
   Museum of Western Art, Fort Worth, Tex., 1979), 44, 47, 102.

9 Gerdts and Ferber, 245; and Ella M. Foshay, "Charles Darwin and
   the Development of American Flower Imagery," *Winterthur
   Portfolio* 15 (Winter 1980): 309.

Robert Spear Dunning

1829–1905

Apples

1869
Oil on canvas
19 ³/4 x 25 ³/8 in. (50.2 x 64.5 cm)

Describing Dunning's *Apples*[1] in a review of the artist's works at the Dunning memorial exhibition in 1911, Bryant Chapin, an artist and a student of Dunning's, wrote: "The old hat is amazingly natural, both in color and texture, and the tree trunk is worked out in infinite detail, but keeps its place in complete subordination to the rest of the picture. Taken as a whole, it is a unique conception and finely handled." Chapin went on to praise Dunning's still lifes for their refinement: "Rich, brilliant and glowing in color, gracious in line, well balanced in composition and through all a subtle quality of tone hardly definable, yet a quality that goes to make them what they are—almost the ne plus ultra of still life painting."[2]

Although he continued to paint local landscapes and stately portraits of prominent members of his community, by 1865 Dunning's main focus was still life, and he inspired other painters as a teacher and leader of a provincial school of still-life painting in Fall River, Massachusetts. *Apples* was painted in the early part of Dunning's career as a still-life painter. Characterized by its pronounced Ruskinian format of a still life in a natural setting, it is one of three types produced by Dunning: the interior tabletop still life with fruit, tableware, and, occasionally, vegetables or flowers, the most common combination; the less frequent outdoor natural-setting still life; and, a unique example, a work that includes a human presence, two people's hands, incorporated into the still-life composition.[3]

Dunning's interior tabletop still lifes are lavish displays. He typically combined a piece of ornate Victorian glass or metalware with a fine tablecloth and an abundance of lush fruit—peaches, pears, grapes, melons, cherries, and oranges, whole or cut open to reveal their succulence—and sometimes added a vase of flowers. To add a touch of the exotic, he would often include an open box of large figs or a sticky honeycomb, arranging these objects on top of a highly polished wood table onto which the elaborate containers and fruit would cast reflections.

Apples depicts a more humble subject—apples spilling out of a soft white bag and a tattered straw hat onto a natural bower of grass and dusty earth at the base of a tree. The straw hat's frayed edges and rough texture contrast with the smooth surface of the cloth bag.[4] The artist captures both the perfection and the imperfection of the objects: the ragged straw hat echoes the dented skin of the worm-holed apples, whereas the pristine white bag is more aligned with the

unmarred, fully ripe fruit. To add to the intimacy of the setting, Dunning compressed the space by cropping the composition on all four sides. The foreground is strongly lit with a raking light that illuminates the textured surfaces of objects—the rough tree bark, the polished apple skins, the prickly straw hat, and the velvety cloth. Beyond the trunk, an impenetrable blackness defines the boundaries of the picture space, forcing the viewer to focus on the foreground still-life arrangement.

Dunning used the same mundane prop—the tattered straw hat—in two other still-life paintings with fruit: *Still Life* (fig. 1; Private Collection) and *Harvest of Cherries* (Terra Museum of American Art, Chicago).[5] An indoor scene, *Still Life* is a close-up view of two hands, an elderly man's and a young woman's. The man is holding the same torn straw hat: his aged hand is dry and wrinkled, symbolizing his years of work. By contrast, the woman's hand is aristocratic—soft, youthful, bejeweled; she holds a bunch of grapes as if she were placing them inside the old man's hat in a charitable gesture of giving.[6] More important than the still life's moral concerns, however, is the narrative in all three paintings of a male/female relationship. In *Harvest of Cherries* (fig. 2), for example, a woman's bonnet and a man's straw hat are juxtaposed at the base of a tree. Similarly, in *Apples*, the soft white bag with its smooth curves and supple form may symbolize the feminine aspect, while the straw hat symbolizes the male. Unlike *Still Life*, however, *Harvest of Cherries* and *Apples* are natural-setting still lifes that lack a human presence, the unseen characters being represented only by their worldly possessions.

The strong narrative elements in these works and their implication of male and female interaction outdoors, have parallels in nineteenth-century British and American courtship paintings.[7] In both countries, advice and etiquette books adumbrated strict rules that governed the behavior of courting couples and the stages of their love relationship. These rules, however, did not preclude intimacy: chaperonage and the strict segregation of the sexes were practiced less frequently than was once believed, and young men and women were given the opportunity to share intimate moments and to decide their own futures with a prospective mate.[8] Charged with sentimentality, English courtship paintings expressed the latent sexuality and frustrated love of the courting couple.[9] An artistic convention that recalled the Virgin in an enclosed garden (the *hortus conclusus*), a solitary woman awaiting her lover in a rustic setting by a fence, country stile,

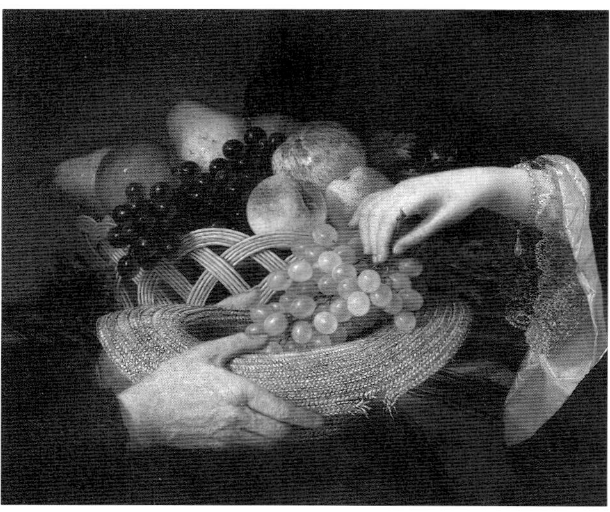

Fig. 1. Robert Spear Dunning, *Still Life*, 1865, oil on canvas, 20 x 24 1/8 in. (50.8 x 61.3 cm), signed and dated l.l. "R. S. Dunning 1865," Collection of Peter G. Terian

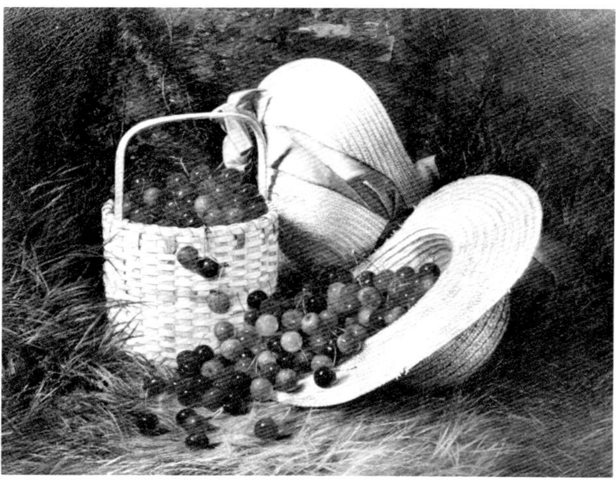

Fig. 2. Robert Spear Dunning, *Harvest of Cherries*, 1866, oil on canvas, 20 x 26 1/2 in. (50.8 x 67.3 cm), Terra Museum of American Art, Evanston, Ill. From Linda S. Ferber and William H. Gerdts, *The New Path: Ruskin and the American Pre-Raphaelites,* exh. cat. (New York: The Brooklyn Museum, 1985)

wall, or tree, suggested feminine purity. When the woman was accompanied by a male, the fence or other barrier became an "inanimate chaperone," a symbol for the couple's propriety and understanding of the rules of courtship. In several instances, the couple was depicted by a "trysting tree,"[10] a romantic meeting place in a bucolic setting; in a gesture of informality and relaxed enjoyment, the man, and sometimes the woman too, might be shown with their hats off and casually placed on the ground. Influenced by European precedents, American artists often depicted courtship outdoors in rural settings at picnics, apple-pickings, and other country events. Both women and nature were assumed to possess salubrious qualities that were viewed as positive influences on the urban middle-class male.[11]

In both *Harvest of Cherries* and *Apples*, Dunning drew upon this romantic iconography by incorporating symbols of courtship: the "trysting tree" along with informally arranged objects that connote masculinity and femininity—the man's straw hat, the woman's bonnet, the soft, voluptuous white bag. Men's straw hats were country attire, worn at picnics, sporting events, or by the sea. In *Apples*, the ragged edge of the hat suggests that its owner is of rural stock—perhaps a peasant or a farmer. The simple cloth bag is also a rustic prop, resembling utilitarian traveling bags or bags used to carry or store agricultural produce.[12] Although it is true that apples were sometimes plucked from the tree and gathered in a hat during apple picking, the absence of the standard objects generally used in paintings of this subject—a barrel or large basket[13]—may suggest that Dunning's *Apples* instead symbolizes the informal countryside tryst of a rural couple, the ripe fruit, a love token, underscoring the painting's romantic theme. Taken one step further, the spilling and mixing together of the apples from both containers, the straw hat and the cloth bag, might be seen as an obvious sexual reference.

Although Dunning's works were produced in the latter half of the nineteenth century, their opulence and sense of bounty is a continuation of a mid-century still-life aesthetic. Painted with thin layers of transparent pigment and a tight, descriptive brushstroke, Dunning's still lifes glow with color and are characterized by their meticulous detail. Only in his later years did he handle his paint more freely and impressionistically, perhaps because of metropolitan influences. Probably because Fall River was so far removed from the still-life developments taking place in the urban centers of

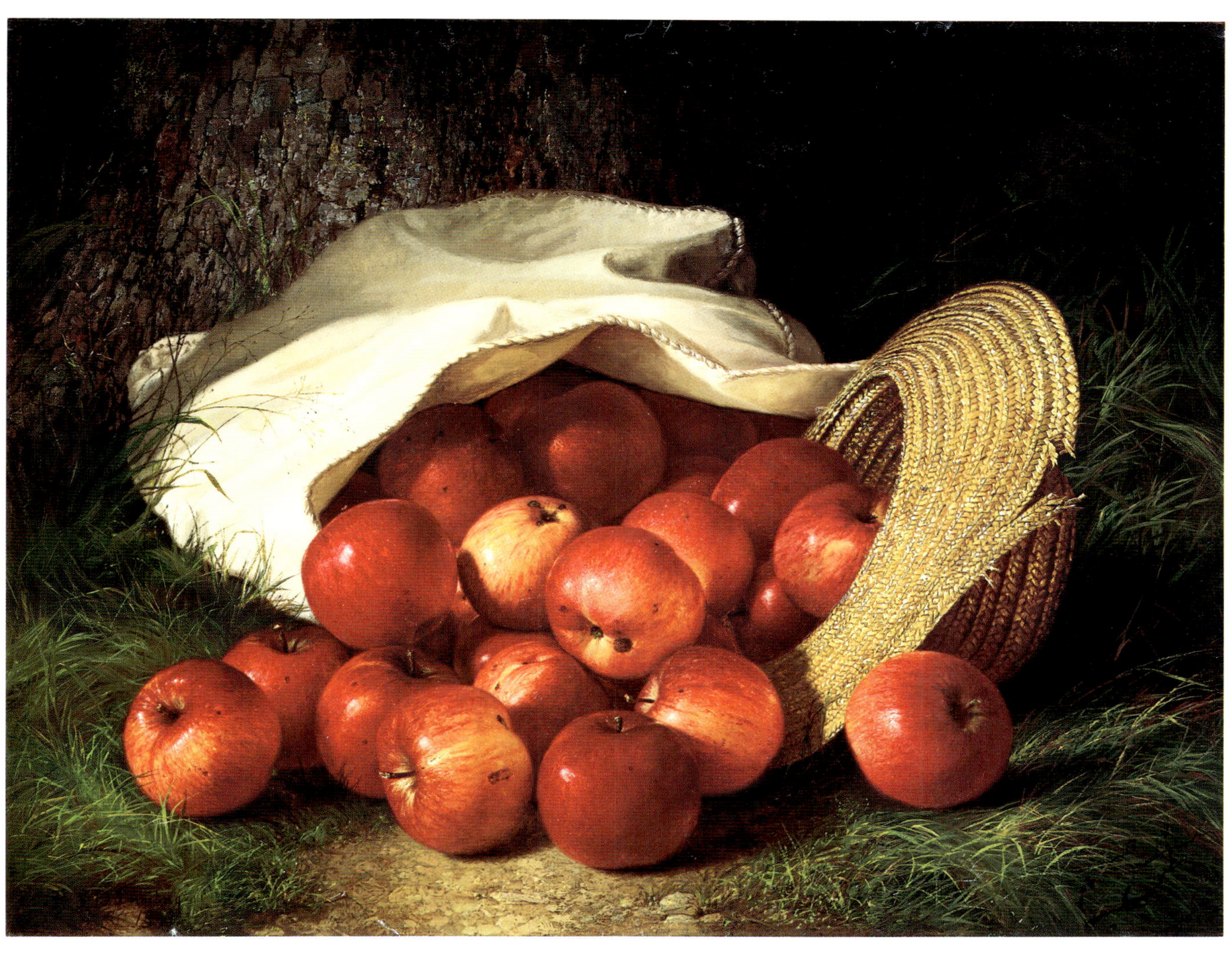

New York and Philadelphia, Dunning and other artists there continued to work in a somewhat *retardataire* but nonetheless sophisticated and high-quality fashion.[14]

BETHANY ASTRACHAN

1 I am indebted to Michael Martins of the Fall River Historical Society for his generosity in sharing with me his knowledge of Dunning and other Fall River artists.
2 Bryant Chapin, "Dunning Exhibit at the Library," *Fall River Evening News*, December 14, 1911, 9.
3 For Dunning, see William H. Gerdts, *Painters of the Humble Truth: Masterpieces of American Still Life, 1801–1939*, exh. cat. (Tulsa, Okla.: Philbrook Art Center/Columbia and London: University of Missouri Press, 1981), 116–17; William H. Gerdts and Russell Burke, *American Still-Life Painting* (New York: Praeger Publishers, 1971), 169–74; and Linda S. Ferber and William H. Gerdts, *The New Path: Ruskin and the American Pre-Raphaelites*, exh. cat. (New York: The Brooklyn Museum, 1985), 252.
4 A common still-life motif of the mid- to late-nineteenth century, the overturned vessel with fruit spilling onto the ground was a symbol of bounty and plenitude. Fruit filling up the inside of a straw or felt hat was another standard still-life convention. See, for example, Levi Wells Prentice's (1851–1935) oil on canvas *Apples in a Hat*, reproduced in Cecily Langdale, *American Still Lifes of the Nineteenth Century*, exh. cat. (New York: Hirschl and Adler Galleries, 1971), 28.
5 I gratefully acknowledge Bruce Weber, Director of Research and Exhibitions, Berry-Hill Galleries, for bringing the similarity of these three works and their relationship to nineteenth-century courtship scenes to my attention. For the symbolism of fruit and the iconography of the hat, and the erotic connotations of both motifs, see Mary D. Sheriff, *Fragonard: Art and Eroticism* (Chicago and London: University of Chicago Press, 1990), 95–113; and Donald Posner, "The Swinging Women of Watteau and Fragonard," *The Art Bulletin* 64 (March 1982): 85.
6 James W. Tottis discusses *Apples* in terms of its moral implications, interpreting the apples in the tattered straw hat as symbolizing an act of charity; see *American Paintings from the Manoogian Collection*, exh. cat. (Washington, D.C.: National Gallery of Art/ Detroit: Detroit Institute of Arts, 1989), 102. See also Gerdts and Burke, 174.
7 For information on nineteenth-century British courtship paintings, see Susan Paulette Casteras, "Down the Garden Path: Courtship Culture and Its Imagery in Victorian Painting," 7 vols. (Ph.D. diss., Yale University, 1977), passim, and Casteras, *Images of Victorian Womanhood in English Art* (London and Toronto: Associated University Presses, 1987), 85–101. For American courtship paintings, see Sarah Burns, "Yankee Romance: The Comic Courtship Scene in Nineteenth-Century American Art," *The American Art Journal* 18 (1986): 51–75; and Elizabeth Johns, *American Genre Painting: The Politics of Everyday Life* (New Haven and London: Yale University Press, 1991), 143–51.
8 See Karen Lystra, *Searching the Heart: Women, Men, and Romantic Love in Nineteenth-Century America* (New York and Oxford: Oxford University Press, 1989), 190. Lystra writes: "A private, unchaperoned, mutually agreed upon relationship, Victorian courtship was an incubator of romantic love. It encouraged the growth of both physical and emotional intimacy." Françoise Barret-Ducrocq also discusses the loosening up of strict rules regulating courtship behavior in England, in *Love in the Time of Victoria: Sexuality, Class and Gender in Nineteenth-Century London*, trans. John Howe (London and New York: Verso, 1991), 86. She writes: "Although most [young couples] were no longer under surveillance in a closed rural society, or supervised by their parents, they still used a traditional frame of reference which prescribed ritual stages for a love relationship." There is evidence, however, that in the last quarter of the nineteenth century there was an increase in adult supervision. As young people began spending time away from home in a world that was becoming more complex, parents exerted tighter controls. See Ellen K. Rothman, *Hands and Hearts: A History of Courtship in America* (New York: Basic Books, 1984), 207–8.
9 Johns describes a basic difference between European and American courtship paintings: "The varieties of subtle shared experience in courtship that had found expression in English and German paintings—shyness, frustrated longing, sexual energy, even sentimentality—were not explored by American genre painters. Rather, American artists interpreted the activity as a proving ground of the middle-class male" (143).
10 Casteras, "Down the Garden Path," 70–76, 268, 122.
11 Johns, 147. By the mid-1840s courtship had become an integral part of many outdoor scenes with male and female activity. Johns writes: "The ostensible purpose of such excursions, which were the pleasures of urban citizens carried out in the country, was to remove men from the fast-paced, corroding influence of the city and place them in the context both of rural nature and of female influence."
12 See Doreen Yarwood, *English Costume: From the Second Century B.C. to 1950* (London: B. T. Batsford, 1952), 206, 215, 237. For information on costume and class distinctions, see Sarah Burns, *Pastoral Inventions: Rural Life in Nineteenth-Century American Art and Culture* (Philadelphia: Temple University Press, 1989), 125, 168–69. One of many paintings that includes rustic bags or sacks is Winslow Homer's depiction of a light-colored cloth bag in his 1870 wood engraving, *Chestnutting* (Bowdoin College Art Museum, Brunswick, Maine).
13 See, for example, the large barrels and baskets in Jerome Thompson's 1856 oil on canvas *Apple Gathering* (The Brooklyn Museum, Brooklyn, N.Y.). The motif of apples in a hat might also symbolize stolen fruit. In one 1802 example, a stipple engraving by E. Scott after George Morland titled *Boys Robbing an Orchard*, four young men are shown fleeing the scene after a farmer has caught them in his orchard; one boy quickly gathers some apples in his hat (reproduced in Sarah Burns, *Pastoral Inventions*, 140).
14 Gerdts and Burke, 169; Gerdts, *Painters of the Humble Truth*, 116–17.

Otto Stark

1859–1926

Gathering Wild Poppies

1885
Oil on canvas
18 x 14 in. (45.7 x 35.5 cm)

A rosy-cheeked young peasant girl is picking blossoms in a field of tall grass and colorful wildflowers. She is perfectly at ease in uncultivated nature, her attitude humble and absorbed. Stark's portrayal draws on a number of influences: his training as an academic painter; the widespread impact of peasant genre themes; and the light palette, gestural brushwork, and planar composition of the Impressionists.

In 1885, Stark arrived in Paris to enroll in the Académie Julian, where he took lessons from the academic painters Gustave Rudolphe Boulanger and Jules-Joseph Lefebvre. *Gathering Wild Poppies* was painted during his first year in the French capital. Stark's academic training is most evident in the realistic representation of the young girl. Using carefully delineated outlines, he has emphasized the girl's face and hands. The play of midday light and shadow on her figure calls particular attention to the outstretched gesture of her right hand and her clasped left hand.

While in Paris, Stark was drawn to the popular peasant genre derived from Jean-François Millet and other Barbizon painters. Peasant imagery, which tended to exalt rural life as dignified and morally uplifting, was pervasive throughout Europe.[1] Many artists looked to peasants and fisherfolk for subjects and found inspiration in the heroic stoicism and timeless quality of lives closely tied to the rhythms of nature. Stark's provincial child, however, does not possess the melancholy and careworn aspect of the monumental peasant images of Millet, Jules Breton, and other French artists. Innocent and serene, she is more attuned to enjoyment than relentless toil.

In many respects, *Gathering Wild Poppies* also relates to the painting of the French artist Jules Bastien-Lepage, whose work was highly praised, especially among American artists in the 1880s.[2] Like Bastien, Stark maintained a basic conservatism with regard to the human figure, which he rendered with draftsmanlike skill while at the same time creating fluently brushed *en plein air* landscapes. The landscape in this work is rendered in an almost impressionistic manner. Gestural strokes of color suggest blossoms and leaves; yet the wildflowers are recognizable—mostly poppies, sweet peas, and Queen Anne's lace. Loosely painted stalks of dried grass in the foreground and dark shrubbery in the background give the painting a minimal sense of depth. The figure is close to the foreground, which produces a sense of intimacy and immediacy; the viewer could almost be standing in the field along with the young girl.

Although Stark did not fully embrace the techniques of Impressionism until the 1890s, he was aware of its tenets during the previous decade. In 1895, he published "The Evolution of Impressionism," one of the first defenses in the United States of the modern style .[3] In this essay, he divided the movement into four stages, which he categorized by color: the first used primarily dark colors such as blacks and browns; the second, inspired by the plein-air movement, concentrated on varying shades of gray, as "air and light were sought after as never before"; the third was a "high-key" era in which a white palette predominated; and, finally, Impressionism evolved into the "color harmony" or "complete color value" technique that became the signature style of the movement. *Gathering Wild Poppies* falls into Stark's second stage of Impressionism, which he categorized as "beautiful in repose, harmonious in tone, [and] generally without shrill notes of any kind."[4]

This emphasis on serenity and Stark's celebration of childhood are consistent with a widespread craving for an idyllic harmony with nature that prevailed in the latter part of the nineteenth century. As technological change and industrialization were taking their toll on society, the idealized image of the country child served as an icon of lost innocence.[5] Popular illustrations and academic paintings increasingly presented rural childhood as a symbol of Edenic closeness to nature and God. Specialized literature for and about children also glorified the insular experience of youth. By the 1860s, the concept of childhood had acquired an enhanced status, and nostalgic renditions of provincial children elicited strong sentiments that masked some of the more disturbing realities of urban life.[6]

A sensitive and evocative work, *Gathering Wild Poppies* relies on a simple subject and compositional format. Yet in this painting Stark brings together the rich artistic currents of the period in a deceptively effortless way.

ALISON TILGHMAN

1 The enormous popularity of the peasant genre began around the time of the 1848 revolution, was revived around Millet's death in 1875, and continued through the end of the century. The general appeal of this genre depended on a sense of continuity and contact with a stable past associated with rural life, especially during times of economic and social upheaval. See Robert L. Herbert, "City vs. Country: The Rural Image in French Painting from Millet to

Gaugin," *Artforum*, no. 8 (February 1970): 44–55; Herbert, "Millet Reconsidered," *Museum Studies*, no. 1 (1966): 28–65; and Herbert, *Barbizon Revisited* (San Francisco: California Palace of the Legion of Honor, 1962).

2 For information on Bastien-Lepage and other French painters who influenced American artists, see H. Barbara Weinberg, *The Lure of Paris: Nineteenth-Century American Painters and Their French Teachers* (New York: Abbeville Press, 1991).

3 Otto Stark, "The Evolution of Impressionism," *Modern Art* 3, no. 2 (Spring 1895): 53–56; also reprinted in Leland G. Howard, *Otto Stark, 1859–1926* (Indianapolis: Indianapolis Museum of Art, 1977): 58–60.

4 Stark's works of the 1890s have a greater intensity of color value and are rendered in a more diffuse manner, consistent with his approximation of the final stage of Impressionism.

5 See Sara Burns, "Barefoot Boys and Other Country Children: Sentiment and Ideology in Nineteenth-Century American Art," *American Art Journal* 20 (1988): 24–50; and Burns, *Pastoral Inventions: Rural Life in Nineteenth-Century America* (Philadelphia: Temple University Press, 1989).

6 Stark did, in fact, have a genuine fondness for children. He was the eldest of seven himself and maintained close contact with his brothers and sisters throughout his life. He married a few months after painting this picture. He and his French wife had four children before she died, within six years of their wedding. Never remarrying, Stark raised his family alone. Much of his career centered around teaching children. He was employed in a technical high school, occasionally gave private art lessons, later acted as an instructor, and eventually became the head of a formal art academy.

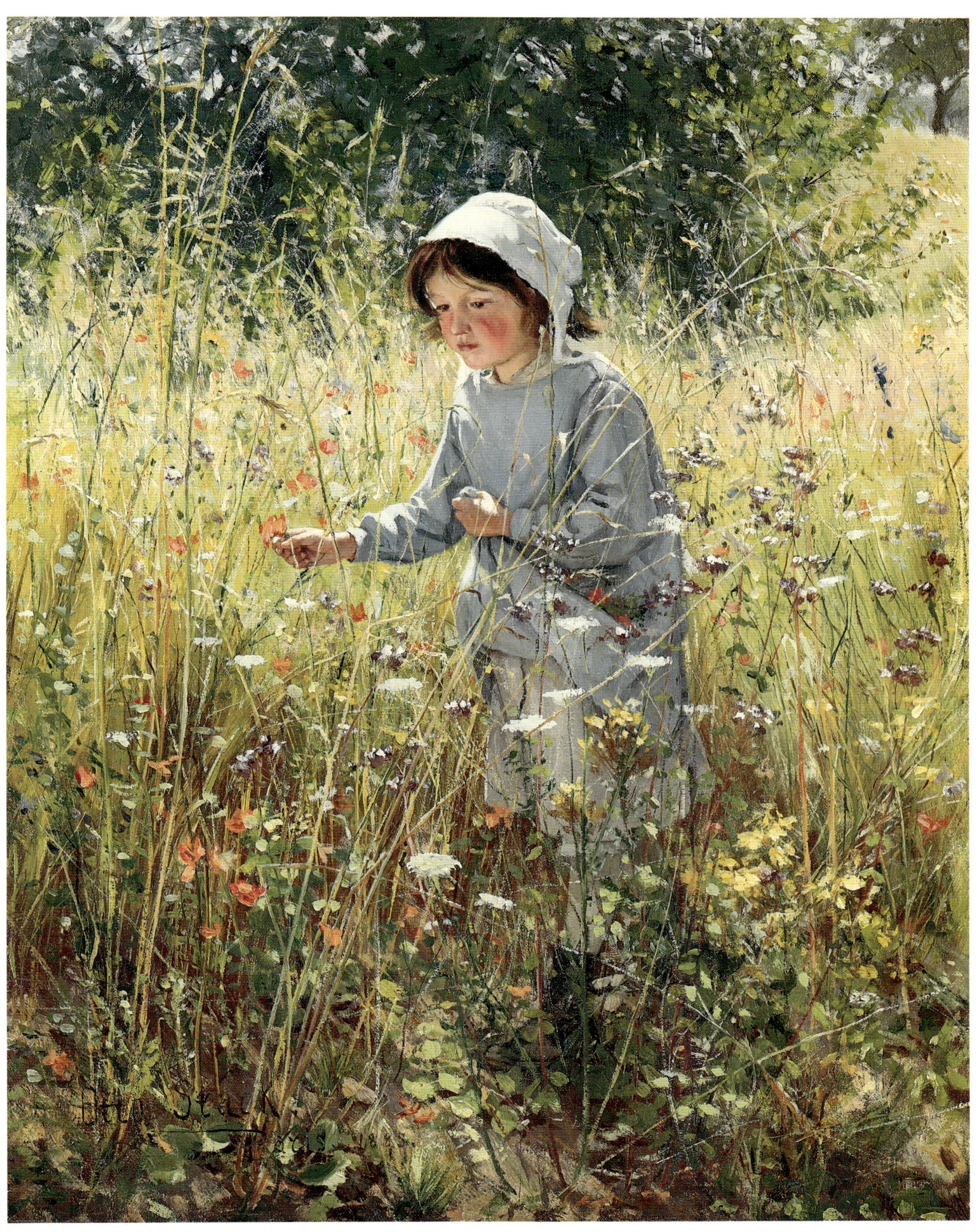

Willard Leroy Metcalf

1858–1925

The Poppy Garden

1905
Oil on canvas
24 ⅛ x 24 ⅛ in. (61.3 x 61.3 cm)

From the late nineteenth to early twentieth centuries, a significant number of American artists painted flowers as they had never been painted before in this country—in full bloom in gardens or growing in the wild.[1] Although hardly new to Western art, no tradition of painting the floral environment had previously existed on this side of the Atlantic. The painting of flower gardens and fields of flowers was especially popular with Impressionist artists.

Artists were not the only Americans during this period to develop a passion for flowers. They were joined by poets, natural scientists, philosophers, and writers. Women of affluence also devoted an increasing amount of their leisure time to flower-related activities. The first garden club in America was founded in Athens, Georgia, in 1890. Floral dictionaries, flower painting instruction books, greeting cards, flower shows, and flower gift books were all the rage. Gardening manuals and seed catalogues also attest to the prominence of flowers at the turn of the century.

Many flower painters had their own gardens that directly involved them in the processes of plant life. Others—for example, William Merritt Chase—were drawn to the subject by visits to public gardens, like the nursery in New York's Central Park (p. 23), or to the parks and gardens of Paris and other fashionable cities. Childe Hassam was repeatedly drawn to depicting the celebrated flower garden of Celia Thaxter at Appledore Island, off the New Hampshire coast.

Drawn by his friendship with Hassam and the colony of artists in residence at Miss Florence Griswold's boarding-house, Metcalf spent the first of several summers in Old Lyme, Connecticut, in 1905. Old Lyme is one of the most beautiful villages in southern New England, and Metcalf, fresh from the success of his first one-man show in New York, approached his craft with particular enthusiasm. His joyful mood is revealed in the "flowers that bloom in profusion on a number of canvases. Dogwood blossoms, laurel, peonies, poppies—suddenly he was in love with them all."[2] *The Poppy Garden* is the best-known painting of the group and is believed to have been painted in the garden of Metcalf's colleague Clark Voorhees. It was first shown at the "Eighth Exhibition of the Ten Americans" the following spring.[3]

Critics were impressed by the "lyrical lightness and charm"[4] of Metcalf's Old Lyme subjects, and in their reviews of this and a slightly earlier exhibition,[5] pronounced them his best works to date.[6] "A capital river view with hedges, some billowy laurel bushes, and a gorgeous poppy garden"[7] was one of the works singled out for praise.

Metcalf had begun to incorporate the impressionist techniques of diffused light and broken color into his landscapes as early as 1895, but he maintained a definition of form and never completely abandoned local color. This summer scene, with its high-key red and green palette, is one of his most animated improvisations on nature, the bright poppies and other blooms appearing as a magnificent blaze of color against the foil of the blue-gray water and the sun-bathed vista and pale-blue sky.

Although Metcalf here took his primary inspiration from the example of Claude Monet, a more direct influence may be found in Hassam's paintings of Thaxter's flower garden, made in the previous decade—some of lush beds of poppies offering a distant view of sea, sky, and the islands beyond. At the same time, Metcalf impressed his own temperament on the subject, for it incorporates the square format and the ingratiating mixture of brushwork—long and broken in the foreground, smooth in the river and sky—that characterize his adaptation of the Impressionist style.[8]

NANCY RIVARD SHAW

1 For an excellent discussion of this subject, see William H. Gerdts, "Down Garden Paths: The Floral Environment in American Art," exh. cat. (Montclair, N.J.: Montclair Art Museum, 1983).
2 Elizabeth de Veer and Richard J. Boyle, *Sunlight and Shadow: The Life and Art of Willard Metcalf* (New York: Abbeville Press, 1987), 83.
3 Metcalf sent six canvases to the exhibition, held at Montross Gallery, New York, March 1906. The other five were: *November Sunshine, The Misty Morn, On the River, Mountain Laurel,* and *Nocturne.*
4 Metcalf Correspondence and Papers, Archives of American Art, Smithsonian Institution, Washington, D.C., roll N70/13, frame 506. "Landscapes by Mr. Willard L. Metcalf," *New York Tribune,* February 6, 1906.
5 Held at Fischel, Adler, and Schwartz Gallery, New York, February 1906.
6 Metcalf Papers, Archives of American Art, roll N70/13, frames 505 and 506.
7 *Evening Post*, March 16, 1906, Metcalf Papers, Archives of American Art, roll N70/13, frames 505 and 506.
8 Most of these elements would appear again in the similarly structured *Purple, White, and Gold,* a river view with a garden of flowers in the foreground, possibly also painted at Old Lyme. Illustrated in *Palette and Bench,* July 1909, color supplement.

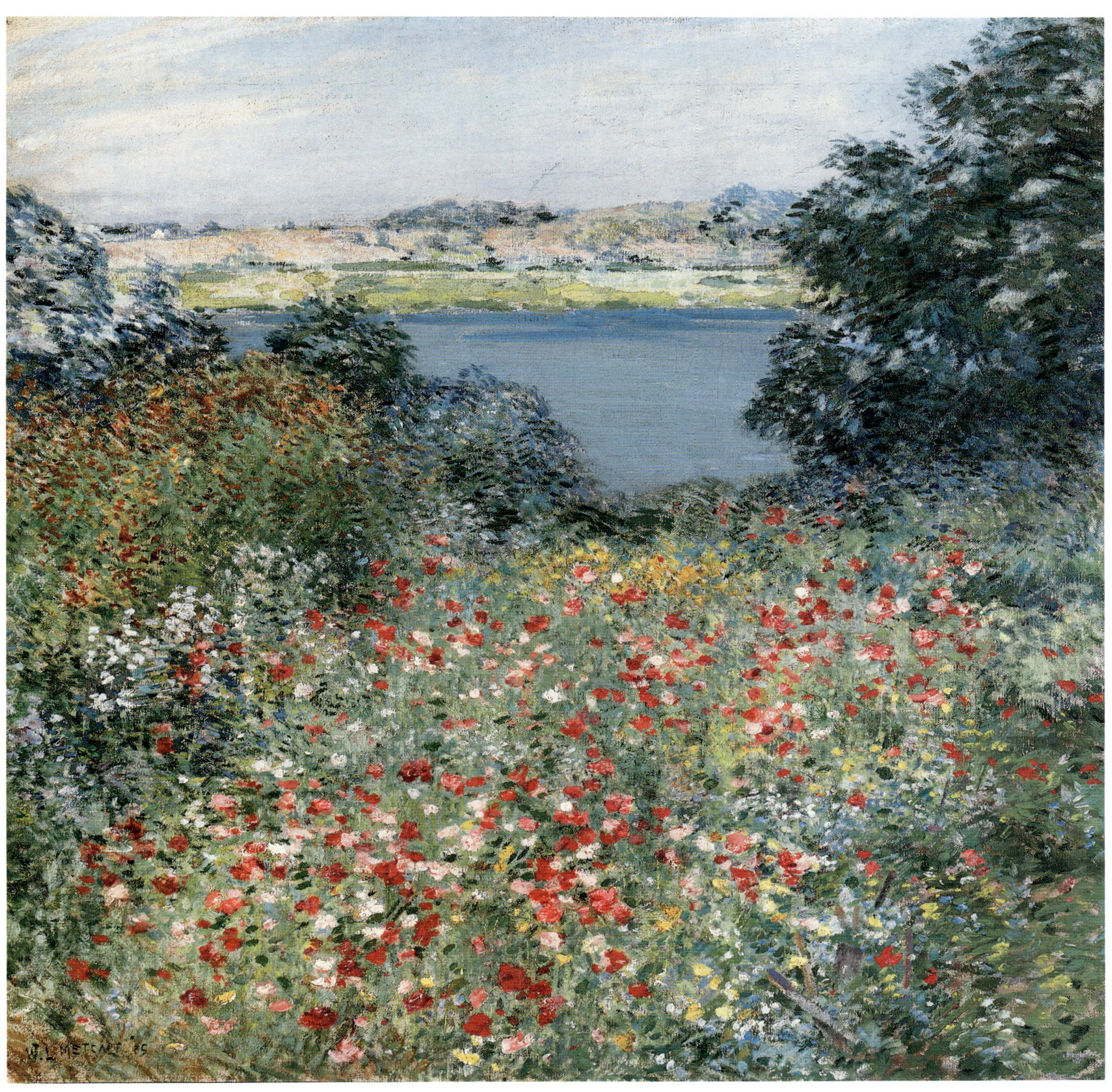

Theodore Robinson

1852–1896

Low Tide

1894
Oil on canvas
16 x 22 in. (40.6 x 55.9 cm)

Low Tide is one of the many paintings and sketches Robinson made in Connecticut during the summer of 1894. Primarily working near and in Cos Cob, he spent most of that summer attempting to capture on canvas the particular beauty of the Connecticut shoreline.[1] In its integration of firm design and draftsmanship with color, *Low Tide* attests to his success.

Robinson's training in America and France instilled in him a fidelity to drawing, while his close friendship with Monet sparked his interest in the pictorial description of light and air. Like many American artists painting in France in the 1880s, Robinson did not abandon his commitment to draftsmanship in favor of the colorist techniques of the Impressionists. Consequently, much of his earlier work displays a tension between color and line. Upon his return to America in 1892, where he would remain for the rest of his life, Robinson resolved to reconcile these conflicting tendencies; *Low Tide* represents his achievement of that goal.

Dividing the composition into three horizontal registers, Robinson consolidated the planes by his use of light and color: the colors of the pink-tinged gray sky are reiterated in the roof of the Riverside Yacht Club and the shadows of the white-hulled boats; the broad band of beige sand with light-blue highlights provides a nice foil to the thinly painted strip of bright-blue water of the middle ground; the flecks of green seaweed mirror the green and brown band of trees on the horizon. Robinson bathed these colors, scattered across the painting, in a clear, soft light that spreads evenly over the canvas. Through his use of a diffuse light source and a restricted and subdued palette, he created the image of a cool, almost idyllic, atmosphere.

The extreme horizontal format of the painting heightens the scene's sense of tranquillity. The low, flat boats, the patches of seaweed, and the strips of reflections on the water and sand fix the image in its wide plane. Paradoxically, the vertical masts of the boats serve to further emphasize the picture's horizontality by cutting across all three planes, as if to link them together. The bands of paint across the canvas add to the steadiness of the image and even evoke the slow, calm lapping of water against the boats at low tide.

These elements—the subdued yet bright bands of colors and the visible brushstrokes—fuse to produce a solidly constructed canvas. But the artist plays with his forms and makes his image quietly but intensely vibrate. No line remains sharp; each stroke of paint seems to bleed into the next.

The image appears to be out of focus. The mist of bright light veils and blurs the distinctness of the lines. The boats, water, and sand move and sparkle in the hazy sunlight, while the trees on the horizon dissolve into the sky.

The broken, dry brushwork and the dependence on light to evoke atmosphere show the influence of Monet; the effects of weather and light on the appearance of landscape fascinated him, as they had his French mentor. Much impressed by Monet's series of Rouen Cathedral seen at different times of day (which he had seen and discussed with Monet at an early stage in the series's conception), Robinson himself experimented with paintings conceived together as a series. Although not part of a series, *Low Tide* may be regarded as a pendant to a similar image of the same scene painted at a different time of day, *Low Tide—Riverside Yacht Club* (Private Collection). In fact, Robinson executed a number of sketches of the same subject also depicting small boats in different atmospheric conditions.[2] He also discussed these marine images done in Cos Cob in a diary entry of June 19, 1894: "Am getting well and strong and work with interest—especially from the R.R. Bridge, late afternoon, the club house and little yachts at anchor, low-tide, patches of sea-grass. It is particularly brilliant at about 5 P.M."[3]

In light of both the number of works depicting similar scenes and this comment about his interest in this particular view, Robinson's paintings of the Cos Cob shoreline seem to suggest an increasing subordination of subject to form. It is precisely this fusion of solid, almost abstract, design—reminiscent of the Japanese prints the ailing artist so admired—with soft atmospheric effects created by his use of color and brushstroke, which makes *Low Tide* one of the most successful paintings of Robinson's career.

JULIA ALEXANDER

1 For a comprehensive discussion of Robinson's other Cos Cob images, see Susan G. Larkin, "Light, Time, and Tide: Theodore Robinson at Cos Cob," *The American Art Journal* 23, no. 2 (1991): 74–108.
2 For reproductions of a few of these sketches, see *Theodore Robinson, 1852–1896*, introduction and commentary by Sona Johnston, exh. cat. (Baltimore: Baltimore Museum of Art, 1973).
3 From the unpublished diaries of Theodore Robinson, quoted in John I. H. Baur, *Theodore Robinson, 1852–1896* (Brooklyn, N.Y.: The Brooklyn Museum, 1946), 68.

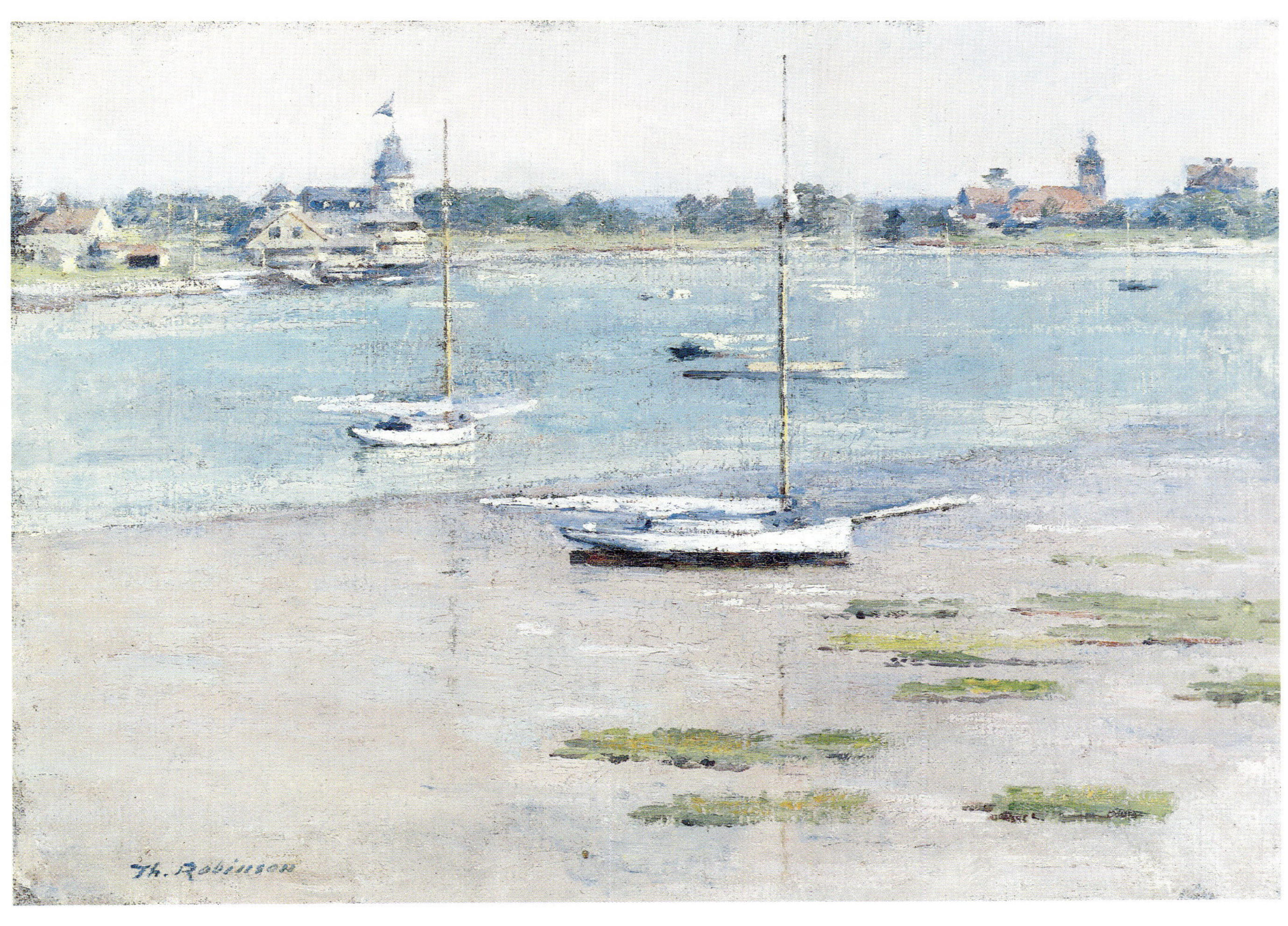

Charles Sprague Pearce

1851–1914

Reading by the Shore

c. 1888
Oil on canvas
11 7/8 x 18 1/8 in. (30.3 x 46 cm)

In 1934 an *Art Digest* article described Charles Sprague Pearce as an artist whose "fame [in America] had faded almost to obscurity," a consequence attributed to his having "spent most of his life in France."[1] Indeed, by the end of his career, Pearce was more associated with French than with American art; like hundreds of fellow New Englanders, he had traveled to Paris during the early 1870s with the intention of training at the prestigious Ecole des Beaux-Arts and participating in annual Salon exhibitions, aspirations realized in 1873 when he was accepted into the atelier of Léon Bonnat, who taught him the fundamental tenets of academic art: interpretation of nature through a consummate technique; study of past works of art; and concentration on historical, mythological, religious, or exotic subject matter.[2]

Typically rendered in a controlled academic style, most of Pearce's subjects—religious martyrs, Arabs, Egyptians, and Normandy peasants—celebrate the foreign as grand and mysterious.[3] *Reading by the Shore*, an intimate portrait of Pearce's wife, is a departure from such exoticism: painted in the late 1880s while the couple was living in a village twenty miles north of Paris, Auvers-sur-Oise, it exhibits a more personal and casual subject as well as a looser, more expressionistic brushstroke. Despite its nonacademic scale, technique, and subject, however, in its synthesis of a dialectic between the natural and the artificial the painting subtly encapsulates Pearce's philosophy of art.

Beyond recording an image of the artist's wife, *Reading by the Shore* aggrandizes the strength and beauty of nature. Pearce captures what nineteenth-century guidebooks praised as the awesome features of the Normandy seacoast: its jagged, precipitous cliffs, rocky shores, violet-gray water and sand, cloud-swept skies, and brilliant light.[4] As he does in several of his paintings, Pearce relegates the horizon line to the uppermost corner of the canvas in order to focus on the land. On the one hand, he suggests the rugged power of the terrain with a vigorous, impastoed brushstroke.[5] The power of the rocky and sloping shore to order the natural elements around it is emphasized by the body of the woman, whose brown boots and roughly painted skirt appear to spring directly from the rocks. Pearce's foregrounding of the land over the sea or sky does not preclude his interest in demonstrating the play of light on the Normandy coast. Exemplifying painting *en plein air*, *Reading by the Shore* displays an overall luminous setting where shaded areas serve to reinforce those more directly illuminated by the sun.

Although Pearce highlights nature, his inclusion of his wife in this particular Normandy setting gives us the first hint of the artificial construction of the painting. During the 1880s, the coastline of northwest France was characterized for the most part by rocky shores interrupted only occasionally by sandy beaches. Areas marked by boulders and sharp rocks were hardly choice spots for leisured activities; in fact, most paintings depicting upper-middle-class vacationers relaxing at Normandy resorts, such as Claude Monet's *The Beach at Trouville* (1870, The National Gallery, London), feature groups of people lounging on sandy expanses, not single figures pretending to be comfortable on rocky ground. On the other hand, the more rugged, dangerous Normandy shores were usually reserved in pictorial imagery for lower-class locals—peasants who were able to endure harsher environmental conditions. For example, the American artists Edward Emerson Simmons, John Singer Sargent, Edward Moran, and Henry Bacon populated their rocky shore scenes with Norman and Breton peasants working, either gathering oysters or unloading ships. James Abbott McNeill Whistler's *Alone with the Tide* (1861, Wadsworth Atheneum, Hartford) shows a peasant woman leaning against some boulders along a Breton beach, but she reclines because she is exhausted from work;[6] by contrast, in *Reading by the Shore*, Mrs. Pearce, wearing a fashionable tailored suit and charming lilac-covered hat, reclines as she indulges in a carefree activity.[7] Thus Pearce's painting, in substituting a refined upper-middle-class woman for the peasant figure traditionally placed along the rugged Norman coast, presents the "unnatural" or unexpected within a natural setting.

Surely one could dismiss the incongruity of a fashionable woman lying on a rough beach; yet the pose that Pearce had his wife assume in *Reading by the Shore* possesses a further air of artificiality. Whatever attempts he made to capture the spontaneity of this scene are unsuccessful: his wife's direct stare at him implies that she is posing for a picture, and her body, aligned with the diagonal furrows of rocks and sand on the beach, is carefully positioned so as not to disturb the formal unity of the painting. Obviously concerned with compositional balance, Pearce has even paralleled his wife's stiff, elongated form, transecting a semicircular band of gray sand at her feet, with the spokes on the floral Japanese umbrella that she holds.

The two accessories that Pearce features in *Reading by the Shore*—book and umbrella—also contribute to the theme of

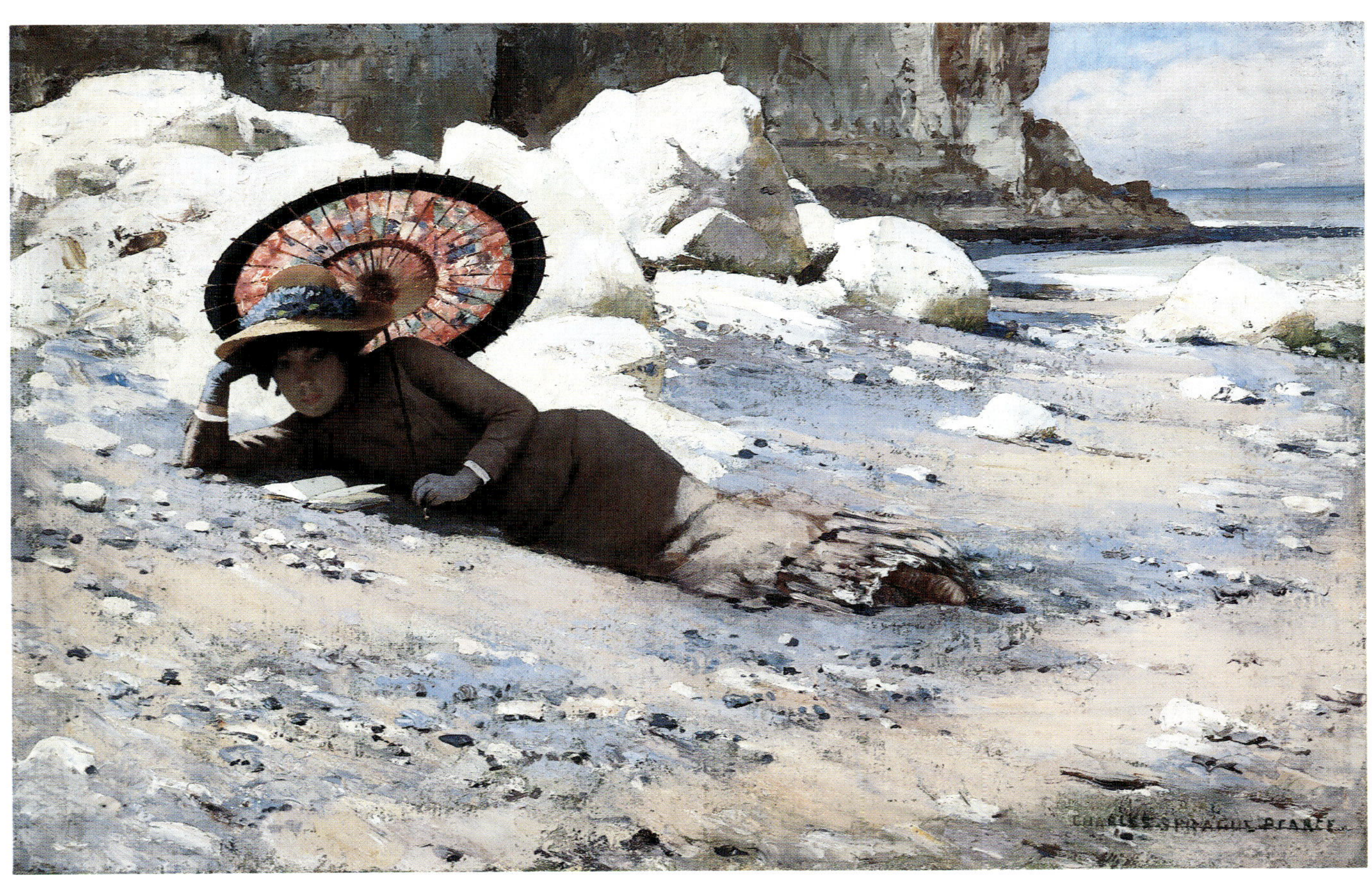

artificiality, as they are transformed from functional objects into decorative props. Indeed, although depicting his wife in an understated, yet fashionable, costume appropriate for the beach, Pearce included the book and the umbrella as conspicuous indicators of leisure and wealth. Resembling hoards of late-nineteenth-century images of upper-middle-class women reading, playing musical instruments, or simply musing, *Reading by the Shore* most likely utilizes the book more as a symbol of the leisure time Mrs. Pearce possessed than of her desire to read.[8] The striking Japanese umbrella also carries certain associations with class and the decorative artificiality often associated with a nineteenth-century woman of leisure. With the opening of trade routes to Japan in the 1850s, many middle- and upper-class Americans, including artists, began to collect Japanese prints, porcelain, costumes, and accessories.[9] Especially at the turn of the century, during the height of interest in Japanese culture, artists often portrayed their wives, mistresses, or friends in oriental costume or surrounded by oriental props; such luxurious and decorative objects both connoted the wealth of their purchaser and enhanced the decorative beauty of their wearer.[10] In *Reading by the Shore*, the Japanese umbrella suggests luxury, and thus Pearce's own distinguished status; at the same time, it transforms Mrs. Pearce into an exotic object of beauty.[11]

By synthesizing the natural—in the form of setting and *plein air* technique—and the artificial—in the form of construction and props recalling the artificiality or decorativeness of leisured women—*Reading by the Shore* merges the two elements of Pearce's artistic style. Closely following the example of his academic master Bonnat, he looked to natural models, both the human body as well as landscape, for guidance in developing a controlled technique. Unlike nineteenth-century Realists, however, Pearce did not depict nature with any "realistic" flaws; rather, he consistently rearranged and transformed nature to effect compositions of pure beauty. *Reading by the Shore*, like the majority of his paintings from the 1880s, emphasizes such decorative, artificial beauty as well as the expressionistic power of brushwork.[12] Nonetheless, his continued interest in the precise rendering of the human body indicates that, even with personal, nonmythological, or nonhistorical subjects, Pearce had not completely abandoned his academic training.

MARY ADAIR WOODALL

1 *Art Digest*, May 15, 1934, 16. Lois M. Fink points out that "objections to works created by painters in Paris pertained, first of all, to the fact of being abroad and therefore disconnected from American cultural values and, second, to the choice of subject matter." Lois Marie Fink, *American Art at the Nineteenth-Century Paris Salons* (Washington, D.C.: National Museum of American Art, 1990), 287.

2 Ibid., 66–67. For an account of Pearce's early school days in Paris, see Barbara Weinberg, *The Lure of Paris: Nineteenth-Century American Painters and Their French Teachers* (New York: Abbeville Press, 1991), 170, and Annette Blaugrund, ed., *Paris 1889: American Artists at the Universal Exposition*, exh. cat. (Philadelphia: Pennsylvania Academy of the Fine Arts, 1989), biography.

3 Exotic subjects certainly were not unfamiliar in Pearce's oeuvre. After an 1873 trip to Egypt, Algeria, and Nubia with the American artist Frederick Bridgman, he became intrigued by foreign cultures and began depicting beautifully costumed Arabs. Such images, together with Pearce's numerous paintings from the 1880s of the peasants around Auvers-sur-Oise, exhibit a Darwin-inspired fascination with cataloguing different peoples or species in their natural environments. For descriptions of the exotic quality of Near Eastern scenes and peasant scenes, see Fink, 193, 73, and 205. For a description of Darwin's influence on exoticism, see *The Quest for Unity: American Art Between World's Fairs, 1876–1893*, exh. cat. (Detroit: Detroit Institute of Arts, 1983), 25.

4 David Sellin, *Americans in Normandy and Brittany, 1860–1910*, exh. cat. (Phoenix: Phoenix Art Museum, 1982), 5. For other descriptions of the Normandy landscape, see Françoise Vibert-Guigue, ed., *Normandie* (Paris: Hachette-Guides Bleus, 1988), 50, 55–57, and *Le Paysage Normand dans la littérature et dans l'art* (Paris: Presses Universitaires de France, 1980), 78.

5 Concerning Pearce's placement of the horizon line, see "Book of American Figure-Painters," *The Art Amateur* 16 (January 1887): 47. D. Dodge Thompson discusses Pearce's brushstroke in *American Paintings from the Manoogian Collection*, exh. cat. (Washington, D.C.: National Gallery of Art/Detroit: Detroit Institute of Arts, 1989), 138.

6 Sellin, 4.

7 Valerie Steele, *Fashion and Eroticism: Ideals of Feminine Beauty from the Victorian Era to the Jazz Age* (New York: Oxford University Press, 1985), 65. During the 1880s, dark tailor-made suits became extremely popular with wealthy women. For comparable examples, see Madeleine Ginsburg, *Victorian Dress in Photographs* (New York: Holmes and Meier Publishers, 1983), 94–95.

8 During the late nineteenth century, a woman reading was often equated with a woman who did not have to work, which, in turn, was equated with a husband who had money. That Pearce associated a woman reading with her decorative properties and her husband's status is also evidenced by his *Lady with a Hat* (c. 1885, Private Collection), in which a woman wearing an elegant furred bonnet and shawl casually thumbs through a novel. Martha Banta, *Imaging American Women: Idea and Ideals in Cultural History* (New York: Columbia University Press, 1987), 345, 357–58.

9 Gabriel Weisberg, *Japonisme: Japanese Influence on French Art* (Cleveland: Cleveland Museum of Art, 1975), 1.

10 *Quest for Unity*, 127. *Japonaiserie* is a category of Western paintings that "incorporate Japanese objects for their associative value or

fashionable novelty." Pearce's painting belongs to this category. *Japonaiserie* must be distinguished from *japonisme*, or elements of Japanese technique and design in Western paintings (Robert Preato, *La Femme: The Influence of Whistler and Japanese Print Masters on American Art, 1880–1917* [New York: Grand Central Art Galleries, 1983], 40, 42). Louis Octave Uzanne underscores that the Japanese sunshade contributed to a woman's decorativeness: "Parasols are now quite indispensable [as a] complement of the toilette for the promenade—[and not only for] protection from the sun," [but because they are a] gracious adjunct of feminine costume; [how beautiful is] a rosy head with dishevelled hair, on the transparent ground of a Japanese sunshade" (Louis Octave Uzanne, *The Sunshade, Muff, and Glove* [London: J. C. Nimmo and Bain, 1883], 61).

11 *Reading by the Shore* is not the only painting in which Pearce dressed up his wife in exotic, decorative finery. In *Portrait of Mrs. Pearce* (1888, Private Collection), for example, he displayed her wearing an Empire-style tunic (c. 1805), a paisley shawl, and a high, feathered bonnet. For similar examples of this costume, see Herbert Norris and Oswald Curtis, *Costume and Fashion: The Nineteenth Century* (London: J. M. Dent and Sons, 1933), 27–28, and Elizabeth Ewing, *Everyday Dress, 1650–1900* (London: B. T. Batsford, 1984), 71, 77.

12 The creation of beauty as an artistic goal in and of itself was central to the philosophy of the Aesthetic Movement, which revolved around the American expatriate James McNeill Whistler. During the 1870s, Whistler renounced moral, historical, or mythological art in favor of a subjective art that demonstrated a "harmony of technique, of abstraction, and of the artist's own person with nature's mood." Whistler based many of his paintings on Japanese prints, whose compositional designs and decorative beauty he admired. In fact, adoring Japanese culture in general, Whistler also included Japanese objects in several of his paintings, a practice Pearce emulates in *Reading by the Shore* (*Quest for Unity*, 18–19, 21).

John George Brown

1831–1913

Sunshine

1879
Oil on canvas
14 1/8 x 20 1/8 in. (35.9 x 51.1 cm)

Celebrated during the 1860s through the 1880s as one of America's most popular genre painters, Brown was best known for his nostalgic and often humorous images of childhood. Although playful country girls and boys and urban bootblacks and urchins proved to be his most marketable subjects, he occasionally painted landscapes and seascapes.[1] *Sunshine*, possibly depicting the Long Island shore not far from Brown's home in New York City, belongs to a small series of beach scenes painted in 1879, 1887, and 1890.[2] The painting is both thematically and stylistically unique in his oeuvre. The fluid, expressionistic brushstrokes in the dunes, as well as the play of light and shadow on the central figure's body, are examples of his transition from rendering forms in minute detail to capturing the more naturalistic effects of painting *en plein air*.[3]

Indeed, seashores provided the ideal settings for mid-nineteenth-century experimentation with outdoor light, as evidenced by the luminous beach scenes of John Frederick Kensett, Winslow Homer, and Samuel S. Carr. The most common of these scenes focused either on the natural grandeur of the shore, offset by vast expanses of sea and sky, or on the social activities of a crowded beach.[4] A variation on such themes, Brown's *Sunshine* features nature and leisure activities not as central subjects but, rather, as backdrops for the physical and social "awakening" of an individual—a girl on the brink of womanhood.

Several compositional elements in *Sunshine* suggest that the young woman is in a state of flux, poised between the two worlds of childhood and adulthood. Stretched out along the diagonal edge of a dune that almost precisely halves the painting into foreground and background areas, her figure is literally placed on a point of transition. On the one hand, her body, solidly buttressed by her left elbow and hip, connotes immobility, as it resists the possibility of rolling off the precarious slope of the dune. On the other hand, as it is framed by windswept sea grass, crashing waves, and moving clouds, her body seems unable to escape the imminence of nature's changes. The light in the painting further underscores this transition or change: exactly between morning and afternoon, the noon sun, shining directly on the young woman from overhead, both warms her body and, as is suggested by her contemplative expression, effects a mental "enlightenment." That she is aware of her physical and mental individuality is indicated by her aloofness from the small family cluster in the left middle ground: distanced from childhood, she no longer romps in the waves or plays in the sand; yet, not

quite an adult, she prefers to lounge on the beach rather than promenade with an escort.

The young woman's costume—an amalgam of straw hat, rugged dress, striped stockings, short boots, and leather accessories—confirms this bridging of childhood and adulthood. Like the seashore beauties of 1870s magazine engravings, Brown's subject sports a simple white cotton dress, typically associated with middle-class teenaged girls at the beach or in the country.[5] The sturdiness of the cotton material would permit its wearer to loll in the sand, yet the garment's ankle-length underskirt and its decoratively ruffled collar and sleeves recall the more elaborate walking dresses worn by older women at the beach.[6] Although boots and striped stockings were shared by both teenaged girls and women, wide-brimmed straw hats with long ribbons and loosely worn hair were much more characteristic of children and young women than of women above the age of twenty.[7] Nonetheless, the curious leather or silver bangles this particular young woman displays, more commonly worn for dinner engagements, hint at her interest in fashion and possible attempt to simulate adult manners.[8]

In addition to her costume, the young woman's body language seems simultaneously childlike and mature. Resembling the smaller children supervised by a mother or nanny near the water, this figure unabashedly reclines on the ground and toys, not with sand, but with a handful of sea grass. However, apparently aware of her own sensuality, she invitingly swivels her hips and throws back her shoulders, offering her maturing body to the viewer, and perhaps to the receptive gaze of another vacationer beyond the picture plane. Her candid expression, whether interpreted as meditative or enticing, also suggests that she is controlling her own body rather than unwillingly subjecting it to scrutiny.

Such a bold display of the body would not have been uncommon in the social landscape of the late-nineteenth-century American beach, which encouraged playacting and relaxed behavior. In the early 1800s, it was only the wealthy who visited beach resorts for therapeutic bathing; yet by midcentury, middle-class Americans were flocking to Newport, Narragansett Pier, the Jersey Shore, Coney Island, and Long Island in order to escape the drudgery of the urban workplace.[9] Although some status-conscious vacationers used the beach as a fashion showplace, many repaired to it for liberation from a formal parlor atmosphere. Indeed, at

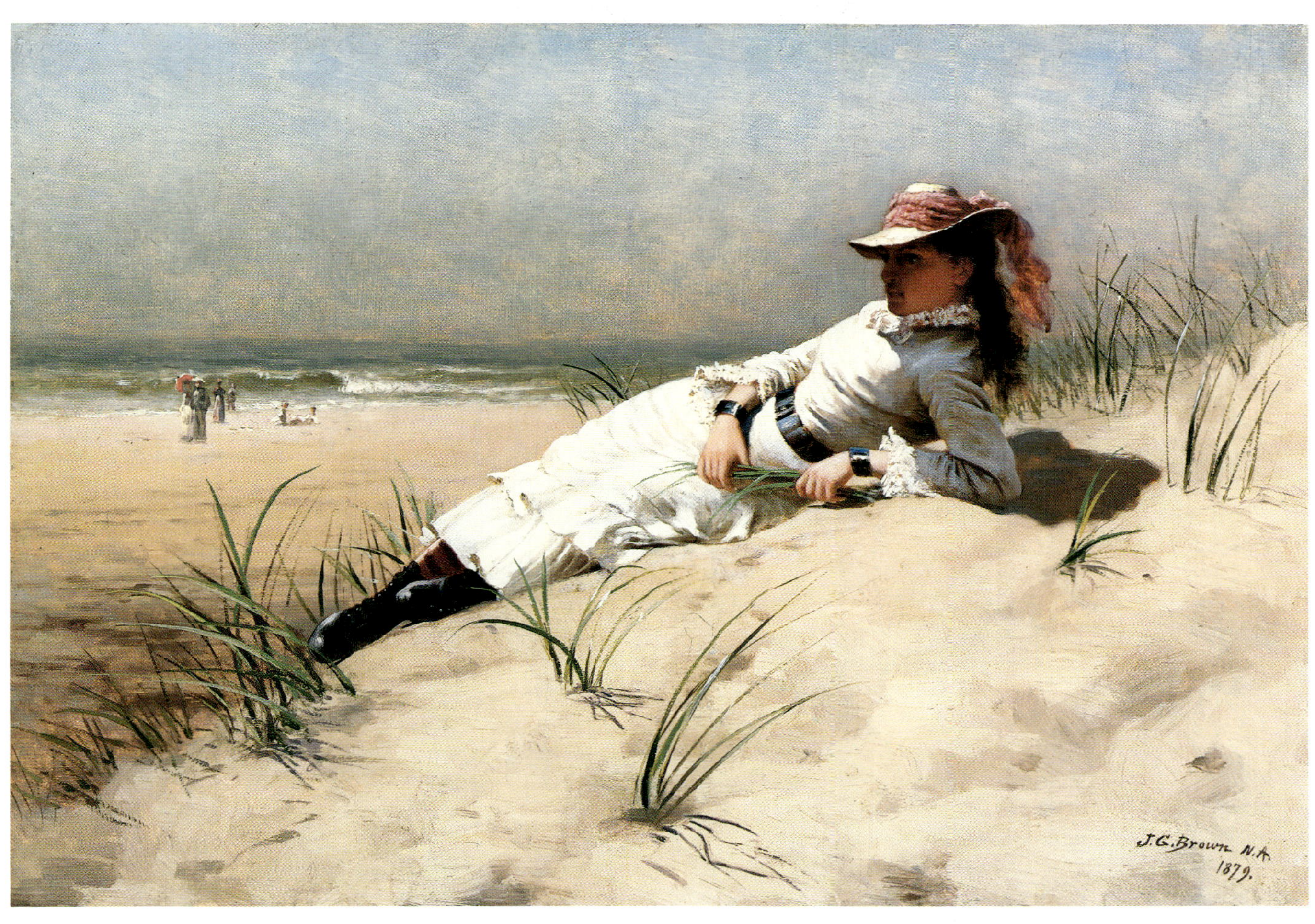

the beach people could "kick back" and assume different identities: they could either bathe in the ocean and frolic along the shore or indulge in various other leisure-time activities such as having photographs made, playing penny games, and watching theatrical shows.[10] The frequent puppet shows that were often performed along the shore, in fact, encapsulated the spirit of play and masquerade engendered by the beach environment.

Not surprisingly, it was at the seashore, a place of metamorphosis, that a nineteenth-century woman could both achieve heightened self-awareness and exercise control over men in a courting context. Kate Chopin's controversial 1899 novelette, *The Awakening*, painted a vivid picture of what a woman might experience at the beach. While spending the summer on the Gulf Coast, the married protagonist recognizes her own sensuality and her longings for a younger man; once she has returned to the city, she proceeds to engage in a series of affairs.[11] Contemporary newspapers and magazines as well as fiction often commented on the relaxed behavior of women by the seaside. One writer reported that the female vacationer not only could shed her constraining everyday dress in order to swim but could actively flirt with men.[12] Indeed, the young woman in *Sunshine*, "awakened" to the power of her maturing mind and body, appears to be practicing such flirting skills with her steadfast and alluring gaze and her provocative reclined position.

Themes of flirtation, courtship, and sexual longing figured largely in other Brown paintings besides *Sunshine*. Most likely in an effort to maintain the lighthearted nature of his work, he typically explored these themes through images of children playacting in adult roles. Subtly addressing this transition between childhood and adulthood are Brown's paintings of young, self-absorbed women isolated in quiet fields or forests. Like the pastoral young shepherdesses imaged by his colleague Winslow Homer, Brown's nature-seeking women evoke nostalgia and innocence, as well as unfulfilled passion and desire.[13]

The settings of most of Brown's 1860s paintings of courting children and pensive women—either Edenic pastures or woods—served to reinforce the nineteenth-century theme of childhood as a state of innocence. Especially after the Civil War, images of children were often used to express the hope that the lost paradise of an earlier, more peaceful time could be recaptured. Whether playing, fighting, wooing a mate, or contemplating bodily changes, the child in a pastoral world

was a reminder of the ease and purity of youth and, by extension, of the past.[14] On the other hand, Brown's emphasis on the moment of sexual or mental awareness, found in many of his paintings, testifies to his recognition that postbellum America could not avoid maturation, acceptance of loss, and Reconstruction. Nevertheless, he utilized the figure of the maturing child, not to presage the ugly reality of the future, but, optimistically, to "prophesy what [the country] could become."[15] *Sunshine*, in particular, probably appeared to nineteenth-century audiences as a symbol of the nation poised between the innocence of the past and the possibilities of the future. Childlike and carefree, this young American woman lounges on the beach; emboldened by the warming sun, she has left behind the other children by the shore and lies comfortably gazing off into the distance, toward the future. By situating *Sunshine* at the seashore, where modern-day leisure activities were taking place, rather than in the more nostalgic atmosphere of a field or forest, Brown also emphasized the contemporaneity of this maturation, both of the young woman and of the nation.

MARY ADAIR WOODALL

1   Martha J. Hoppin, *Country Paths and City Sidewalks: The Art of J. G. Brown* (Springfield, Mass.: George Walter Vincent Smith Art Museum, 1989), 1, 6.
2   Ibid., 6. Brown moved permanently to New York City from New Jersey in 1869. The exact location of this beach scene is not known; the only recorded information about the painting is from a *New York Times* review on April 20, 1879: "*A Sunny Day* [is] . . . a full-length miniature portrait of a young girl lying on a sandy hillock on the beach." The dates of Brown's beach scenes are found in Katharine M. McClinton, "John George Brown: Sentimental Painter of the American Scene," *Connoisseur*, April 1974, 245.
3   For information about Brown's experimentation with various styles, see the following: Linda S. Ferber, "Ripe for Revival: Forgotten American Artists," *Art News*, December 1980, 72; Daniel Grant, "Remembering a Neglected Artist," *American Artist*, September 1989, 115; and Hoppin, 9. Hoppin, in particular, points out that Brown's emphasis on "accurate recording and descriptive detail" during the 1860s most likely stemmed from his "contact with American Pre-Raphaelite painters."
4   William H. Gerdts, "Surf and Shore: Nineteenth-Century Views of the Beach," in *At the Water's Edge: Nineteenth- and Twentieth-Century American Beach Scenes* (Tampa, Fla.: The Tampa Museum of Art, 1989), 25–29.
5   Philip C. Beam, *Winslow Homer's Magazine Engravings* (New York: Harper and Row, 1979), 176, 178, 195, 197, 216. For similar examples of outdoor costumes worn by teenaged girls, see: *Winslow Homer, 1836–1910: A Selection from the Cooper-Hewitt Collection* (Washington, D.C.: Smithsonian Institution Press,

1972), plate 30; Priscilla H. Dalrymple, *American Victorian Costume in Early Photographs* (New York: Dover Publications, 1991), plates 135, 172; and Stella Blum, *Victorian Fashions and Costumes from Harper's Bazaar: 1867–1898* (New York: Dover Publications, 1974), plate 7.4.

6 For examples of outdoor walking costumes, as exhibited by the woman with the parasol in the background of *Sunshine*, see: Evelyn Ackerman, *Dressed for the Country: 1860–1900* (Los Angeles: Los Angeles County Museum of Art, 1984), 16–17; Madeleine Ginsburg, *Victorian Dress in Photographs* (New York: Holmes and Meier Publishers, 1983), 59, 62; and Blum, plate 8.25.

7 For discussions about the meaning and use of striped stockings and boots, see: Valerie Steele, *Fashion and Eroticism: Ideals of Feminine Beauty from the Victorian Era to the Jazz Age* (New York: Oxford University Press, 1985), 66; and Ginsburg, 182. For discussions about hairstyles, see Steele, 119, and Ginsburg, 183.

8 Margaret Flower, *Victorian Jewellry* (New York: A. S. Barnes and Company, 1967), 185. Here Flower reviews the various types of Victorian silver bangles and the occasions on which they were worn. In books on Victorian jewelry, no mention is made of leather cuffs, although fashionable young girls occasionally wore leather capes to the beach.

9 Russell Lynes, "At the Water's Edge: Changing Perspectives on the Beach." In *At the Water's Edge: Nineteenth- and Twentieth-Century American Beach Scenes* (Tampa, Fla.: The Tampa Museum of Art, 1989), 18–20; James Walvin, *Beside the Seaside: A Social History of the Popular Seaside Holiday* (London: Penguin Books, 1978), 13.

10 James Walvin, *Leisure and Society, 1830–1950* (London: Longman Group, 1978), 77.

11 Kate Chopin, *The Awakening*, in *Literature of the Western World*, ed. Brian Wilkie and James Hurt (New York: Macmillan Publishing, 1988), 1361–1457.

12 Walvin, *Seaside*, 71–72; Thomas E. Jordan, *Victorian Childhood: Themes and Variations* (Albany: State University of New York Press, 1987), 202. That girls and women at the seashore were allowed to indulge in amorous pursuits is indicated by the following popular midcentury poem: ". . . Young Cupid, 'tis said, lies hid in yon main,/And philters each wave that roles to the shore/A draught daily drunk by the rich and the poor,/The ladies well pleased by a potion so sweet,/Come here in groups their fond lovers to meet,/And gentlemen too, who are friends to the fair,/Come under pretense to enjoy the fresh air."

13 For example, comical courtship scenes such as *Pay Toll* (1862, Private Collection) and *Walk In* (1875, Hirschl and Adler Galleries, New York) foreground the very moment at which innocence becomes experience. In *Pay Toll*, the female member of a juvenile couple prepares to cross over a literal threshold to meet her receptive and even seductively coaxing male partner, while in *Walk In*, a young woman entices the viewer to pass through her garden gate. *Waiting for a Partner* (1872, Collection of Jo Ann and Julian Ganz, Jr.) presents a similar scenario: in the center of a wooded grove populated by various types of courting couples, a virginal girl dressed in white contemplates her own choice of mate from a ring of children surrounding her; "awakened" by an overhead spotlight, she seems ready to break through this symbolic circle of childhood into the world of love beyond. For a description of *Waiting for a Partner*, see *American Narrative Painting*, exh. cat. (Los Angeles:

Los Angeles County Museum of Art, 1974), 140–41. For examples of Brown's pensive women, see Hoppin, plates 6, 7, 34, 36, and 46. For examples of Homer's shepherdesses, see *Winslow Homer, 1836–1910*, 38–40.

14 Sarah Burns, "Barefoot Boys and Other Country Children: Sentiment and Ideology in Nineteenth-Century American Art," *The American Art Journal* (1988), 25–28. Here Burns looks at the nineteenth-century notion of innocence associated with the country child, in particular, with the barefoot boy.

15 Linda Ayres, "The American Figure: Genre Paintings and Sculpture," in *An American Perspective: Nineteenth-Century Art from the Collection of JoAnn and Julian Ganz, Jr.*, exh. cat. (Washington, D.C.: National Gallery of Art, 1981), 57. Quoted by Henry Tuckerman from 1867.

Edward Henry Potthast

1857–1927

In the Surf

1914
Oil on panel
12 x 16 in. (30.5 x 40.6 cm)

Almost every notable artist of the late nineteenth and early twentieth centuries has, at one time or another, been attracted to the seaside—an ideal setting in which to explore the various elements of color and form and composition. Perhaps the best-known American artist to have investigated this theme is Edward Potthast, of whom it was said, "When a man paints a theme as well as Potthast paints seashore scenes, we forgive him for sticking to it to the exclusion of other subjects."[1] Potthast's interest in this motif may have been inspired, at least in part, by the work of Maurice Prendergast, whose vivacious watercolors of seashore life were being widely exhibited in various American cities during the 1890s. To immerse oneself in a particular kind of subject matter was characteristic of turn-of-the-century American artists, especially American Impressionists, of whom Potthast was one.

When Potthast moved to New York in 1896 he was nearly forty years old and had already been earning a living as a commercial artist. Like Robert Henri, John Sloan, and others, he used his experience as an illustrator to enter the mainstream of city life and to refine his art. Working for various publishers, including *Scribner's* and *The Century*, Potthast developed a system of notation that enabled him to transcribe scenes "on-the-spot," quickly and adeptly; he applied this approach to his oil paintings as well. According to his nephew, Potthast was ambidextrous and would often amuse his fellow artists by using both hands at once, though he seems to have favored the left.[2] He is said to have worked entirely out-of-doors, preferring to make small oil sketches on wood panel or canvas mounted on board, which he often incorporated into larger studio compositions.[3] Rendered in both crusty, light-charged impasto and free-flowing washes, Potthast's plein-air beach scenes, particularly, won the favorable attention of his contemporaries and the admiration of later collectors and critics. In his own mind, these were "only sketches,"[4] but insofar as they are his simplest and most direct paintings, they are often the most personal and expressive statements in his work.

Potthast's dexterity in manipulating pigment is evident in this work of 1914, a colorful depiction of women and children enjoying the sun and surf on a breezy day. The figures are typically indicated in broad strokes, with no attempt to individualize their features. They are just a few joyous grace notes in a quietly happy composition. The artist must have been pleased with this painting, as a label affixed to the back

indicates that he submitted it to the 1915 Panama-Pacific Exposition in San Francisco.[5]

Potthast painted his lively beach scenes during summer visits to various East Coast resorts, including Provincetown and Gloucester, but at the time of this work his favorite watering place was Coney Island. In the early years of this century a trip to Coney was an exotic and thrilling experience. As Sarah Howell notes, visitors to Luna Park "could drift in a gondola past the facade of the Doge's Palace, or ride a camel through the Streets of Cairo to the clashing of cymbals and the howls of Arab swordsmen . . . . [They] could visit an island in the Philippines complete with fifty-one head-hunting savages, watch volcanoes erupting and dams bursting, go on a trip to the moon, or stroll under an arch made by the huge wings of a naked stucco goddess into Dreamland. Bands played without pause and there was dancing all night in gilded ballrooms." For more athletic types, there was Steeplechase Park, so-named for the wooden horses "that took their riders along a track running all around the fifteen acre park, up and down slopes and in and out of pavilions."[6] Coney Island grew even more crowded after the subway reached it at the time of World War I.

With its many attractions, it is only natural that, in the era before air-conditioning, thousands of middle-class New Yorkers would flock to Coney Island's public beaches to escape the heat. Family groups picnicking and bathing at Brighton and Manhattan Beach provided Potthast with an infinite variety of subject matter and figure compositions that he recorded in oil sketches and studio works. The combinations of these themes were inexhaustible, and Potthast never tired of new variations. The beach life of New York became his virtual trademark.

NANCY RIVARD SHAW

1 Quoted in Arlene Jacobowitz, "Edward Henry Potthast," *Brooklyn Museum Annual*, 1967–68, 122–23.
2 Potthast Papers, Archives of American Art, Washington, D.C., roll N738, frame 400.
3 Ibid., frame 445, "The Week in Art Circles," n.d. (probably 1927).
4 Ibid., frame 428, "In Studio and Gallery," n.d. (probably 1896).
5 This painting does not appear in the catalogue for the exhibition. Instead, Potthast is represented by three examples of his earlier, pre-Impressionist period. They are: *The Ox Team* (no. 370); *The Village Carpenter* (no. 636); and *Milking Time* (no. 571). The date, 1914, is handwritten on the exposition label.
6 Sara Howell, *The Seaside* (London: Studio Vista, 1974), 166–67, 170.

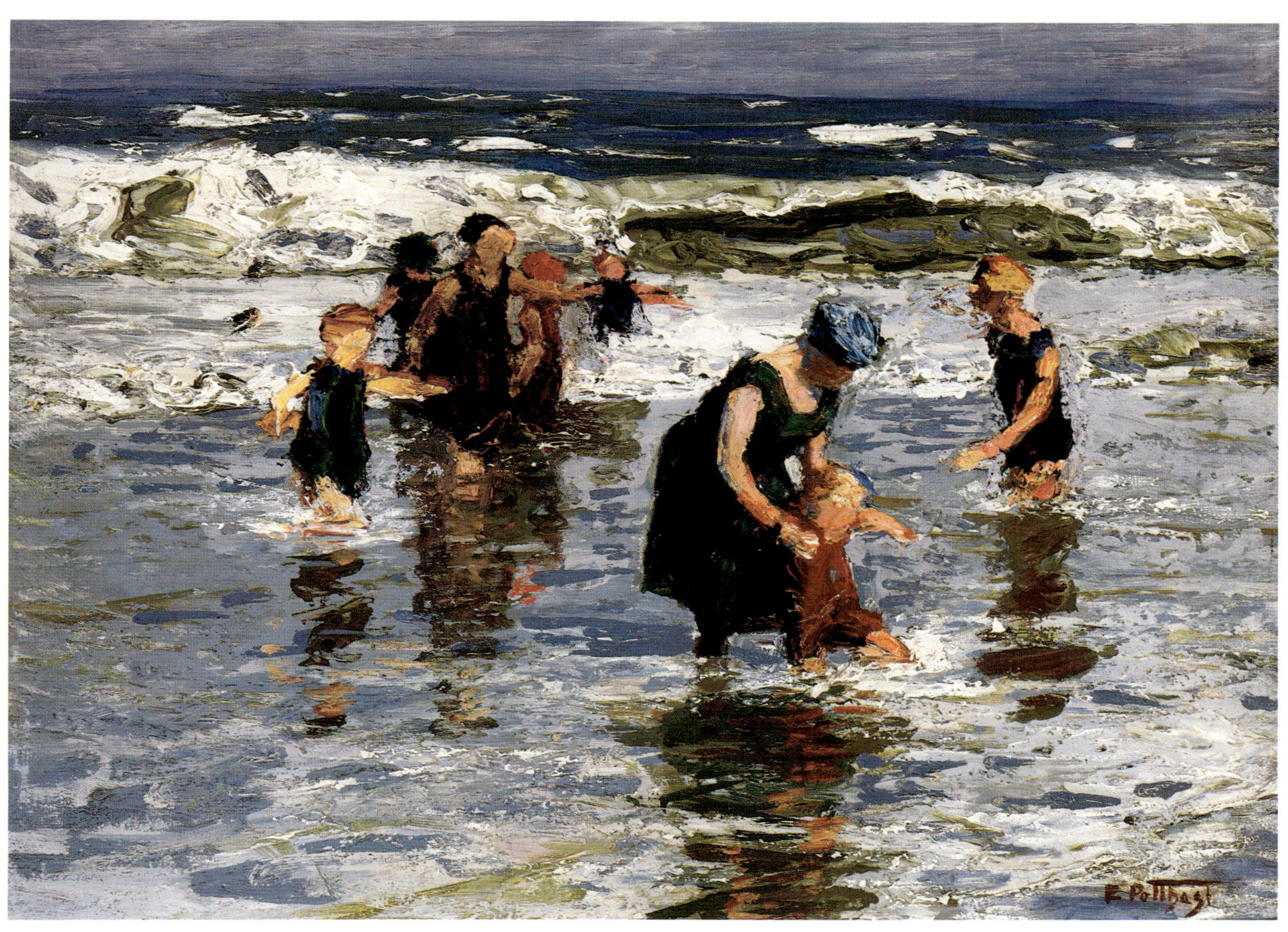

Maurice Brazil Prendergast

1858–1924

Handkerchief Point

c. 1896–97
Watercolor and pencil on paper
13 1/2 x 9 5/8 in. (34.3 x 24.5 cm)

"Mr. Prendergast was born to paint fêtes and he carries a whole Fourth of July in his color-box," wrote a critic in 1899 upon seeing a group of Prendergast's watercolors. "What an irresistible spirit of happy holiday activity pervades his scintillating . . . scenes [of] waves rippling, sun shining over all, brilliantly dressed throngs of men, women and children, all moving, here and there, in a veritable kaleidoscope of life."[1]

Wherever he painted, whether in the parks of Boston and New York, along the boulevards of Paris and the canals of Venice, or on the beaches of New England and Brittany, Prendergast was drawn, not to the private activity, but to the color and movement of crowds of fashionably dressed city-dwellers at their leisure.[2] His thematic focus was a modern one, derived from the French Impressionists, particularly Edouard Manet and Edgar Degas.[3] It was an interest that reflected broad cultural developments in Europe and America.

Following the Industrial Revolution, as ever greater numbers of people moved from the country to the cities, public recreational facilities became essential elements of urban life and culture. In America's cities, the influence of Frederick Law Olmsted and the park movement resulted in the conversion of large tracts of land into parks, playgrounds, and public beaches. With more leisure and money at their disposal, an emerging middle class turned increasingly to these public entertainments for amusement. Fostered by the development of easily accessible and inexpensive public transportation—train, streetcar, boat—a new weekend and vacation culture evolved.[4] More than the work of any other American artist of his time, Prendergast's subjects reflected the great variety of public entertainment available to city-dwellers at the end of the nineteenth century.[5]

In both subject and style, Prendergast was perhaps the first American artist to reflect fully the lessons of French modernism. While the greatest European impact on his work would come in the period from 1909 to 1912, he was, from the time of his first visit to Paris in 1891 to pursue formal art training at the Atelier Colarossi and the Académie Julian, influenced by the tonalities, pattern, and compositional arrangements of James McNeill Whistler, and especially by the imaginative and decorative values of color used by the Nabis, an avant-garde group whose members included Pierre Bonnard, Edouard Vuillard, and Maurice Denis. Soon after returning to Boston in late 1894 or early 1895, Prendergast

began to receive enthusiastic praise for his watercolor views of Paris and French beaches, the critics calling special attention to his manipulation of color and light. Almost overnight he became one of Boston's most celebrated artists,[6] described as the "rage of the town . . . unable to keep pace with the demand."[7]

In Boston's public parks and nearby beaches, Prendergast rediscovered the urban life he had previously found in Paris.[8] *Handkerchief Point*, signed but not dated, can probably be dated to 1896–97 and identified as a view of Nantasket Beach, based on its stylistic and subject similarity to a number of watercolors of Nantasket's rocky headlands done at the same time, among them *Low Tide, Nantasket*, 1896–97 (Williams College Museum of Art, Williamstown, Massachusetts), *Handkerchief Point*, 1896–97 (fig. 1; Museum of Fine Arts, Boston), *Rocky Shore, Nantasket*, 1896–97 (Collection of Mr. and Mrs. Granville M. Brumbaugh), and *Handkerchief Point, Nantasket Beach, No. 2* (Collection of Mr. and Mrs. Meyer P. Potamkin). As there is no recorded point on either the South or North shores of Boston bearing the name Handkerchief Point, one may presume that the name was a local one, no longer in use, given to a spot on Nantasket where people would stand to wave at the passing steamers.[9] In the 1890s Nantasket was a popular seaside resort. A short distance south of Boston and easily reached by steamer or rail, it was renowned for the picturesque beauty of its long, smooth beach and the adjoining rocky headlands, where water surged in among the rocks, casting showers of sparkling spray into the air. People came for a few hours or a few days. Newly built hotels bustled with activity, bands played, and the beach presented the appearance of a town on holiday, as crowds of people arrayed in fine clothes promenaded on the shore and sat or walked on the rocks.[10]

Handkerchief Point is one of a group of watercolors created from 1896 to 1898 (when Prendergast left for Italy) in which many of the characteristics of his later watercolor style are already established: surface pattern, high horizon, empty foreground, and a large number of figures, most of them grouped in the middle ground in complicated spatial interrelationships.[11] Through fluid brushwork, flowing decorative shapes, and exquisitely balanced pools of color, he seems effortlessly to capture the lighthearted mood of city-dwellers on a holiday excursion.

The appearance of spontaneous execution is, however, deceptive. A prolific watercolorist, Prendergast frequently

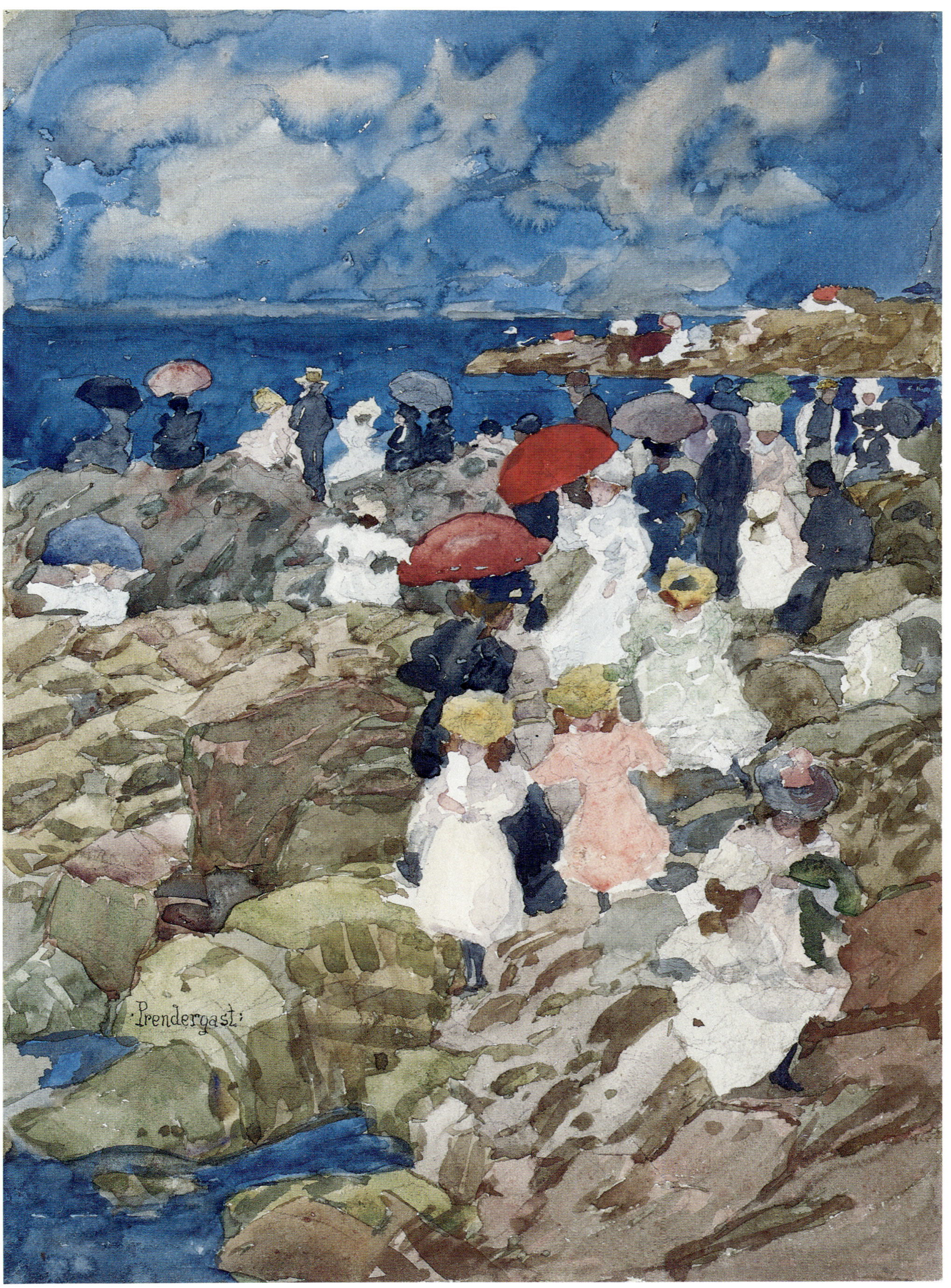

Prendergast

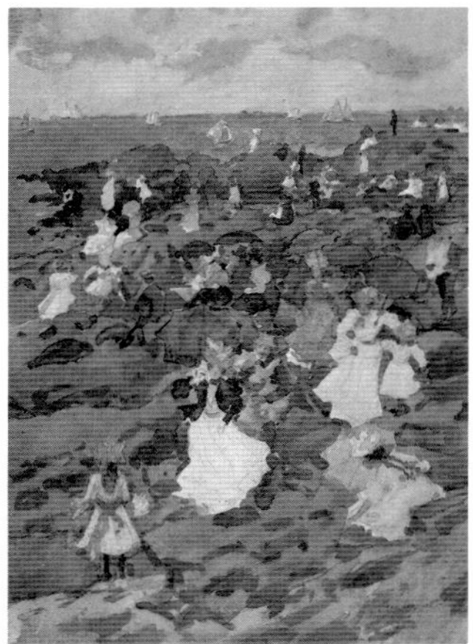

Fig. 1. Maurice Brazil Prendergast, *Handkerchief Point*, 1896, watercolor and pencil on paper, 19 7/8 x 13 3/4 in. (50.6 x 34.9 cm), Museum of Fine Arts, Boston, Gift of Francis W. Fabyan in Memory of Edith Wescott Fabyan

painted the same subject over and over, often working from sketches and varying the composition slightly by changing the vantage point (see, for example, fig. 1). Like all his watercolors, *Handkerchief Point* is an amalgam of observed and imagined images rather than a realistic record. It is built upon a solid foundation of color, tone, draftsmanship, and rhythmic organization. The handling of the watercolor is loose, transparent, and largely unsaturated. With audacious economy he lays down cool shades of blue, indigo, and ochre, with accents of red, in broad, loose washes over summary pencil lines that sparkle against the translucent white of the reserved areas and are orchestrated into patterns that inform the meaning of the picture. The figures in recession are placed vertically, as if climbing up an incline, their serpentine pattern and patchwork of color suggesting the casual, weaving movement of the crowd. The forms are simplified, and the drawing—in pencil as well as brush—is an important graphic element on its own, reinforcing the wash but not subservient to it, capturing individual gestures through animated, quick strokes.

Although presented as if seen from a distance, and despite the generalized, anonymous character of the group, Prendergast's throng is made up of individuals—one can readily distinguish differences in dress, activity, and relationships. Under a bright blue sky filled with scudding white clouds (which Prendergast created by dropping pools of water into the wet blue paint), men, women, and children in pairs or small groups mingle, move precariously among the rocks, or watch the activity on the water. In the lower right foreground, about to move out of the picture, a young woman in a pale pink dress lifts her skirt to step carefully over the rocks. In the center a woman in dark blue accompanied by two young girls in pink, steps gracefully toward a young woman in a billowing white dress who turns to face her, her expression solicitous as she watches the descending figure of another young girl. Both women carry red parasols, and all three girls wear pale ochre hats in the same style, suggesting that this central group of five figures belongs to one family, perhaps a mother and four daughters. The curved forms of the two bright parasols, placed in almost the center of the picture, create a dynamic focal point, drawing

together, through their color and shape, the myriad tones and curves that punctuate the composition and underscore the human relationship of their owners. With such devices, Prendergast brings the whole sheet to life, drawing the viewer into a colorful holiday spectacle.

Paris had established Prendergast's interests in the currents of contemporary life and art. In works like *Handkerchief Point*, he filtered avant-garde European techniques and a subject matter centered on figures seen as color shapes placed in a holiday setting through an American sensibility. Style and content are joined in a seamless fashion. Through fluid, shifting forms and colors, he expresses simultaneously the fleeting brilliant glimpses of a New England holiday crowd on a summer's day and, more subtly, the rapidly changing nature of an urban middle class in flux at the turn of the century.

HELEN A. COOPER

1 "Twelfth Annual Exhibition of the Water Color Club," *Boston Evening Transcript*, March 4, 1899, 10.
2 Hedley Howell Rhys, *Maurice Prendergast* (Cambridge, Mass.: Harvard University Press, 1960), 16.
3 See Milton W. Brown, "Maurice B. Prendergast," in Carol Clark, Nancy Mowll Mathews, Gwendolyn Owens, *Maurice Brazil Prendergast, Charles Prendergast, A Catalogue Raisonné* (Williamstown, Mass.: Williams College Museum of Art, and Munich: Prestel-Verlag, 1990), 15–16; also Carol Clark, "Modern Women in Maurice Prendergast's Boston of the 1890s," in ibid., 23–24 passim. Both chapters are excellent discussions of Prendergast's modernity.
4 Brown, in Clark et al., 16.
5 Clark, in Clark et al., 32.
6 Dominic Madormo, "The 'Butterfly Art' Artist: Maurice Prendergast and His Critics," in Clark et al., 60.
7 Review in *Artists Exhibition and Sale*, C. O. Elliett Gallery, Boston, April 2–May 4, 1897; quoted in ibid.
8 Clark, in Clark et al., 27.
9 I am indebted to Carol Troyen for this information. Ann Greenwood, Dr. John B. Pearce, and Patricia Rausch also assisted in the search for "Handkerchief Point."
10 Dexter Smith, *Cyclopedia of Boston and Vicinity* (Boston: Cashin and Smith, 1886), 232.
11 Brown, in Clark et al., 19.

Artists' Biographies

John George Brown
1831–1913

Brown was born near Durham, England, on November 11, 1831. Apprenticed to a glass cutter at an early age, he began to study art in the evenings with William Bell Scott at the Newcastle School of Design in 1840. Scott was associated with the British Pre-Raphaelite school of painters, and his influence can be seen in the meticulous rendering of illusionistic detail characteristic of Brown's mature painting style. Brown continued part-time studies in antique drawing with the historical and biblical genre painter Robert Scott Lauder upon moving to Edinburgh in 1852. After a summer in London, he emigrated to the United States in 1853, settling in Brooklyn and finding employment at the Brooklyn Flint Glass Company. Two years later he married the daughter of his employer and left the glass works to begin his career as a professional artist. In 1858, he enrolled in classes at the National Academy of Design, where he began exhibiting the following year. Brown would continue to be represented in the National Academy's annual art exhibitions every year, except 1871, until his death.

Around 1860, Brown moved his studio to the Tenth Street Studio Building in Manhattan, an address that many well-known American artists would establish as their workplace over the coming decades. Elected a full member of the Academy in 1863, he also served as that organization's vice president from 1899 to 1903. In addition, the American Watercolor Society made a him a member in 1867 and the society's president from 1887 until 1940. An active and prominent participant in the academic art circles of New York City throughout his artistic career, Brown was also founding member of the Brooklyn Art Society and the Brooklyn Art Association. Many of his depictions of children, particularly the shoe-shine boys of New York City or young girls in the countryside, grew popular from their reproduction, publication, and distribution as chromolithographs. Beginning in the 1860s, he spent his summers away from New York, working in more natural New England surroundings such as the Catskill Mountains, western Massachusetts, or the south shore of Long Island. He enjoyed a large degree of commercial success and wide public recognition for his painting over much of his career. He died on February 8, 1913, in New York City.

William Mason Brown
1828–1898

Brown was born in Troy, New York, in 1828. When he was fourteen years old, he was employed by Thomas Grinnell, a local ornamental painter, and studied portraiture with Abel Buel Moore. In 1850 Brown moved to Newark, New Jersey, with Grinnell, and there began to paint landscapes characterized by the kind of romantic naturalism found in works by the Hudson River School painters. In 1858, he moved to Brooklyn, New York. He continued to paint landscapes, but in the 1860s moved on to still lifes of fruits and flowers depicted in a natural outdoor setting or on a tabletop with elegant glassware, metalware, or Victorian bric-a-brac. His still lifes are characterized by their precise detail, high finish, and vivid color.

Active in the arts community, Brown exhibited regularly at the National Academy of Design from 1859 to 1891, the Brooklyn Art Association from 1865 to 1886, and the Pennsylvania Academy of the Fine Arts from 1869 to 1891. He received wide recognition as a still-life painter in the 1860s, when his work *Basket of Peaches Upset* (where?) was purchased by the prominent New York art dealer William Schaus for two thousand dollars. This painting and other of his still lifes of fruits and flowers were then widely distributed through the process of chromolithography. Brown died in 1898 in Brooklyn from complications caused by sunstroke and its accompanying paralysis.

Samuel S. Carr
1837–1908

Although we know that Carr was born in England on October 15, 1837, it is not known when he emigrated to the United States. In 1865, he attended a class in mechanical drawing at Cooper Union in New York City. From 1870 to 1907, he lived in Brooklyn with his sister and brother-in-law, sharing studio space with the painter Clinton Loveridge. Exhibiting frequently at the National Academy of Design, the Brooklyn Art Association, and the Brooklyn Art Club, he at one time served as president of this last organization.

Carr apparently made a living from his paintings of pastoral landscapes with domesticated animals and natural settings populated by leisurely figures. Such subjects were largely inspired by seventeenth-century Dutch genre painting and nineteenth-century French works of the Barbizon School. His representations of leisure activities and rural landscapes appealed to popular American tastes of the period. His wide views of well-dressed beach strollers at Coney Island and other locations along the south shore of Long Island provide a unique record of prosperity and entertainment in late-nineteenth-century America.

A bachelor until his death on February 25, 1908, Carr left behind little documentary information about his personal life. His paintings create a vision of American society that remains the most complete record of this artist's life.

William Merritt Chase
1849–1916

A dynamic force in American art of the late nineteenth century, Chase was born in Williamsburg (later renamed Ninevah), Indiana. After early training with a local painter, Barton S. Hays, Chase enrolled in the National Academy of Design in 1869. While supporting himself as a still-life painter in St. Louis, he found patrons willing to finance his study in Munich, a major art center in the 1870s. There he studied at the Royal Academy under Alexander von Wagner and Karl von Piloty and came under the influence of the realist Wilhelm Leibl. Chase adopted the somber palette and bravura brushwork typical of the Munich school. He also traveled to Venice in 1877–78, accompanied by the American painters Frank Duveneck and John H. Twachtman.

In 1878 Chase returned to America and acquired the most desirable space in the Tenth Street Studio Building in New York City.

Lavishly decorated, the studio became a celebrated salon and the setting for some of his most ambitious paintings. He soon abandoned the dark tones of his Munich years, gradually combining an animated surface with a lighter palette. During the early 1880s, Chase took several trips to Europe, visiting Spain, Holland, France, and England. In 1886 he had his first one-person exhibition at the Boston Art Club.

That same year Chase married his model, Alice Gerson. His domestic life increasingly occupied his artistic attention, for his family—eventually including eight children—became the subjects of many of his paintings depicting their leisure life. Around the time of his marriage, Chase also began to paint innovative views of New York City's urban parks, his first sustained efforts at landscape. His palette became increasingly impressionist in tone, culminating in the light-filled 1890s landscapes made at Shinnecock, Long Island, near the Chase family home. His Shinnecock interiors, often featuring family members, are only now being appreciated for their spatial and psychological complexity. Throughout his career, Chase also painted masterful portraits and still lifes. His freely executed still lifes of fish received much critical acclaim in the closing decades of his life.

Perhaps the most influential teacher of his generation, Chase was one of the first instructors at the newly formed Art Students League, where he taught from 1878 to 1885, from 1886 to 1896, and again from 1907 to 1912. In addition, he held teaching positions at the Brooklyn Art Association (1887, 1891–95) and the Pennsylvania Academy of the Fine Arts (1896–1909), and also conducted summer classes in Europe in the early 1900s. His dedication to teaching led to the founding of two of his own schools: the Shinnecock Summer School of Art (1891–1902), the first important school of open-air painting in America; and the Chase School of Art (1896–1907), later renamed the New York School of Art and now known as Parsons School of Design. Although he disapproved of modernist tendencies, Chase's emphasis on technique fostered a generation of avant-garde modernists, including Joseph Stella, Charles Sheeler, and Georgia O'Keeffe.

Chase further shaped the course of American art through his prominent role in artistic politics. He was a founder and for more than ten years president of the Society of American Artists (1880, 1885–95), and a member of both the prestigious Ten American Painters and the social Tile Club. Elected an associate member of the National Academy of Design in 1888, Chase became an Academician two years later. As a founder and contributing member of the Society of Painters in Pastel, he helped to elevate the status of the medium. He experimented in various media, including oils, pastel, tempera, and prints. His works were exhibited widely in America and Europe, and won many awards and medals. As an artist, teacher, and personality, Chase achieved international stature, becoming one of the leading spokesmen for his generation's belief in the dignity and importance of the artistic profession.

Charles Courtney Curran

1861–1942

Born in Hartford, Kentucky, in 1861 and brought up in Ohio, Curran enrolled in the Cincinnati Academy of Design in 1880 before going to New York the following year to study at the Art Students League. He began exhibiting at the National Academy of Design as early as 1883. His 1888 contribution, *A Breezy Day* (Pennsylvania Academy of the Fine Arts), garnered him a Hallgarten Prize and election to Associate status. One of several rural genre scenes executed in 1887–89, it depicts two laundresses spreading sheets out to dry on a windy day. The real subject, the solidly drawn women seen in bright sunlight and the strongly articulated surface patterns, would remain Curran's primary concerns throughout his career. He was already a confident painter in 1889 when he entered the Académie Julian to work under Lefebvre, Constant, and Doucet. He exhibited at the Salon from 1889 to 1891, receiving an honorable mention for *Lotus Lilies* (Terra Museum of American Art) in 1890, which depicts women in a rowboat surrounded by enormous lilies. In addition to scenes, like *Chrysanthemums* (p. 00), that recorded and interpreted contemporary life, in Paris Curran also began painting poetic, Symbolist-related images of nudes and flowers—for example, *Scent of the Rose* (Private Collection).

After his return to New York in 1891, his paint handling became somewhat looser, perhaps in response to the impressionist concerns of his contemporaries, although his primarily female figures were still carefully delineated. On occasion, they were also more prettified than in his earlier work. Curran won a medal at the World's Columbian Exposition, as well as the Clark Prize in 1893. He was awarded the Hallgarten Prize again in 1895 for *At the Sculpture Exhibition* (Yale University Art Gallery), but the prize was later withdrawn because it was reserved for artists under thirty-five, the age Curran turned during the exhibition. An unusual choice of subject matter for him, the painting documents the 1895 National Sculpture Exhibition in New York and records the presence of the artist and his wife. Curran was active in the fray of the New York art world, teaching at Brooklyn's Pratt Institute in 1895–96 and conducting the antique and life classes at the Art Students League from 1901 to 1904. He was assistant director of the American art exhibitions at both the Paris Exposition of 1900 and the Pan-American Exposition in Buffalo, New York, in 1902. In 1904 he was elected to full membership in the National Academy of Design, serving as secretary of that institution for about twenty years.

Around this time Curran discovered Cragsmoor, New York, in the Shawangunk Mountains, a few miles from Ellenville. An art colony had been established there in the 1880s by genre painter Edward Lamson Henry, and at the turn of the century many painters, writers, and musicians were drawn to it. Cragsmoor's spectacular scenery and proximity to New York City made it ideal for artistic life, and Curran and his wife, Grace, became important members of the art colony. From October 1907 through December 1910, they both contributed regularly to *Palette and Bench*, an arts magazine affiliated with Keramic Studio in Syracuse and edited by Adelaide Alsop-Robineau. Grace Curran contributed feature articles and served as assistant editor, becoming editor for the December 1910 issue. Charles Curran wrote a regular series, "Class in Oil Painting." Together they cultivated a garden renowned for its beauty around their home in Cragsmoor.

During his lifetime, Curran was considered a chronicler of contemporary life, a painter of domestic genre scenes, a landscapist, and a prolific portraitist. But first and foremost he was a painter of the ideal female figure, the embodiment of health and beauty. At Cragsmoor, he specialized in rendering women and young girls posed high on cliffs, dramatically silhouetted against patterned skies. One of the best known of these paintings is *On the Heights* (1909, The Brooklyn Museum).

Robert Spear Dunning

1829–1905

The principal painter of the Fall River School of still-life painting, Dunning was born in Brunswick, Maine, on January 3, 1829. The son of Joseph and Rebecca Spear, he moved with his family to Fall River, Massachusetts, when he was five years old, where his father is reputed to have built the first marine railway. He was educated in the local school system and, as a young man, worked in the textile mills of Fall River and spent three years at sea on coastal vessels. Sometime in the early 1840s, Dunning began his art training with James Roberts of Thomaston, Maine, and in 1849 he went to New York to study with Daniel Huntington at the National Academy of Design. During his New York years, Dunning exhibited genre and portrait paintings at the American Art-Union in 1850 and at the National Academy of Design in 1850–51.

In 1852 Dunning returned to Fall River, where he remained for the rest of his life, establishing a studio in Providence, Rhode Island, and marrying Mehitable D. Hill in 1869. In Fall River, Dunning painted landscapes, seascapes, and portraits of the mayors, congressmen, and other prominent members of his community. In 1865, however, he started to paint still lifes, which he concentrated on for the rest of his career, exhibiting locally and in Boston, Providence, and again in New York at the National Academy in 1880. He taught private art classes at his studio and, beginning in 1870, at the Fall River Evening Drawing School. Under Dunning's influence, other artists in Fall River turned to still life, becoming prominent painters in their own right; among them were Bryant Chapin, Franklin H. Miller, Albert F. Munroe, and Abbie Luella Zuill. In 1892 Dunning was commissioned by the Washington Society of Fall River to copy the full-length portrait of George Washington by Gilbert Stuart that was located in Newport, Rhode Island, in the senate chamber of the old state house. Today, the portrait hangs in the Fall River Public Library. Dunning died of apoplexy at his summer home in Westport Harbor, Massachusetts, on August 12, 1905.

De Scott Evans

1847–1898

Born March 28. 1847, in Boston, Indiana, Evans was the son of Dr. David Souder Evans and Nancy Davenport Evans. In the early 1860s, he attended Miami University in Oxford, Ohio, and by 1865, he had begun his art training in Cincinnati, under the tutelage of Albert Beaugureau. In 1872, he married Alice Josephine Burk(e) and embarked on a teaching career. During that year, Evans was an instructor of music and art at Smithson College in Logansport, Indiana, and from 1873 to 1875 chairman of the fine arts department at Mount Union College in Alliance, Ohio. In 1874, he opened a studio in Cleveland, where he was active in the art community as a portrait and genre painter, becoming one of the founders of the Cleveland Art Club in 1876.

From 1877 to 1878, Evans went to Paris to study with the renowned academic painter, Adolphe-William Bouguereau (1825–1905). Upon his return to the United States, he continued to teach, becoming one of the founders of the Cleveland Academy of Art, where he served as codirector and art instructor. In 1881, he showed his first works at the National Academy of Design in New York, and exhibited there regularly for the rest of his career. During the 1880s, he painted *Winter Evening at Lawnfield* (Western Reserve Historical Society, Cleveland), a commemorative portrait of President James A. Garfield and his family.

In 1887, Evans left the Midwest and opened a studio in New York City, establishing his family residence in Yonkers. Active in the New York art community and a member of the Salmagundi Club, he continued to exhibit genre paintings at the National Academy of Design. He also sold paintings in Cleveland and exhibited at the Brooklyn Art Association and Gill's Art Galleries in Springfield, Massachusetts. In the mid-1890s, he moved his family residence to Plainfield, New Jersey, spending his winters in Jamaica in 1893–94 and 1896–97. On July 4, 1898, Evans and his three daughters died in a shipwreck of the French liner *La Bourgogne* on their way to Paris, where he was commissioned to paint a ceiling and frieze decoration.

Evans's earliest canvases are signed D. S. Evans or D. Scott Evans, shortened versions of the name given to him at birth, David Scott Evans. After studying in France, he evidently wished to be identified with that country and changed his name to De Scott Evans. His trompe l'oeil still-life paintings, for which he apparently received no acclaim throughout his career, are signed with a variety of pseudonyms, including S. S. David, Stanley David, Stanley S. David, Scott David, or simply David. Without the support of firm evidence to prove otherwise, these works have been assigned to De Scott Evans, based on their strong similarity to one another in terms of technique, style, and subject matter.

William Glackens

1870–1938

Born in Philadelphia in 1870, Glackens first professional experience was an as illustrator for *The Record*. He later moved to *The Press*, another Philadelphia newspaper. It was during this early period that he became associated with other artist reporters, specifically, John Sloan, George Luks, and Everett Shinn. It was Shinn who encouraged Glackens to join him in attending evening classes at the Pennsylvania Academy of the Fine Arts. In 1894 Glackens began to share a studio with Robert Henri, who had also become his mentor. A year later Glackens traveled to Europe where he studied many of the old masters, especially Frans Hals, and was drawn to the work of Edouard Manet. Upon his return to the States he settled in New York, where his old friend and associate George Luks arranged for him to take a position at *The World*.

Glackens worked as a freelance illustrator until 1915; but his major focus from the turn of the century was painting. In 1906 he traveled to Europe for an extended visit, returning in 1908 to participate in The Eight's exhibition at Macbeth Galleries. Organized by Henri, this show included works by Sloan, Luks, Shinn, Ernst Lawson, Arthur B. Davies, and Maurice Prendergast. After the close of this show, Glackens's style began to show the influence of the spirit of Impressionism, leaving behind his Henri-inspired realism. By the Armory Show of 1913, he appears to have been completely under the stylistic influence of Pierre-Auguste Renoir.

In 1913 Glackens served on the selection committee for the Armory Show, having spent the previous year in France assembling the basis of the Barnes Collection. Dr. Albert Barnes was a childhood friend and sent Glackens abroad to act as his advisor and agent. Glackens continued to travel frequently to France and paint successfully, adding to his considerable ouevre until his unexpected death in 1938.

John Haberle

1853–1933

Haberle was born in New Haven, Connecticut, in 1853 to German immigrants. In 1870, at the age of fourteen, he apprenticed with Punderson and Crisand, local lithographers and engravers, following which he remained in New Haven as a lithographer, possibly for W. F. Hobson. After working for two years as a lithographer in Montreal, Haberle moved on to Providence, Rhode Island, and then to New York City from about 1878 to 1880. In 1880, he returned to New Haven, where he worked for the paleontologist Othniel Charles Marsh, founder of the Peabody Museum at Yale University. While Haberle cleaned fossils and made plaster castes, he continued with lithography, possibly for some of Marsh's books and for local clients. He was also a draftsman and a painter at this time, and two of his earliest drawings from 1882 contain examples of trompe l'oeil.

After a year at the National Academy of Design in New York City in 1884, Haberle returned to New Haven and his job with Marsh. As a founding member of the New Haven Sketch Club, he taught drawing, without pay, and exhibited his paintings there. At the same time, he established a studio in his home. By about 1886, he

had fully embraced a trompe l'oeil style and exhibited some of these works at the National Academy of Design, the Art Institute of Chicago, and the Pennsylvania Academy of the Fine Arts. By 1893, however, Haberle's failing eyesight was becoming an impediment to his painting of trompe l'oeil, by the mid-1890s he had begun to paint still lifes and animals in a more impressionistic style, although his last trompe l'oeil was produced in 1898 (*Japanese Corner*). Haberle died in New Haven in 1933.

William Michael Harnett

1848–1892

Perhaps the best known of the late-nineteenth-century American trompe l'oeil painters, Harnett had a short but very productive career. Born in Clonakilty, County Cork, Ireland, on August 10, 1848, he emigrated to Philadelphia with his family when he was a baby. He was raised in a family that valued good craftsmanship: his father was a shoemaker; his brother, a saddlemaker; and his mother and three sisters, all seamstresses. As an adolescent, Harnett worked to help support his family after his father's untimely death by drowning. At seventeen he took a job as an engraver, a profession he would follow while studying art until he could establish his own painting studio.

Harnett began his studies in 1865 at the Pennsylvania Academy of the Fine Arts. At twenty-one he moved to New York, where he attended classes at Cooper Union and the National Academy of Design while employed as an engraver for both Wood and Hughes and Tiffany and Co. In 1875 he set up a studio at 104 E. Eleventh Street, where he concentrated on his highly precisionistic still-life arrangements. About a year later he returned to Philadelphia, took a studio at Wistar House, 400 Locust Street, and continued his academic pursuits at the Pennsylvania Academy. Under the tutelage of Thomas Eakins and others, Harnett's fellow students included Kenyon Cox, Thomas Anshutz, and John Frederick Peto. By exhibiting on a regular basis in New York, Philadelphia, and elsewhere, Harnett managed to save enough money to go to Europe in 1880.

After a brief stay in London, Harnett painted a series of commissions for a wealthy patron in Frankfurt. He spent the next four years in Munich diligently studying the still-life techniques of the seventeenth-century Dutch masters. This proved to be a prolific period, during which he held his own in the competitive art market of Munich, where he managed to show and sell paintings from his st udio to both traveling Americans and European buyers. His still lifes were exhibited on a weekly basis at the Kunstverein, an artist cooperative in Munich, and a number of his works were still being shown in various venues in United States. Responding to criticism about the merits of his ability, Harnett moved to Paris in 1885 to prepare for his Salon debut. He spent three months working on one painting, the fourth version of *After the Hunt* (1885), and was ultimately rewarded with critical recognition at the Paris Salon.

The following year, Harnett returned to New York via London to begin the most lucrative period of his career. He found his work to be highly popular with the public, even though art critics of his day tended to denigrate his engaging illusionism. Although failing health curtailed the number of paintings Harnett was able to produce over the next six years, the lessons he had learned in Europe enabled him to achieve notable success with a number of important works. The forty-four-year-old Harnett died after a brief illness at New York Hospital on October 29, 1892.

Childe Hassam

1859–1935

Born in Dorchester, Massachusetts, into a prosperous and old New England family, that included both the writer Nathaniel Hawthorne and the painter William Morris Hunt, Frederick Childe Hassam (at the suggestion of a friend he later dropped the Frederick) would become in his own lifetime one of the leaders and best-known members of the American Impressionist movement. After making a reputation as an accomplished illustrator, Hassam was determined to hone his skills in drawing and painting, studying anatomy from the anatomist and self-taught painter, William Rimmer, at the Lowell Institute and taking painting lessons from the well-known Ignaz Gaugengigl. By 1882, Hassam had his first one-man exhibition at the Williams and Everett Gallery in Boston.

In 1883 Hassam embarked on a trip to Europe, during which he became enamoured of such the early-nineteenth-century British painters as John Constable, J. M. W. Turner, and Richard P. Bonington. In fact, Hassam claimed throughout his career that his works, both in oil and watercolor, owed more to these English artists than to the French Impressionists. By 1885 he had begun to paint more frequently in oils, and by 1886 he had at last gained a reputation as a professional artist.

In the same year, Hassam and his new bride, Kathleen Maud Doane, left again for Europe. The couple settled in Paris, where Hassam had spent little time on his earlier trip. Like many of his American colleagues, he studied at the Académie Julian, under the supervision of Gustave Boulanger and Jules-Joseph Lefebvre, and made occasional visits to the French countryside outside Paris. During this time, he exhibited at the annual salons, winning a medal at the Salon of 1888. After the Exposition Universelle in Paris in 1889, in which he exhibited, Hassam returned to the United States and settled in New York City, where he maintained a residence for the rest of his life.

During the 1890s his friendship with such artists as Willard Metcalf and John Twachtman grew steadily. Already an active member of the New York Watercolor Club and the Pastel Society, Hassam, along with Metcalf and seven other prominent artists, withdrew from the Society of American Artists to found a group that came to be known as the Ten American Painters. Their aim was to create a more hospitable and less competitive environment in which to exhibit their works. By the last exhibition of the Ten in 1918 (the first was in 1898), and due in large part to the participation of Hassam and the other leaders of the American Impressionist movement, this group itself had begun to be regarded as an academy of American Impressionism.

By 1895, Hassam had established a pattern of spending winters in the city and summers vacationing in artists' colonies along the Connecticut and Long Island shores (he and his wife bought a home in East Hampton, Long Island, in 1917). His involvement in such colonies as those established by the writer Celia Thaxter in Appeldore on the Isle of Shoals off the coast of New Hampshire, and by Frances Griswold in Old Lyme, Connecticut, has since become legendary. His regular participation in these informal artistic "summer camps" fostered Impressionism in American painting at the turn of the century.

An extremely prolific artist, Hassam excelled in many media, including oils, watercolors, pastels, and prints. As he grew older, he began to work more and more in prints, creating exquisite etchings and lithographs of his favorite subjects: tree-lined landscapes and urban scenes. By his death in 1935, He had gained a national reputation through numerous major exhibitions across the country. He bequeathed all his works to the American Academy of Arts and Letters and stipulated that the proceeds from their sale be used to create a fund which would allow the institution to purchase works by other American artists. A generous, cheerful, and sociable man, Childe Hassam remains, in the eyes of most critics, the father of American Impressionism.

Martin Johnson Heade

1819–1904

Heade was born on August 11, 1819, in Lumberville, Pennsylvania, a small town in Bucks County. His father, a prosperous businessman, encouraged his son's early interest in art. Heade studied as a young man with the Quaker naive painter Edward Hicks, but also benefited from the Philadelphia milieu of the Peales, Thomas Sully, and Thomas Doughty. The artist's career until his move to New York City in 1859 has not been exactly charted. He appears to have been a competent, academic-style portraitist and genre painter working in Philadelphia, Trenton, and Providence. Unlike most of his peers, however, Heade traveled to Europe at a young age, spending two years in Italy, France, England, and possibly Spain in the late 1830s. He returned to Europe at least once during his career and was an inveterate traveler throughout North America and, in the 1860s and 1870s, in South America and the Caribbean.

Heade's arrival in New York associated him quickly with Frederic Edwin Church, who worked in the Tenth Street studio that had already become a center for New York landscapists and in which Heade soon worked. His landscapes from the 1860s possess a luminist spirit also embraced by such contemporaries as John Kensett and Sanford Robinson Gifford and are most numerously represented by marsh scenes of New England and seascapes. Heade's simple, horizontally stratified landscapes, with limited tonal range, have been viewed as the archetype of luminism, though in the moody weather effects, of, for instance, *Sudden Shower, Newbury Marshes*, he evokes, too, the landscapes of Constable.

Heade first traveled to Brazil in 1863, attracted there probably by Church's success in depicting the exotic South American landscape. There he produced the *Gems of Brazil*, a series of small paintings of hummingbirds and at least one butterfly and the forebear of his important series of paintings of hummingbirds and orchids or passion flowers. He went to Nicaragua in 1866, and in 1869 and 1870 to Colombia and Jamaica, developing for the remainder of the century images of tropical enchantment, represented mostly by flowers and birds but also including such larger tropical landscapes as *Sunset: A Scene in Brazil*. His spectacular orchid and bird scenes were often purchased by travelers and collectors with strong interests in science, while his domestic marsh scenes appealed more to bourgeois tastes. Heade, though not a natural scientist, was correctly regarded as having a deep understanding of the mechanics of nature as well as a personal fascination with birds, about which he wrote extensively. Among the major landscapists of the period, only Heade produced still lifes as a serious element of his oeuvre. The artist's late work is distinguished particularly by a remarkable series of flower still lifes, a major example of which is *Magnolias on a Blue Velvet Cloth*, in which large tropical blossoms are arrayed suggestively on velvet, evoking an enigmatic languor.

Heade was neither famous nor rich in his lifetime, and by the time of his death the advent of Impressionism to the United States and the success of Ashcan imagery had driven his work into even deeper obscurity. It was not until the 1940s that he was rediscovered and until the 1960s that extensive scholarship on his paintings was undertaken. His own achievement of security and modest financial success began only with his marriage in 1883, his resettlement in St. Augustine, Florida, and his new friendship with his only major patron, the oil magnate Henry Morrison Flagler. Flagler, the pioneer of Florida real-estate speculators, established St. Augustine not only as a major resort but as an artist colony in which Heade thrived for the remainder of his life. Heade enjoyed an active old age in which he wrote and painted until only weeks before his death on September 4, 1904.

Edward Lamson Henry

1841–1919

Henry was born in Charleston, South Carolina, where he lived until he was seven years old. By 1848 his family had moved to New York City, and he lived for some time in Connecticut with his grandparents, the Stows. From an early age he showed an interest in drawing, and he began his art training in New York in 1855 with Walter M. Oddie. In 1858 Henry moved to Philadelphia, where he continued his studies at the Pennsylvania Academy of the Fine Arts, exhibiting his first work there in 1859. The following year he went to Europe, studying art in Paris with Marc-Charles-Gabriel Gleyre and Gustave Courbet and taking the grand tour. He traveled abroad again in 1871, 1875, and 1881.

When Henry returned to New York City from his first trip to Europe in 1863, he set up his studio at the Tenth Street Studio Building, where he worked until 1885. In 1864 he left New York temporarily to serve as a captain's clerk in the Union army, a position that allowed him to sketch Civil War scenes. Some of these sketches he later turned into finished paintings. An avid collector of antique carriages, costumes, furniture, glass, engravings, pottery, and architectural ornament, Henry used both his artifacts and photographs as visual resources for his paintings. His meticulously finished genre paintings of both contemporary and historical subjects appealed to a wide audience, and from an early age he achieved financial success. Throughout his career he exhibited regularly at the National Academy of Design, the Pennsylvania Academy of the Fine Arts, and the Brooklyn Art Association. He

was elected an associate of the National Academy in 1867 and a full member in 1869, and was awarded medals at the world expositions in Chicago, Buffalo, Charleston, and St. Louis. The fact that many reproductions of Henry's works were produced in the 1880s attests to his wide popularity.

In 1875, Henry married Frances Livingston Wells, and in 1883 the couple established their summer residence in Cragsmoor, New York, an agricultural community near Ellenville in the Shawangunk Mountains. His enthusiasm for Cragsmoor, its simple way of life and pristine nature, attracted many New York artists there, and the village became a summer art colony. Using the indigenes of Cragsmoor as models for his artwork, Henry produced genre paintings of contemporary rural life. He was an active member of the Century Association, the American Watercolor Society, and the Salmagundi Club. In 1919, he died of pneumonia in Ellenville, New York.

Otis Kaye

1885–1974

A latter-day proponent of trompe l'oeil painting, Otis Kaye was born in 1885 in Neemah, Michigan, where his German immigrant father, Werner Kaye, had a lumber business. After his father died in a mill accident, Kaye moved with his mother, Frieda Millabeke Kaye, to New York in 1904. Stimulated by the art he saw there, he frequented the New York School of Art but never enrolled as a student. Around this time, he met Nicholas A. Brooks, a trompe l'oeil artist, who most impressed him. Kaye acquired two of Brooks's paintings and, years later, paid him homage by imitating his style and subjects.

After living in New York for a year, Kaye and his mother moved to Dresden, Germany, where he studied engineering. Here he was exposed to the precision draftsmanship that he would later use in his artwork. After he graduated, the family relocated to Hamburg, where Mrs. Kaye died in 1916. After World War I, Kaye moved back to the United States. He settled in Pittsburgh until the mid-1920s, when he married Dresden resident Alma Goldstein.

Although he earned a profitable living as an engineer, Kaye speculated in stock investments; when the market crashed in 1929, he lost his financial security. While he was unemployed during the Great Depression, he and his wife, son, and daughter moved to Chicago to live with relatives. During World War II, Kaye and his cousin, Paul Banks, formed a successful civil engineering firm called J. J. Billsby and Company.

Kaye's art production was a private hobby rather than a vocation. He never exhibited his work publicly and sold only two paintings during his lifetime. His earliest known paintings date to around 1917, when he returned to the United States after the war. While living in Chicago nearly a decade later, Kaye took a few art lessons. He taught himself etching by copying the works of Rembrandt and Whistler, but always included objects of contemporary life in his copies, giving them a personal, often humorous, touch. He produced between twenty to thirty small still lifes in oil on wood panel, more than a dozen large canvases with figurative subjects or more complex still-life compositions, and a prodigious number of intricate drawings and etchings portraying animals, insects, and birds.

Kaye was particularly drawn to trompe l'oeil painting, probably because of its close relationship to his technical training and his exposure to the art of Brooks, Harnett, Peto, and Haberle. His paintings often included puns and "in-jokes" that relate to the work of Dada artists, to whom Kaye may have been exposed in Germany. A substantial number of works focused on currency and had ironic titles such as *A Fool and His Money*, *Hidden Assets*, *Money to Burn*, and *The Only Constant Is Change*.

Kaye continued painting in oil, ink, and watercolor into the early 1950s. In 1966, he moved back to Dresden, possibly to locate his missing son, who may have died during the war. By the time of Kaye's death in Dresden in 1974, most of his works were in the possession of his family and friends.

William Leroy Metcalf

1858–1925

Born in Lowell, Massachusetts, Metcalf served a brief apprentice-ship to a wood engraver then, in 1876, entered the studio of the landscape painter Charles Loring Brown while also attending life-drawing classes at the Lowell Institute. He advanced his training at the Massachusetts Normal Art School and the School of Fine Arts, Boston.

To support his art education, Metcalf turned to illustration, and in the early 1880s he traveled twice to the Southwest to sketch the Zuni tribe for popular periodicals. With his earnings as an illustra-tor and from the sale of some paintings, he went to Europe in 1883, first visiting England and then Paris, where he studied at the Académie Julian under Gustave Boulanger and Jules-Joseph Lefebvre. During the summer months he sketched and painted in the countryside at Brittany, Grez-sur-Loing, and Giverny, the home of Claude Monet. An 1887 visit to Tunis and Morocco inspired the large painting *Arab Market* (location unknown), which received an honorable mention at the Salon in 1888.

In 1889 Metcalf returned to Boston, then moved to New York where he taught at the Art Students League and the Cooper Institute. Along with nine other prominent artists, who came to be known as the Ten American Painters, Metcalf was one of the first to sign the Ten's agreement to secede from the Society of American Artists, and he exhibited with the group regularly after 1897, but his work (chiefly portraits in the 1890s) did not receive satisfying critical attention until after 1903, when he underwent a personal crisis and turned anew to landscape painting. The success of what Metcalf termed his "first personal exhibition," held at Fischel, Adler, and Schwartz Gallery, New York, the following February, was immediate. The critic Royal Cortissoz praised all twenty-one paintings as evidence of Metcalf's "new spirit" and "truth to the very soul of the American landscape." From that time on the artist devoted himself to recording the changing moods and seasons of the New England countryside.

Francis Davis Millet

1846–1912

Born in Massachusetts, Millet graduated from Harvard in 1869, after which he worked as an editor for three Boston newspapers, *The Daily Advertiser*, the *Courier*, and the *Saturday Evening Gazette*. In 1871 he left New England to study art at the Royal Academy, Antwerp, under Joseph van Lerius and Nicaise de Keyser, yet he soon abandoned the painterly style he learned there for a more precise realism. During the 1870s Millet established himself in the United States as a portraitist and painter of domestic scenes. He also worked on several mural programs, including one under John La Farge for Trinity Church, Boston, and another under Louis C. Tiffany for the Seventh Regiment Armory, New York. By the early 1880s, Millet was dividing his time between London and New York: he served as a daily correspondent for the *London Daily News* and the *New York Herald*; published art criticism and fiction; and exhibited paintings at the Royal Academy, London, and at the National Academy of Design in New York.

From 1882 until 1892, Millet was part of an American artists' colony in Broadway, Worchestershire, England, a village described by Henry James as "lying among meadows and hedges, in the very heart of the country, . . . the perfection of the old English rural tradition." Of the members of the "Broadway Group," which included Edwin Howland Blashfield and John Singer Sargent, Millet and Edwin Austin Abbey were most fascinated with imag-ing the English past of the seventeenth and eighteenth centuries. Millet's interest in the past also prompted him in 1892 to organize the restoration of Broadway's oldest domestic building, the four-teenth-century Abbot's Grange.

From 1882 until 1888, most likely influenced by the work of his close friend Lawrence Alma-Tadema, Millet painted genre scenes with classical Greek and Roman subjects. His focus on classicism reflected the goals of the late-nineteenth-century American Renaissance movement that stressed the adaptation of classical and Renaissance styles to American art. He contributed to this move-ment both by lecturing on Roman costume and by participating in Renaissance-inspired mural projects in St. Paul, Newark, Cleveland, Jersey City, and Baltimore.

Apart from painting and teaching, Millet served on the administra-tive boards of various artistic organizations, most notably the Society of American Artists, the American Federation of Arts, the National Academy of Design, and the American Academy in Rome. He was particularly active as a judge and organizer for sev-eral world's fairs, including the 1873 Vienna Exposition, the 1878 Paris Exposition, and the 1893 World's Columbian Exposition. By the time of his death in 1912 on the *Titanic*, Millet had already achieved a noteworthy career and was, as Henry James pointed out, "very modern, in the sense of having tried many things and availed himself of all the facilities of his time."

William McGregor Paxton

1869–1941

Born in Baltimore on June 22, 1869, Paxton grew up in Newton, Massachusetts. While still in high school, he attended evening art classes at the Cowles School of Art in Boston. Gaining a scholarship there in 1887, he studied with the American academic painter Dennis Miller Bunker. In 1889, he left for Paris to study at the Ecole des Beaux-Arts with Bunker's former instructor, the French realist Jean-Léon Gérôme. Spending four years in Paris under Gérôme's tutelage, Paxton developed the finely hewn illusionism and carefully controlled composition that marks his mature style. He returned to Boston in 1893 and married the artist Elizabeth Okie in 1899. He began painting the interior scenes reminiscent of seventeenth-century genre pictures by the Dutch master Vermeer for which he is best known. Paxton's interest in Vermeer was shared by a group of painters known as the Boston School, which also included Frank Weston Benson (1862–1951), Joseph Rodefer DeCamp, Philip Leslie Hale, and Edmund Charles Tarbell.

An instructor at the Boston Museum School early in the century, Paxton resigned his position in 1913. He was made an associate of the National Academy of Design in 1917 and a National Academician in 1928. His professional career brought many opportunities to exhibit and a long succession of awards, including a bronze medal at the 1904 St. Louis World's Fair and the "Popular Prize" at juried shows more frequently than any other American artist of his day. Although Paxton gained early fame and recognition for his realistic portraiture and naturalistic renderings of elegant settings, his painting style and depictions of upper-crust society went out of fashion with the Great Depression. He died at the age of seventy-two on May 13, 1941, a virtually forgotten figure of American art.

Raphaelle Peale

1774–1825

William Dunlap, the nation's first biographer of American artists, mentions Peale only in a footnote in his three-volume history of American art, published just nine years after the artist's death. Acknowledged today as the first major American still-life painter, and embraced as one of the country's finest artists of the early nineteenth century, he was considered a failure in his own lifetime.

Born in Annapolis, Maryland, on February 17, 1774, Raphaelle was the eldest child of Charles Willson and Rachel Brewer Peale. His father, a skilled painter and inventor, helped raise his son in a household that prized art, hard work, and learning. As multitalented as his father, Raphaelle worked variously as director and taxidermist for the Peale Museum; as a painter of portraits, miniatures, and still lifes; as a poet; and even as an inventor. At the time of his death he held several patents for various processes to preserve ship timbers, desalinate seawater, and even for the design of an efficient and inexpensive stove, which he and his father had built to aid the poor. Unfortunately, none of his ventures provided him with a steady income.

Peale was well known for his sense of humor and irreverent wit. An advertisement he placed in a local newspaper offered to paint dead relatives under the heading of "still lifes," while another reassured potential portrait sitters of "No Likeness, No Pay."

Despite his father's urging that he dedicate himself to portraiture, as had his younger and more financially successful brother, Rembrandt, Raphaelle turned his energies increasingly toward still lifes, beginning in 1797. But still lifes remained in relatively low demand in postrevolutionary America, making it difficult for the artist to support himself. It is unlikely that he could have made a living at all had it not been for his father's agreement to purchase every unsold canvas.

Peale's comparatively short life was plagued by ill health as a result of gout and alcoholism, as well as by financial problems. In later life his gout attacks became increasingly prolonged and debilitating, preventing him, at times, from even holding a brush. Despite much adversity, he created stark, precise works, setting the standard for American still-life painting and becoming—in our time, if not his own—one of America's most admired painters.

Charles Sprague Pearce

1851–1914

During the early years of his career, Pearce worked as an amateur artist in Boston, home of his wealthy and prominent family. In 1873 his colleague William Morris Hunt encouraged him to study formally in Paris, where he entered the studio of Léon Bonnat. Under Bonnat's close instruction Pearce began to make religious paintings and portraits that synthesized painterly and linear modes and featured one or two figures close to the picture plane. Because of a respiratory illness, Pearce was forced to spend his winters in a warmer climate, and in 1873 and 1874 he traveled to Egypt with the artist Frederick Bridgman and, in 1875, to Algeria with William Sartain. While living in Arabic quarters on these trips, Pearce became fascinated by Middle Eastern peoples, whose costumes, habitations, and activities he translated into exotic genre paintings.

Like other American artists, such as Daniel Ridgway Knight, Walter Gay, and Gari Melchers, Pearce also discovered exotic qualities in the peasants of Normandy and Brittany, and in order to experience their life-style, in 1885 he settled permanently with his wife in Auvers-sur-Oise, a small village one hour north of Paris by train. Pearce's critically acclaimed Norman peasant scenes, typically portraying coupled or lone shepherdesses wearing contemplative expressions, were sentimental and quasi-religious. Stylistically, these works demonstrated Pearce's interest in painting *en plein air*, an effect he was able to achieve all year round by working in the glass studio he had built onto his house.

Pearce's career was marked by numerous accomplishments and awards. Debuting in the 1876 Paris Salon with a portrait, he went on to receive an honorable mention in 1881 for *The Beheading of Saint John the Baptist* (location unknown). He also exhibited at the Royal Academy, London, in 1876, and, in America, at the Society of American Artists in 1878, the National Academy of Design in 1883, and the Pennsylvania Academy of the Fine Arts from 1883 to 1909. Active in various artistic organizations, Pearce helped found the Paris Society of American Painters, served as a juror for the

1889 Exposition, and coordinated American fine arts submissions to the 1894 Antwerp World's Fair. During the late 1890s he joined a group of twenty artists, including fellow Bonnat students Henry O. Walker and William Brantley, decorating the Library of Congress in Washington, D.C. Pearce's seven tympanum murals for the library's Jefferson Building celebrated the American family. In 1894, he was named a Chevalier of the Legion of Honor, the last great award he received before his death in Paris in 1914.

John Frederick Peto

1854–1907

Born in Philadelphia on May 21, 1854, Peto was the son of Thomas Hope and Catherine Ham Peto. One of four children, he lived with his maternal grandmother, Mrs. William Hoffman Ham, and her four unmarried daughters until he was in his mid-twenties. Peto's father was involved in various careers throughout his life. As an honorary member of the Philadelphia fire department, he was a dealer in fire department supplies. In the 1850s and early 1860s, he was also listed in the Philadelphia City Directory as a gilder and dealer in picture frames, a career that exposed the young Peto to the art world at an early age.

Peto produced watercolors and drawings as a boy, and his first recorded picture is dated 1875, when he was twenty-one. The following year, he was listed as a painter in the Philadelphia City Directory, and for most of the 1880s his studio was located in various buildings along Chestnut Street, a neighborhood where many artists had their studios during these years. In 1877, he enrolled as a student at the Pennsylvania Academy of the Fine Arts, where he studied for two years, periodically submitting works to the academy's annual exhibitions throughout the 1880s. During these years, he began to paint still lifes; his friendship with William Michael Harnett probably influenced his focusing on this genre. Peto supported himself in Philadelphia by producing painted office boards and portrait photographs for patrons. Probably his acquaintance with William Bell, a Philadelphia photographer who married one of his aunts, led to his interest in this medium.

In 1887, Peto traveled to Cincinnati, where he had apparently been commissioned to paint a still life for the Stag Saloon. There he met his future wife, Christine Pearl Smith from Lerado, Ohio, and the two were married on June 16, 1887. Around this time, he started commuting to Island Heights, New Jersey, where he played the cornet at camp revival meetings. In 1889, he built a house in the small resort community and moved there permanently with his wife and their only child, Helen. In Island Heights, Peto was isolated from the major artistic centers. Although he stopped exhibiting his work in Philadelphia, he continued to paint still lifes, selling his work at inexpensive prices to tourists or visitors to his home.

Two maternal, unmarried aunts also lived at the Peto residence in Island Heights, and a third aunt was a frequent guest in their home. This living arrangement proved to be difficult: the three aunts were a burden on the artist's immediate family. Another source of stress in his later years was his involvement in a protracted lawsuit over family property along the Hudson River. On November 23, 1907, Peto died at the early age of fifty-three from complications caused by Bright's disease.

Edward Henry Potthast

1857–1927

Potthast was born in Cincinnati, Ohio, the son of a chair and cabinet maker. As a youth he worked as a lithographer and attended the McMicken School of Design. Around 1882, he went to Antwerp, where he studied with Charles Veriat, and afterward to Munich, where for three years he studied under Nicholas Gysis, Ludwig von Loefftz, and possibly Carl Marr. Potthast returned to Cincinnati in about 1885 and enrolled in the evening classes at the Cincinnati Museum Association Art School. Having accumulated enough funds to finance six years abroad, he returned to Europe in 1887, this time to France. There he studied in various art colonies, including those at Barbizon and Grez, and in the studio of Fernand Corman in Paris. During this period he was introduced to French Impressionism by the American artist Robert Vonnoh and the Irish artist Roderic O'Conor. He exhibited at the Salon, and later at Munich, where he was awarded a bronze medal.

Potthast returned to Cincinnati around 1893. Settling in New York in 1896, he worked for a number of years as a free-lance lithographer before devoting his full time to painting. In 1899 his fellow artists awarded him the Clarke Prize for the best figure painting shown in the National Academy of Design. Other honors came to him as well. He was elected a member of the American Watercolor Society in 1895 and given the Evans Prize in 1901. He won a silver medal at the St. Louis Exposition in 1904 and was elected a member of the National Academy of Design in 1906. By 1908, he had a studio in the Gainsborough Building overlooking Central Park, which he often painted. In the summers, he painted on the New England coast.

Potthast is best known for his dazzling impressionist beach scenes, particularly the beach life of New York, which became his specialty after about 1910. A bachelor, he died alone in his studio from a heart attack, just three months before his seventieth birthday.

Maurice Brazil Prendergast

1858–1924

Born in St. John's, Newfoundland, on October 10, 1858, the eldest son of people of modest means, Prendergast grew up in Boston, where he and his brother Charles (later celebrated as a frame designer and decorator) attended Rice Grammar School. At fourteen, Maurice left school and took a job wrapping packages at a dry-goods store. Around 1879 he joined a firm that produced painted show cards and devoted his spare time to sketching landscapes. In the summer of 1887, Prendergast and his brother visited England and Wales, where Maurice did some minor watercolors. Determined to become an artist, he returned to Boston, intending to stay at his job only until he had saved enough money to return to Europe to study. It took him six years.

In 1891 the brothers arrived in Paris. Prendergast studied first at the Académie Colarossi, where his teacher was probably the academic painter Gustave Courtois, and then moved to the Académie Julian, where drawing from antique casts was stressed. But his real education lay outside the classroom. He spent his afternoons sketching the ebb and flow of life in the cafés, the public gardens, and along the boulevards. It was a theme that, with variations, would continue throughout his career. He became a close friend of the Canadian painter James Wilson Morrice, who shared and encouraged Prendergast's interest in the color and movement of urban life and whose artistic style of simplified arrangements in blocks of color, derived from Whistler, influenced his own style. Prendergast was also greatly affected by the theories of the Nabis, an avant-garde group whose style was characterized by flattened perspective, bright colors, and decorative forms.

When Prendergast returned to Boston in the fall of 1894, he devoted himself to painting, principally in watercolor. His main interest was capturing the color and movement of figures in Boston's parks and nearly beaches. He is first recorded in an exhibition in 1895 at the Boston Art Club and in 1897 began to exhibit in New York at the Water Color Club, where his watercolors and monotypes received high praise. In 1898, he made his third trip abroad, to Italy, where he spent about eighteen months. Venice particularly caught his imagination. There, inspired by the Renaissance masters, the splendid natural and architectural settings, and the colorful crowds in the Piazza San Marco, he produced some of the most sparkling watercolors of his career.

After his return in 1899, Prendergast's reputation grew rapidly. In 1900 he had his first major one-man exhibition in New York, at the Macbeth Gallery. In 1901 he won a bronze medal for watercolor at the Pan-American Exposition in Buffalo. Although he continued to live in Boston, he made frequent trips to New York City, most often choosing Central Park as his subject.

Prendergast spent the summer of 1907 in France, visiting Paris, Versailles, and St. Malo, creating watercolors that were more abstract in style, in which color, line, and movement no longer bent to the demands of representation. A group of the St. Malo watercolors was included among the works he showed at the Macbeth Gallery in New York in 1908 as a member of The Eight— Robert Henri, William Glackens, George Luks, John Sloan, Arthur B. Davies, Everett Shinn, and Ernest Lawson—who joined in reaction against the conservative art and exhibition practices of the National Academy of Design. The more sensational press characterized the eight artists as rebels and proclaimed their work shocking and eccentric. Prendergast's work was referred to as "unadulterated slop" and "an explosion in a color factory."

The years from 1909 to 1914 were difficult for Prendergast. He was past fifty and almost completely deaf. Despite the continuing appreciation of a small group of critics, he received relatively little widespread acceptance. It was thanks to the continued financial support of Charles, who by now had a successful frame-making business, that Prendergast was able to devote himself to his art. He went on to explore different subjects and techniques; painting portraits, nudes, nymphs in imaginary landscapes, and working on mural decorations.

Feeling a need for renewed contact with Europe, Prendergast returned to Venice in the late summer of 1911; but he had little chance to work, for soon after his arrival he fell ill and had to undergo prostate surgery. On his return to New York he joined the Association of American Painters and Sculptors to organize the Armory Show, which opened in 1913. His watercolors were praised as being among the most "advanced" works exhibited. Stimulated by the art he saw at the show, he started working on a series of still lifes and flower studies which, in their organization of space and form, show Cezanne's influence. In the summer of 1914 Prendergast traveled again to Paris and St. Malo; on his return he and Charles settled permanently in New York.

For the last decade of his life Prendergast fell into a quiet routine that alternated between painting in his studio in Washington Square during the winters and visiting his beloved New England coast to do watercolors. His oil paintings increasingly assumed the character of dreamlike tapestries of his life, expressed in sensuous color, weaving together—through fact and fantasy—the many strands of his interests and experiences. In watercolor his brushwork grew freer and broader, the representation more summary, and the color more intense. In 1922 his health began to fail. He was in the hospital, unable to attend in person, when the Corcoran Gallery in Washington awarded him the Corcoran Bronze Medal. He died on February 1, 1924, in New York City.

Levi Wells Prentice

1851–1935

Born on a farm in Lewis County, New York, west of the Adirondacks, Prentice moved in 1870 with his family to Syracuse. Self-taught, he started to paint there and is listed in the city directories as a landscape painter with a studio on Johnson Street. During these years, he also made furniture, picture frames, and art supplies for his own use and worked as a portrait and ornamental painter. He had an active career in art, exhibiting his landscapes in department-store windows and his studio. These small exhibitions received favorable press coverage, and from 1875 to 1880 Prentice's artwork was advertised in E. R. Wallace's *Descriptive Guide to the Adirondacks*, a publication for tourists who visited Upper New York State. In 1879 he moved to Buffalo, perhaps searching for a new market in the region surrounding the picturesque Niagara Falls. He remained for four years, marrying Emma Roseloe Sparks there in 1882.

In 1883 Prentice moved to Brooklyn, where he stayed until 1901. Probably influenced by the active group of still-life painters there, which included William Mason Brown and Joseph Decker, Prentice began to paint still lifes; his earliest is dated 1884. He continued to paint landscapes, often combining landscape and still life; but his main focus during his Brooklyn years was on the painting of fruit. In contrast to the critical acclaim he had received in Syracuse, in Brooklyn, Prentice received no press coverage and is not listed as an exhibitor in the major exhibitions of the Brooklyn Art Association or the National Academy of Design. The illusionism and minute detail of his work, however, probably appealed to young art students, who were attracted to their realism, and Prentice's family recalls that he ran a small art school in Brooklyn in the late 1890s.

After 1901 Prentice moved to Philadelphia with his family and also spent a good deal of time in his Bridgeport, Connecticut, studio, which he built for himself. Sometime around 1923, he had eye surgery for cataracts; he died in 1935.

Robert Lewis Reid

1862–1929

Born in Stockbridge, Massachusetts, on July 29, 1862, Reid's adolescence was disrupted by the failure in 1878 of the school his father had founded. Shuffled off to various relatives' homes in Massachusetts and Connecticut, Reid finally settled in Boston in 1880 in order to enroll in the newly established School of the Museum of Fine Arts. In Boston, he acted as part-time instructor for three of his four years at the Museum School. In addition to his teaching and studying, he founded a journal, *Art Student*, for which he and several other young artists wrote articles.

Reid left Boston in 1884 for New York City, where he joined the Art Students League. Dissatisfied with his training, in 1885 he left for Europe and settled in Paris. Like many of his contemporaries, Reid chose to enroll in the Académie Julian, to submit entries to the annual Salons, and to make the pilgrimage to Giverny, the home of Claude Monet. In 1889, he returned to New York.

In the following years Reid experimented with various painting techniques he had learned abroad. In order to earn extra money, he painted portraits, a practice he continued throughout his career. In 1893 he began to teach at the Art Students League and Cooper Union. Like his friend, artist Childe Hassam, Reid taught during the summers in various informal art colonies, among them Cos Cob and Farmington, Connecticut.

During the 1890s Reid received numerous commissions and won several prizes at the Society of American Artists and the National Academy of Design. In the mid-1890s he began to concentrate on large mural work, neglecting his easel painting, and only late in the decade did he return to exhibiting his smaller paintings.

The year 1898 proved a pivotal one for Reid: he exhibited his work at the first show of the then controversial group of artists who were to become known as the "Ten American Painters" and at his own successful one-man show at the gallery of the international dealer Durand-Ruel, one of the major forces in bringing Impressionism to America. By 1910, Reid was established as a "decorative impressionist," whose murals, stained-glass windows, and easel paintings depicted women in highly decorative settings.

Reid's career and reputation flourished throughout the first three decades of the twentieth century. Although successful financially, in large part because of his portrait commissions, he quickly spent his earnings on the newest fashions, lavish dinner parties for his friends, and his passion, gambling. Married briefly, Reid remained on his own for most of his life. After some years in Colorado Springs, during which he helped to found the Broadmoor Art Academy, Reid returned to New York, where in 1927 he suffered a stroke that paralyzed his right side. Subsequently, he taught himself to paint with his left hand and even exhibited from time to time. He died in Clifton Springs, New York, on December 2, 1929.

Theodore Robinson

1852–1896

Born on July 3, 1852, in Irasburg, Vermont, Robinson grew up in Evansville, Wisconsin. Having expressed an early interest in drawing, by 1870 he had decided to pursue a career as a painter and had moved to Chicago in order to attend art school. Afflicted with chronic asthma, he was forced to leave Chicago shortly after his arrival. From Chicago he followed the clean air—first to Denver, and then to his parent's home in Evansville. His illness did not thwart his artistic drive, however, and while nursing his health, he earned enough money from drawing crayon portraits from photographs to set him up in New York, where he moved in 1874.

Two years' study at the National Academy of Design prepared Robinson for a European sojourn. In 1876 he left for France and finally settled in Paris in order to study with some of the leading artists of the day. During his three years abroad, and like many of his American compatriots, he studied in Paris under the tutelage of Carolus-Duran, Jean-Léon Gérôme, and possibly Benjamin Constant.

Robinson returned to the United States in 1879 and spent a brief time with his parents in Evansville. By 1881, through a friend, he had landed his first job as an art teacher at Mrs. Sylvanevus Reed's school in New York. Robinson worked for and with artists such as John La Farge and Prentice Treadwell, on their decorative commissions. Consequently, during these early years of the 1880s, he began to experiment with a more decorative style in his own work; his paintings of the period—which remained, on the whole, firmly constructed, broadly painted, realist images—demonstrate a growing interest in atmospheric and lighting effects.

In 1884 Robinson decided to return to Europe. For the next eight years, he spent most of his time between France and America, wintering in New York and leaving for France in the springtime. While in France in 1888, he became friendly with Claude Monet. With the exception of Theodore Butler, who married one of Monet's stepdaughters, Robinson became the only American artist to develop a close working relationship with the older painter. Although he and Monet shared ideas about painting, and despite the substantial influence the Frenchman had on the young American, Robinson never fully adopted Monet's Impressionist style. Back in America, his paintings of these "French" years gained him a solid reputation.

Robinson moved back to the United States permanently in 1892, never again to return to Europe. During these last years of his life he sought to apply all he had learned in France to the painting of American scenes. He spent much of his time with his friends John Twachtman and J. Alden Weir and with his family, in both New York and Connecticut. In 1895 Robinson's one-man show at the Macbeth Gallery in New York received laudatory but, overall, unenthusiastic critical attention, and sales were disappointing. In his last year, he returned to his native Vermont in the hope of finding renewed inspiration in the landscape of the Green

Mountains. The stay proved to be more beneficial personally than professionally. Disappointed by his summer's work, he wished to return to Vermont the following spring in order to ameliorate his paintings. Sadly, before he could achieve this goal, on April 2, 1896, Robinson died of an asthma attack in New York. He was forty-five years old.

John Singer Sargent

1856–1925

Sargent was born in Florence to American parents, Dr. FitzWilliam Sargent, a surgeon, and Mary Newbold Singer Sargent. His mother's small independent income allowed the family—often plagued by real and imagined illnesses—to remain in Europe, continually moving locale in search of a healthier climate. As a result, much of Sargent's early education was acquired through sight-seeing and tutoring, his formal training being sporadic.

The cosmopolitan Sargent attended the Accademia delle Belle Arti in Florence in 1873–74. In May 1874 he entered the Paris atelier of the successful portraitist Emile Auguste Carolus-Duran, and also matriculated at the Ecole des Beaux-Arts in the fall. Following Carolus-Duran's approach, based on direct observation, Sargent developed the brilliantly fluid handling of paint that characterized his style throughout his career. The young artist first exhibited at the Salon in 1877, and in 1879 won an Honorable Mention for his portrait of his master (Sterling and Francine Clark Art Institute). Sargent's virtuoso brushwork was further reinforced by his copying of the paintings of Velázquez and Hals on trips to Spain and Holland in 1879 and 1880, respectively. Based on his continuing travels to Venice and Morocco, among other places, Sargent created innovative and vivid genre scenes in oils and watercolor during the 1880s and throughout his career. He gained his greatest fame and notoriety, however, for his portraits. *Madame X (Madame Pierre Gautreau)* (The Metropolitan Museum of Art), a portrait of an American beauty with lavender-powdered skin, created a scandal when it was exhibited at the Salon in 1884. The controversy marked the end of his Parisian career.

In 1885 Sargent stayed with the family of Francis Davis Millet in Broadway, Worcestershire, in the company of other American expatriates, including the writer Henry James and painter Edwin Austin Abbey. In the Millets' garden Sargent began painting *Carnation, Lily, Lily, Rose* (The Tate Gallery), completing it *en plein air* over two successive summer seasons. A personal blend of impressionist and Japanese influences, it was the sensation of the Royal Academy exhibition in 1887. Sargent's experiments with outdoor landscape painting remained an important part of his art, particularly in 1888–89.

In 1886 Sargent moved his studio to London and soon found international recognition as the leading society portraitist of his time. For the next two decades he concentrated much of his energy on the growing demand for portraits of fashionable members of primarily English and American society. He continually experimented with new poses, infusing the Grand Manner tradition with a decidedly contemporary informality. But Sargent longed to be free of the constraints of commissioned portraiture. After 1900, he

increasingly used watercolors—a primary medium early in his career—to paint dazzling, personal records of his travels.

Throughout his career, Sargent made many trips to America, the first in 1876. In the 1890s he received major mural commissions from the Boston Public Library, the Museum of Fine Arts, Boston, and other institutions. Carrying out the research for the symbolic murals based on religious thought entailed trips to Greece and the Middle East. In the nineties he was elected an Academician at the National Academy of Design in New York and the Royal Academy in London, and was made an officer of the Légion d'Honneur in France. At the time of his death, Sargent's exalted reputation was based, not only on his substantial artistic accomplishments, but also on the aura of international glamour that had seemed to surround the expatriate artist from the very beginning of his career.

Otto Stark

1859–1926

Born in Indianapolis, Indiana, Stark began his artistic career in the mid-1870s. He was first introduced to commercial woodcarving in Indianapolis, then to commercial lithography in Cincinnati, Ohio. His formal training in painting began at the University of Cincinnati, where he studied from 1877 to 1879. He moved to New York City later that year and supported himself as an illustrator, designer, and lithographer, while attending classes at the Art Students League. His teachers included William Merritt Chase, J. Carroll Beckwith, and Walter Shirlaw. He apparently also studied under Thomas Dewing.

After six years in New York, Stark was financially able to move on, and in 1885 he traveled to Paris, selecting the Académie Julian for further study. He also worked for about a year in the atelier of Fernand Cormon. In France, Stark absorbed many influences; his palette ranged from dark to bright, and the techniques he used, which included impressionism, were as varied as the spectrum of his subjects. Returning to New York in 1888, he worked in commercial art and exhibited the products of his French experience at the National Academy of Design. In 1890 he moved to Philadelphia, then back to Cincinnati, where he found work as a designer for a lithography company. He returned to Indianapolis in 1893 and opened a studio the following year on East Market Street, where he taught classes in oil and watercolor.

Until about 1890 Stark's subjects were primarily landscapes, portraits, and narrative and figure paintings. During the decade his palette lightened and became more impressionistic. In 1899 he was appointed supervisor of art at the Emmerich Manual Training High School in Indianapolis, and in 1902 he became an instructor at the John Herron Art Institute. Following his retirement in 1919, Stark lived and painted in the woods near Leland, Michigan, with excursions to Florida and Indiana. Although he continued to exhibit until the end of his life, Stark's later work lacked the vision of the years during and soon after his return from Europe. He died of a stroke at his daughter's home in Indianapolis in 1926.

Lemuel Everett Wilmarth

1835–1918

Born in Attleboro, Massachusetts, in 1835 Wilmarth attended
school in Boston, and in the 1850s he moved to Philadelphia,
where he earned a living as a watchmaker. During these years, the
young Wilmarth enrolled in evening drawing classes at the
Pennsylvania Academy of the Fine Arts. In 1858 he went to Europe
to continue his academic art training, studying with Wilhelm von
Kaulbach at the Royal Academy of Munich from 1859 to 1862, and
with Jean-Léon Gérôme at the Ecole des Beaux-Arts in Paris from
1864 to 1867. While living in Paris, Wilmarth sent paintings back to
New York, where they were shown at the annual exhibitions of the
National Academy of Design. Achieving critical acclaim and financial success as a genre and still-life painter, Wilmarth continued to
exhibit regularly at the National Academy until 1893 and at the
Brooklyn Art Association from 1866 to 1884. He set up a studio in
New York in 1867 and began his teaching career. His own academic method of instruction was shaped by his European training,
with a focus on drawing and painting from antique casts and models. He was hired as director in charge of the schools of the
Brooklyn Academy of Design in 1868. Two years later, he became
director of the schools of the National Academy of Design, a position he held until 1890, except for the years 1875–77, when he was
the first president and acting professor of the Art Students League
of New York. In 1871 Wilmarth was made an associate member of
the National Academy, and in 1873 he was elected an Academician.

Wilmarth's home was in Brooklyn, but in 1882 he purchased a farm
on the Hudson River where he lived during the summer months.
During later years he suffered from failing eyesight, and this condition probably accounts for his concentration on still-life subjects,
which did not require the detailed precision of his genre scenes. He
also grew increasingly religious, writing articles on religious life
and becoming one of the founders of *New Earth*, a Swedenborgian
publication. He died in 1918.

Index of Artists
and Works in the Exhibition

Edited by Barbara Wells Folsom

Design and typesetting: Greer Allen and Ken Scaglia

Printing: Northeast Graphics

Binding: Mueller Trade Bindery and Acme Bookbinding Company

Production Supervision: Yale University Printing Service